Creating Scholartistry: Imagining the Arts-informed Thesis or Dissertation

Edited by J. Gary Knowles, Sara Promislow
and Ardra L. Cole

Volume 4
Arts-informed Inquiry Series

Backalong Books
&
Centre for Arts-informed Research

Creating Scholartistry: Imagining the Arts-informed Thesis or Dissertation (Volume 4, Arts-informed Inquiry Series)

Edited by J. Gary Knowles, Sara Promislow and Ardra L. Cole

Copyright © 2008 Backalong Books and individual chapters by author(s)

Published by Backalong Books
P.O. Box 33066
RPO Quinpool Centre
Halifax, Nova Scotia
Canada B3L 4T6
www.backalongbooks.com
An imprint of Northwest Cove Productions

Cover photograph and design by Sharon L. Sbrocchi
Type set in AGaramond Pro.
Printed in Calgary, Alberta by Blitzprint

ISBN 978-1-894132-30-5
List Price $33.95 US $34.95 Canada

Creating Scholartistry:
Imagining the Arts-informed
Thesis or Dissertation

Table of Contents

Finding and Working with Form

Scholartistry in Relation

1. Inspiration to Imagine:
An Invitation and an Introduction

by J. Gary Knowles and Sara Promislow

Creating Scholartistry: Imagining the Arts-informed Thesis or Dissertation, the fourth volume in the Arts-informed Inquiry Series, has contributions from thesis and dissertation writers who successfully completed graduate degrees. It also has contributions from supervisors who guided or facilitated some of this new "scholartistry" (Neilsen, 2002). The various chapter authors offer insights into the art and craft of creating exciting arts-related work that is transformational in process and representation, and regenerational in possibilities and influence. They offer insights into the nature of journeys anticipated, experienced, and reflected upon. There are chapters which evidence scholartistry grounded in the visual, performing, new media, and literary arts. Issues associated with imagining, developing, and completing non-traditional, qualitative, social science research projects are brought forward as well as some of the barriers, complexities, challenges and rewards of guiding and facilitating such exciting work.

The voices of contributing authors reveal that the task of completing a non-traditional thesis or dissertation grounded in the arts has the possibility for many surprises, promises, and pitfalls. Pain and perseverance may be part of the experience for new researchers. Completing a successful thesis is often lonely work, especially when and where one's commitment to alternative genre research is tested to the hilt. But chances are, for those who persevere and remain true to their inspirations and aspirations, arts-related researchers will feel considerable satisfaction with their completed projects. And rightly so, when the work nudges at the boundaries of research conventions, extending notions about process and representation, it creates spaces where new and wider audiences can access the articulation of new knowledge.

Parallels between beginning teachers and beginning or emerging researchers are striking. New researchers may have experiences akin to beginning teachers who — as so often reported in research literature — find themselves tested by students, more experienced teachers, and administrators in their first weeks and months on the job. Sometimes these new teachers find themselves with their backs against the wall, as it were, defending their practices, perspectives, pedagogies, and fundamental definitions of self from testy and challenging students, arrogant and omniscient teachers, authoritarian and bureaucratic administrators, and protective

2

parents. Beginning arts-informed researchers are often tested in myriad ways: by relational circumstances and challenges (e.g, difficulties in finding and convincing a faculty supervisor to support the work); theoretical groundings and frameworks (e.g., finding the orientation that fits the work and circumstance and having the theoretical and methodological freedom to explore); institutional barriers and bureaucracies (e.g, meeting institutional requirements regarding form and media), to name a few. But more crucial may be the challenges to a new researcher's authority and identity — questions about fundamental elements of self associated with what it means to be a researcher and scholartist.

One of the central issues for new teachers revolves around the conception of self as teacher. The inability of a new teacher to define his or her teacher identity — an underlying philosophy and way of being in the classroom, not to mention perspectives on places called schools, views of parents and community and ideas about curriculum development, for instance — ultimately invites students to be coercive and shape a new teacher's practice. Such pressures may push the teachers to merely cope with the affairs of the day according to the policies or rules of engagement delineated by students (or peers, administrators, or parents).

The crucial question of identity for new practitioners — whether it be the beginning teacher or the emerging researcher — is this: Who am I? As teacher? As researcher? For the aspiring scholartist, the question is paramount for the continued existence of an inquiry project as conceived. If clarity and assurity to these questions cannot be established then the heart of a new researcher's scholartistry may be brought into question. More than anything the scholartist is first and foremost the instrument of the research and, ultimately, of the thesis or dissertation.

This book sprung from conversations at the Centre for Arts-informed Research at the University of Toronto. It became apparent that, in contrast to the experiences of those working in the

Centre, new researchers in many university contexts experienced reduced or little faculty and peer support, resources, or examples of arts-informed work (such as successful completed theses and dissertations). Of course there are institutional exceptions — usually those locations where advocates of various arts-related methods reside (see, Knowles & Cole, 2008, for example, for a range of arts-related researching perspectives, the scholars who advocate them, and their institutions). With the growing prominence of arts-related approaches to researching (for example, arts-based, a/r/t/ography, as well as arts-informed, the latter being the particular orientation and framing expressed through many of the research projects emerging from the Centre) comes the responsibility of articulating the nuance of meanings, purposes, and processes associated with each orientation and its various contexts. As more experienced scholartists delineate and clarify the unique theoretical and practical elements of their orientations, possibilities for new and emerging scholartists will enlarge. This volume demystifies some of what it means to do research related to the arts.

The collection was developed with three main audiences in mind: first is new researchers, graduate students, who are or are about to make their way through the labyrinths of institutional requirements, methodologies, and research relationships and are interested in arts-related qualitative research; second, faculty members whose interest is piqued by the possibilities of the arts in research; and third, faculty members who may be in supportive roles with new researchers infusing the arts into their research.

New scholars who know before they apply to graduate school that they want to do arts-related research locate institutional contexts and faculty who are supportive. Most new researchers do not have such foreknowledge. Those who come to use the arts in qualitative research often do so as a result of being inspired by peers, academic texts, performances, and conference presentations.

Chapters within the *Handbook of the Arts in Qualitative Research* (Knowles & Cole, 2008) present a range of enabling perspectives and methodologies for arts-related researchers.

To infuse the arts into inquiry is to break out of conventional ways of researching. It is to be inspired by the arts, with regard to process and representation. Such inspiration may be serendipitous or happenstance. To do this work is to act as a visual artist, poet, painter, photographer, dancer, dramatist, performer, and so on. Process is informed not only by bringing to bear one's creativity given the art form but by knowing how artists work. It is about fusing into one's scholarship the inspiration of an art and its processes and representations: How does a fiction writer work? What is a writer's source of data? What is involved in readying to write, developing storylines, plot? How does a photographer work? And a film maker? How does a playwright work? How does a dancer work? The answers to these questions partially reveal the heart of what it means to do arts-related research. This knowledge of process is infused into researching procedures in ways that make inherent sense and enhance the possibilities for gathering a different quality of information, analyzing and interpreting and presenting it creatively (Cole & Knowles, 2000, 2008).

Is it essential for scholartists to consider themselves "artists"? Being a scholartist, one who draws on the arts, implies a familiarity with an art form to the level that makes inherent sense for the project in question. There is usually no preordained "arts" coursework, for instance. Nor are there measures of artistic ability or set paths to becoming a competent scholartist. Knowing how artists of a specific genre engage with and represent subject matter is crucial for success. To become a scholartist is to possess a creativity and artfulness about inquiry and scholarship. It is to possess a willingness to take risks and not be bounded by conventions of academic discourse and research while being grounded in them. These are places from which to begin imagining.

To complete a thesis or dissertation is a formidable task in itself and scholartists and their supervisors face challenges that make the thesis / dissertation journey full of surprises. Risk taking, courage, openness to unknowing, and tolerance for ambiguity — on the part of both emerging scholars and their supervisors — are prerequisites for developing an arts-related project. Securing a supportive supervisor (and committee) is not always an easy task for new scholars. As for completing such a project, there are no models and maps to follow. Indeed, research projects drawing on the arts are likely to be entirely idiosyncratic endeavours with regard to process, form, and representation. Creativity is at the heart of the enterprise (not to imply that other research paradigms are not reliant on researcher creativity). This may be scary for a novice researcher unsure of her step and whose first socialized action is to seek reassurance from completed theses already stacked neatly on university library shelves.

There may be individual and institutional obstacles and challenges to infusing the arts into research methodologies (Knowles & Promislow, 2008). Individual obstacles and challenges include: becoming confident about exploring the unknown; uniting research methods with processes and representations; developing related artistic skills and knowledge; and, having the energy, time, skill, technical and financial resources to do the inquiry work. Institutional obstacles and challenges include: locating a suitable supervisor / guide and negotiating actual and perceived institutional constraints (such as that the form, structure, and medium for theses and dissertations is predetermined by universities).

The dominance of conventional views of empirical research is one obstacle to arts-related research. Even though alternative research methodologies are available (texts on arts-related inquiries exist and journals increasingly publish articles which express alternative orientations to qualitative research), incoming graduate school students have limited access to the range of epistemologies and methods possible. Where faculty actively support arts-related research there may be efforts to reveal alternative possibilities. In other contexts new researchers may become aware of arts-related research and have to seek supportive faculty (since faculty may not promote arts-related work because they think it not credible or acceptable at their institution or because they lack supervisory expertise).

Creating Scholartistry: Imagining the Arts-informed Thesis or Dissertation is divided into four sections; however, these divisions are porous and multilayered, and the issues portrayed therein are inextricably intertwined. The sections, as do the chapters, embody a blurring of boundaries reflective of artful inquiries, scholartistry, and as discussed throughout the book focus on: communities and supervisors; finding and working with form; method, theory, and process; and, representation.

Disrupting Traditions

In this section authors discuss issues related to creating and putting forth non-traditional theses and dissertations. The journeys recounted in these chapters reflect bumpy roads travelled, risk-taking, and experimentation as part and parcel of undertaking artful kinds of work. Representation is one of the ways in which traditional research is disrupted. However, the art forms that embody and / or shape the thesis / dissertation representations in these chapters are often central to the research inquiries and the representations are inseparable from the processes in which they are brought into existence. For example, Peter Gouzouasis and Karen V. Lee (Chapter 2) offer a humourous yet serious account of the negotiation between supervisor and thesis writer to create and represent a non-traditional piece of work. Theory, form and method are reflected upon as Karen convinces Peter to support her artful thesis concept. Daria Loi's Thesis-as-Suitcase (Chapter 8) is an artifact that embodies "What the thesis discusses", enables what it promotes, and demonstrates "In Action", the concepts developed in her research. The process of creating a research representation is integral to her research method, the theory behind her work, and the processes associated with it. Daria discusses the obstacles she overcame in order to create and represent a groundbreaking form — the suitcase. She provides advice to novice schol-artists who wish to follow in her footsteps.

Method, Theory, and Process

Authors in the chapters that follow reflect on issues related to research methods and theoretical frameworks as shaping and / or shaped by artful research processes and journeys. Issues such as subjectivity, researcher presence, the intersection of art, life, and research, creative and artful learning processes, among others, are discussed. Interconnections with other sections in this book are exemplified in Elizabeth de Freitas' chapter (Chapter 15) the process of artful storying, of working with the form of fiction, is intertwined with her development as an arts-informed scholar as well as the method and hermeneutic framework of her research. Liz reflects on the shaping of her method as crucial to the development of her theoretical framework. She states, "Fiction writing allowed me to explore an imagined world of contingent and partial truths." Sharon Sbrocchi (Chapter 16) reflects on her doctoral research processes: "the position of the researcher within the text" and, "as a researcher". In her thesis stories, photographs, archival materials, and memory maps come together to help explore and represent the relationship between self and place. Memory maps structure the thesis text, provide coherence to its representation, and are a metaphor for the process of inquiry.

Finding and Working with Form

Individual experiences of finding, developing, and working with arts-related forms are discussed in this section. Form as evolving in and through one's research, form as informing one's work, processes of working with artful forms throughout and / or at different stages of a research project, are among issues discussed. Form is never far from process and / or method and / or theory in these chapters. Nor is it often separate or excluded from the research representation. For example, Nancy Halifax-Davis (Chapter 18) describes her desire "to write a text that wholly supports an emergent manner of encountering the world from within it. Not a work of linear perspective but a work of imagination and multiple perspectives." It is through this desire and the research process and method that she stumbles upon the form(s) that illuminate her inquiry. Kevin Kirkland and Carl Leggo (Chapter 22) reflect on the difficult and often painful process through which Kevin, with the support and guidance of his supervisor, Carl, discovered form. They discuss how artful forms, theories, and processes "can facilitate a scholarly engagement with all experiences, including personal experiences that are frequently silenced." Drawing on mythopoetics and narrative inquiry, and the form of a fairy tale, Kevin was able to go forth with the subject matter that he was determined to explore and to uncover complex and multilayred knowledge.

Scholartistry in Relation

Supportive contexts and relationships are often central to the development of artful theses and dissertations. Reflections on supervisor-thesis / dissertation researcher relationships, the process of supervision, artful research communities and courses, and the work that is often inspired by them are the focus of these chapters. Intersections with other sections in this book are common. For example, the a/r/tography group at the University of British Columbia (see Chapter 28) is not only a supportive context for the development of artful inquiries but is also a research group which developed a unique research method and process: "The a/r/tographical process is one of intimacy and vulnerability; a living inquiry that breathes and moves through difficult spaces of un/knowing." In Antoinette Oberg's and Laura Cranmer's account (Chapter 29), Antoinette's "methodless method" is both a pedagogical and research approach that serves as a guide for supervising and conducting research. Antoinette and Laura provide a glimpse of this open-ended and emergent method in practice. They reflect on their work together, as supervisor and student, and Laura's research process — from developing research questions, finding and working with form, to representing her research — within the "methodless method". The supervisor-student relationship and the role of the supervisor in artful inquiries are found in additional chapters in other sections of the book for example, Chapters 2 and 9 (by Peter Gouzouasis and Karen V. Lee, and by Pauline Sameshima and J. Gary Knowles, respectively).

One of our hopes for this compilation is that it may encourage emerging scholars to complete arts-inspired theses and dissertations. We see it as a reference point offering insights and implying possibilities. There is no one path to follow. The unique elements of this kind of inquiry centre on the qualities of researchers themselves: vision, perseverance, and commitment to an art form, for example. There is support for arts-related work in universities and professional / research organizations. Paths taken by scholartists are idiosyncratic, often hinge on serendipity, exposure to other scholartists, grounding in the arts, so that the art, or arts, becomes a catalyst and means for achieving exciting new work. The definitive means for judging the success of scholartistry in theses and dissertations may be audience response and the potential for making a difference.

We will judge this collection of reflections about the work of completing arts-informed or related theses or dissertations to be successful, if it stimulates the imagination, inspires action and propels new researchers to complete arts-related inquiries.

References

Barone, T., & Eisner, E. (1997). Arts-based educational research. In R. M. Jaeger (Ed.), *Complementary methods for research in education* (2nd edition). Washington, DC: American Educational Research Association.

Cole, A. L., & Knowles, J. G. (2008). Arts-informed research. In J. G. Knowles & A. L. Cole (Eds.), *Handbook of the arts in qualitative research: Perspectives, methodologies, examples, and issues* (pp. 55-70). Thousand Oaks, CA: Sage Publications.

Cole, A. L., & Knowles, J. G. (2001). *Lives in context: The art of life history research.* Walnut Creek, CA: AltaMira Press.

Knowles, J. G., & Cole, A. L. (Eds.). (2008). *Handbook of the arts in qualitative research: Perspectives, methodologies, examples, and issues.* Thousand Oaks, CA: Sage Publications.

Knowles, J. G., & Promislow, S. (2008). Graduate studies and thesis / dissertation development. In J. G. Knowles & A. L. Cole (Eds.), *Handbook of the arts in qualitative research: Perspectives, methodologies, examples, and issues* (pp. 515-530). Thousand Oaks, CA: Sage Publications.

Neilsen, L. (2002). Learning from the liminal: Fiction as knowledge. *Alberta Journal of Educational Research, 48*(3), 206-214.

About the Authors

J. GARY KNOWLES is Professor of Education and Co-director of the Centre for Arts-informed Research, Ontario Institute for Studies in Education of the University of Toronto.

SARA PROMISLOW holds a PhD from the Ontario Institute for Studies in Education of the University of Toronto (OISE/UT). She was editor of the Centre for Arts-Informed Research's online publication *arts-informed* for five years.

Disrupting Traditions

2. Sticky Knot Danish

by PETER GOUZOUASIS AND KAREN V. LEE

"But how does a person systematically investigate truth?" Rain rumbles on a gray, blustery day. "I don't know, Peter. But story writing is research. And it's arts-informed," says Karen. "But how does it relate to current music research? What's your purpose and problem?" Peter walks quickly on the sandy grass at the beach. "You know what I mean, KV?" He looks behind him. "Where are you?"

"Karen, what the hell happened?" She hangs onto Peter's arm. "You scared the heck out of me, KV." She staggers but stands. Peter wipes chunks of wet grass off her sleeve. He holds her left arm and they walk. "Let's go sit in my car." Dazed and drenched they walk toward Peter's car. "Are you okay? Are you ill?" Karen looks down. "Karen?"

"Maybe it was that cigarette, Peter." "Huh?" He opens the door as Karen looks over her clothes. Wet pants stick to her legs. Her coat is drenched. Strands of hair drip water. She pulls her hair over her right ear. "I'm soaked. There's wet grass all over me." "Never mind, just get in. It'll be okay. I'll turn on the heater." With the ignition, the car stereo begins. "Let's listen to some music. Maybe you'll feel better." Karen nods.

Wes Montgomery plays *West Coast Blues*. "This tune really gets me. Even before Wes moved to the "left coast" he must have seen the Pacific Northwest when he wrote it. You know, the rhythmic persistency of his solo is like the rhythms created by the falling rain." "I like it." "Want another cigarette?" Peter laughs and bumps Karen's arm. Karen takes the cigarette but frowns.

"I brought you here to think more freely. You know, getting away from the campus and distractions and academic guidelines helps me. But I didn't mean to get you bent out of shape. This arts-based stuff seems somewhat," Peter pauses, "subversive. Know what I mean? Research needs to be systematic." "What do you mean?" "That there must be some sense of rigour. A clearly defined purpose and problem. A certain structure — an introduction, a lit review, a methodology, tangible results, and conclusions, and all of those components linked through various substructures in the thesis. Structural corroboration, not multiplicative corroboration. I mean, how can you hand in a thesis that's merely a series of stories?"

"Why not? Arts-based inquiry involves different forms of representations. There are aesthetic qualities or elements that infuse the writing. That's what Tom Barone (1995) talks about. It's a more pluralistic view. Knowledge is embodied in different ways. I'll have music, stories, poetry, photos, autobiography. Alternative forms of research. In the end, the character in my stories changes or grows from events that occur. There's a new vision of educational phenomena. I'll get you some articles on the topic."

Peter takes a quick drag on his cigarette. "Listen to the hypnotic chromaticism of the improvisation. Listen to these twists and turns. I'd swear he's plugged into the guitar." Rain dances on the windows. Peter continues, "You know, listen to the changes. Tonic, flat subtonic, tonic, two-five of seven, sliding down to a two-five of flat seven. Isn't that cool? A two-five of flat five that sneaks through three straight measures of two-fives that slide down chromatically. And that funky turnaround."

Wes Montgomery plays in the background

"Sounds just like how you slid when you fainted." He chuckles and nudges Karen. "I've got most of Wes's recordings on vinyl. One of my guitar teachers once told me that Wes Montgomery regretted not learning how to read music fluently and play guitar with a plectrum. Gets me thinking. His signature is that beautiful tone he got by plucking and strumming the strings with his thumb. Highly unorthodox but he took the craft to a whole other level. You know, I stopped performing seriously for a few years in the late eighties because I thought I could never play as well as Wes. The lineage, from Eddie Lang to Pat Martino, and what I thought I had to do was too much for me to handle. Too much history and too many guitar players in one town for a humble kid like me. But you know what I always say, if I didn't love music and the guitar so much, I wouldn't be sitting here right now."

Karen finally changes the subject. "I wanna talk more about my thesis. Art makes a different kind of truth claim than science. That's what Joe Norris (1988) says." "What truth claim? How can an inanimate thing claim anything?" "Arts-based research promotes doubt about values and interests with knowledge. Our framework. Our worldview." Peter messes with the car stereo and loads another CD. "What worldviews? Come on. You know that paradigms and worldviews have been replaced by a broader perspective of research programs. Go back and read Stephen Pepper (1942), Larry Laudan (1977), and Willis Overton (1984), and all those other things we read in my class."

"This stuff has been marginalized. But can't you see? It just plays into the discourse about validating art. That art is a form of epistemology. That aesthetic experiences can bring transformations. Norman Denzin (1989) calls it epiphanies." "I'm still not convinced. How about what other people (e.g., Bowman, 1991) think about aesthetics in music education?" "Okay. You have a point." She takes a puff. "But, I've started this short story and crafted a metaphor to raise questions. I brought a few pages to show you. The first is a postcard." "A postcard?" "Yeah. The character in the story is a computer whiz who e-mails postcards to his girlfriend during his gig on a cruise. There are photos."

Peter turns up the music. "Here's a really cool section. Check it out. Listen to the octave solo in this tune. It's Sundown, another Wes Montgomery tune." He closes his eyes and winces at the virtuosity.

Karen uses both hands to rustle the wet papers. "Here, Peter." Slowly, he unfolds the sticky pages. "What's the name of this story?" "*Unlikely Character*". It's about a bass player in turmoil over teacher education. Gigging for a living versus teaching for financial security. His girlfriend supports him being a musician more than being a teacher. But he's lonely on the cruise ship and E-mails the University of British Columbia Teacher Education about applying." She points, "Take a look."

Karen continues, "That's the beginning and it goes on and on. In the end, the girlfriend accepts a nursing position out of town. They break up." "Oh."

Casual fun on a Royal Caribbean cruise.

Royal Caribbean
INTERNATIONAL
Get out there.

TO: kathryn@hotmail.com
FROM: ma@alvarezrecords.com

Hi Kathryn,

This week isn't going well. The 64-year old band leader is fighting with the other musician over repertoire. They have completely different notions of style. I'm in the middle and don't like it.

The guys in the band speak Spanish all the time. *Hablo un poco de español* but not much. They are both so hot-blooded.

It's hard to make music when they're acting so hostile towards each other. I try to be professional, but I'm in a precarious position.

I keep reminding myself I make $500/wk US.

Love Michael

Figure 1. Karen V. Lee, 2004. *Royal Caribbean Cruise.* Postcard. 3 cm x 5 cm.

"But he's happy and moves on to teacher education. He has such a strong identity as a musician." She takes more papers out of her pocket.

"*Sundown*'s a more unique 12 bar blues that has even more chromatic features than the first tune. Jazz composers and improvisers break rules all the time. It's much more fun playing outside of the chord changes than inside. I love that crunchy sound of playing a blues from the flat five to the flat five of the scale." Karen shakes her head, "I want to start my thesis with a poem. I might read it at my defense."

We begin new music
By a walk through the leaves
At the mercy of the trees
Imagine the future
Sounds we share
Time against us

A car drives by and splashes Peter's window. "Gee, I wish this storm would let up. Damned weather. Liquid sunshine." "This is typical Vancouver, Peter." "Yeah, typical. Do you feel better now?" "Kind of." She crushes her cigarette in the ashtray. "When you fainted, I thought you were gone. I was thinking," he whispers, "this would look so bad. What have I done?" "I would say one of our heated debates knocked me out!" Peter laughs.

"Well, you get me all started about this arts-based stuff. I know you believe in this form of work and want to write your thesis with your own voice, not mine. You have my support but you've got to understand where I'm coming from. I was trained in a totally different way. My own doctoral supervisor was an American who mostly did quantitative research. University of Iowa, home of dustbowl behaviourism. It was enough work for me to get him to think about his research program from an organismic perspective. I read a lot of philosophy — Kant, Leibnitz, Hegel, Pepper, Kuhn, Laudan, Overton — but he never really embraced my ideas. And back then people in music doctoral programs were never encouraged to publish while they were in graduate school. My reviews of his studies and challenging questions forced him to articulate the weaknesses in his work. He felt he was too far into his career to change his theoretical stance."

"Wow." Karen pauses. "Well, what do you think?" "You're pushing it. But I feel a sense of responsibility toward your research. You are my doctoral student." "Isn't it like Wes? Breaking rules?" "Look, Karen, there are pressures that come with following and breaking traditions. I mean, the blues are tradition. And even a basic blues has a fundamental structure that can be worked and reworked to have little resemblance to the original structure. Look at *West Coast Blues* and *Sundown*. Wes is so artful with the nuance of the changes. His art's based on years of knowledge, experience, and even research in a sense — lived experiences in dirty dive bars and smoky clubs. But, maybe it's time to be subversive, make new rules, new structures. Create new research traditions in music." Buckets of rain pour down. Peter hangs his left arm out the window to feel the heavy drops. "Before I fainted I was explaining how stories have been validated as credible research. Read Jerome Bruner, Tom Barone, and Elliott Eisner. I heard Eisner (see, Barone & Eisner, 1997) speak at a conference last year. He was really powerful. You'd like him Peter. He's such an artsy guy." "Really?" "I'll give you some of Tom Barone's articles" (e.g., Barone, 1995).

"Alternative forms of representation. Arts-based research. That's the discourse. And you're a great storyteller! You're always telling me stories. Over the years, you tell me story after story. That's your truth. I know you can write narrative. It is a whole other way of knowing. It's a form of ontology and epistemology."

"It just seems hippy-dippy right now." "But there are multiple ways of learning, Peter. Through art, music, poetry, story, and autobiography. Doesn't a poem tell you something? Last year, someone (Raspberry, 1998) wrote his thesis as a poetic transcription. He passed. And another (Dunlop, 2000) is writing a novel." "Sure, and I've heard mixed reports about those projects, Karen. You know my concerns. Postmodernism and relativism. There's so much contradiction in many postmodernist writings. Plus, this is all still so new that many people, especially in music education, are going to challenge what we're doing." "I'm ready!"

"What a rainstorm this has been," Peter grumbles. "When we left UBC it was barely raining." "It'll pass. Give it a few hours." Peter looks through the lifting fog. The musty aroma of low tide wafts through the cracked windows. "I remember when I wrote my master's thesis. I had all this great observational data that I wanted to include. And reflections on each day that I spent at day-care centers teaching music to little ones. Stories on each child's reactions to the activities. My committee told me that all of that stuff was incidental, not central, to my thesis so I ripped it out of my findings. I argued for months to include some of it in an appendix. And any ideas that were related to that data could only be placed in a discussion section, after my conclusions." "Things change, Peter. Arts-based inquiry is a new way of doing research. It's great progress." "Okay, I'm always willing to listen. I'll need a copy of this story." "I'm not finished yet." "When you're done."

"Tell me what you are looking for in research. I need your help." "Ah-huh. Well, when I first met Orrin Keepnews, in 1985, he drove me from the radio station KJAZ in Alameda over to Fantasy Records in Berkley. After some polite chit-chat he asked me what I wanted to talk about. So I asked him to tell me stories. His eyes lit up when I said 'So how did you discover Wes?' What fantastic stories he told me that afternoon." "You'll have to share some."

Peter wipes the mist off his window. "You know, three years later he published a book, *The View From Within* (Keepnews, 1988), after I convinced him how important his stories were to our understanding of the evolution of the music. That's a seminal text in jazz history."

"The view from within. Reminds me about that sticky knot danish you ate last summer." "What?" "Remember? When the Hong Kong students visited? We took them to the docks to walk around. We went to the Steveston Bakery. I watched you eat two of those sticky knot danishes. They were sticky and gooey with corn syrup and molasses dripping off them!" "You're too funny, KV."

"Those sticky knot danishes made you happy." Peter chuckles, "It's fun to unravel those suckers."

"So, I need my research to unravel the musicians' stories. To capture the essence." "The crux of the sticky knot? Truth about sticky knots? How about Lee's theory of the relativity of sticki-ness?" "Huh?" "Okay, E-mail me the rest of this story. I'm ready to get relatively sticky." Peter lights a cigarette and hands one to Karen. She lights it and slowly inhales. Clouds of smoke rise out of the cracked open windows. The rain has slowed to a fine but steady drizzle.

"What a rainstorm."

"What a brainstorm."

References

Barone, T. (1995). The purposes of arts-based educational research. *International Journal of Educational Research, 23*(2), 169-180.

Barone, T., & Eisner, E. (1997). Arts-based educational research. In Richard M. Jaeger (Ed.), Section II of *Complementary methods for research in education* (pp.73-116). Washington, DC: American Educational Research Association.

Bowman, W. (1991). An essay review of Bennett Reimer's "A philosophy of music education." *Quarterly Journal of Music Teaching and Learning, 2*(3), 76-87.

Denzin, N. (1989). *Interpretive interactionism.* Newbury Park, CA: Sage Publications.

Dunlop, R. (2000). *Boundary Bay: A novel.* Winnipeg, MB: Staccato Chapbooks.

Keepnews, O. (1988). *The view from within: Jazz writings, 1948-1987.* London, UK: Oxford University Press.

Laudan, L. (1977). *Progress and its problems: Towards a theory of scientific growth.* Berkeley, CA: University of California Press.

Lee, K. V. (2004). *Riffs of change: Musicians becoming music educators.* Unpublished doctoral thesis, University of British Columbia, Vancouver, BC, Canada.

Norris, C. (1988). *Deconstruction and the interests of theory.* London, UK: Pinter.

Overton, W. (1984). World views and their influence on psychological theory and research: Kuhn-Lakatos-Laudan. *Advances in Child Development and Behavior, 18*, 191-226. New York, NY: Academic Press.

Pepper, S. C. (1942). *World hypotheses.* Berkeley, CA: University of California Press.

Raspberry, G. W. (1998). *Imagining the curious time of researching pedagogy.* Ottawa, ON: National Library of Canada. Retrieved August 18, 2004 from http://www.nlc-bnc.ca/obj/s4/f2/dsk3/ftp05/nq27231.pdf

About the Authors
Peter Gouzouasis is Associate Professor, Department of Curriculum Studies, University of British Columbia (UBC) and coordinates the Fine Arts and New Media in Education (FAME)

cohort. He actively promotes arts-based educational research with the a/r/t/ography Research Group (UBC). Peter considers himself a lifelong learner of music and still pursues serious studies, studio work, and performance. He is former music director of WRTI / JAZZ 90 radio station, Philadelphia, and has written and produced television and radio commercials.

Karen V. Lee is Faculty Advisor and co-founder of the Teaching Initiative for Music Educators cohort (TIME) at the Faculty of Education, University of British Columbia. She teaches undergraduate and graduate courses in both classroom and online learning contexts. Her research interests include issues of musician identity, teacher identity, music education, teacher education, and arts-based approaches to qualitative research. She is a writer, musician, music educator, and researcher.

In her doctoral thesis, *Riffs of Change: Musicians Becoming Music Educators*, Karen explores the inherent shifts and extensions in musicians' identities as they transform into school teachers. We begin new music / by a walk through the leaves / at the mercy of the trees / imagine the future / sounds we share /time against us. Karen wrote eight short stories and an autobiographical account of her experience. The stories confront, challenge, and steer readers into critical places and unexpected spaces.

3. Crossing Borders:
Wandering into Unknown Territories

by ALEXANDRA CUTCHER

Getting to the destination, actually, was a bit of an anti-climax. Once I arrived I felt somewhat let down. My own true story had been printed, bound, pawed over, and sent half a world away to await its fate. And I, I who was now exhausted, took to my bed, with a strong libation and a head full of nothings. What was I going to do now? I had spent the past five years joined at the hip with this — this *thing* — on a journey that we made together and now it was over, its destiny taking it elsewhere. I was bereft.

"What now?" I pondered. The images of a projected future

would not come easily, so I left them, unyielding and abandoned, I turned instead to the past — the immediate past and the beginning of this voyage which had changed me so much. And as I looked backwards I thought about the journey, the changes and the thing (Was it a thesis? Was it an artwork? Was it a travelling companion?).

During the entire expedition, chance, serendipity, and fate had been my escorts. And now I was at the summit, I was at once exhilarated and glum. All I wanted to do was wallow.

So I did.

•

In the beginning, there was nothing.

Well, almost nothing. I knew that I had chosen to undertake what I saw as a bit of a gargantuan task, that of trying to get my doctoral degree while I was working full time and raising, with my husband, two small girls. But I was much encouraged.

My supervisor was enthusiastic about my work and it was a bit of a personal quest as well. I had chosen to do a multigenerational, autobiographical study of my Hungarian family's migration experience and assumptions of belonging. I knew that the methods I proposed were a bit "out there" for my very conservative university but I had faith that my inner voice (a companion that I was to rely on more heavily in the months and years to come) was guiding me in the right direction.

I realized, though, that something was not quite right when my supervisor said, "You're not going to do one of those ridiculous postmodern things are you?" I just demurred and smiled, what I thought was an enigmatic smile, not realizing the substance of her agenda. For that matter I had not yet realized my own. Things, however, were about to get tricky.

My naïveté at this stage was perhaps charming but quite an advantage in the long run. Because I had no idea what to anticipate my mind was completely open. I expected that my supervisors would, at least, show me the way if not the means. I searched everywhere for a thesis that was something (anything!) like what I had in mind and came up empty-handed. This was a good thing but it did make me sound somewhat clueless at my doctoral research proposal defence — when everything came to a head.

I knew that, somehow, I wanted to incorporate the visual arts into the research. At the very least I wanted "portraits" of the participants because I had used this device in my master's degree research as a way to characterize the protagonists in the narratives. I knew that I wanted to push the boundaries of the way that I conducted research a little further. I knew that I wanted to paint and print and photograph but was not sure about what the end product would look like and how much art I was actually going to (be allowed to) do. This was educational — not visual arts — research after all.

I walked into the room armed with my anxiety, visual diaries, master's thesis, and doctoral research proposal. Both my supervisors were there and the faculty had thought to include in the discussion one of the visual arts lecturers.

What transpired was very interesting indeed. Heated argument sputtered across the table between the parties leaving me somewhat bemused. The whys, the hows, and the wherefores were debated at length. How was I going to present such a proposed body of research? Why would I want to do it this way anyway (what was the point of it)? And, of course, wherefore the assessment procedure and demands?

As a result of our discussions my supervisor resigned — having some difficulty supporting such an unconventional research proposal. Luckily, my associate supervisor replaced her. The conversation around the table that day was animated and discomforting but, ultimately, fruitful in the ideas that were yielded and my new supervisor and I saw completely eye to eye. This was the first of many difficult borders to be crossed and I was beginning to learn the languages of my method.

It was obvious to all involved in those discussions that I had complete faith in the use of art to inform the inquiry. I could not articulate how, or what; I was unable to fully defend my choice in language and adequately justify my intuitive knowing. Instinctively, I knew that this was right for me and it was right for the research. During the entire research journey I learned to listen to my instinctive voice, harness it, and use it in constructive ways. Thinking back, I realized that when I began, I felt quite comfortable taking a mental step backwards, opening up and exploring the available literature and trusting that the ideas would come. And they did.

Thinking back, lying in my bed, the warmth of a beverage soothing my tension, I chuckled to myself as I remembered discussing my plans with my (non-artist) friends, family, and colleagues. I garnered much criticism — the work was not scientific, not truthful, too self-indulgent, it wasn't "real" research. I did expect this and, to a large extent, the criticisms mirrored those evident in the literature surrounding the form. These criticisms were very useful because they helped me engage in the debate and helped me clarify what I believed in doing (or not doing).

During the entire process I persisted in the belief that the outcomes would reveal themselves. This was a strength in my research journey. Because my deadlines were unclear I felt that I could push through with different parts of the inquiry when one part failed or stalled. I trusted the process and this intuition never failed me. Instinct, imagination, and creativity became very effective research tools.

All research is interpretive but arts-informed inquiries are very self-conscious. I was constantly aware of the method, how I should, could, and would use it, what criticisms it would engender and how I would present the information. Just as I am doing now, it was like navel gazing, a highly underrated enterprise. To be able to do this consciously I had to make space for serendipity and chance to play their part in the journey, and create mental spaces for the truths to bubble to the surface.

I am convinced now, as I suspected then, that making art makes me a better researcher. Making research makes me a better artist. And making artistic research and artistic forms makes me an infinitely better teacher.

I lay there, navel gazing, all afternoon. My drink soothed me and I slept. It was the sleep of exhaustion and of relief. And as I drifted off it occurred to me that the journey was not yet over.

•

Many months later I was to fully realize what was in front of me. The degree had been awarded but my work was not finished. When my "spare" thesis copy was finally returned to me I took a moment to cogitate. I had realized myself, and it was confirmed by my examiners, that the work was good but I had not had the thesis in my hands for almost a year and I could barely remember the details.

That night I waited until the house was quiet. I sat, wordlessly, caressing its black bound skin. It was the touch of a fellow traveller, a soothing contact. On reflection, I realized that I wanted to drink the work in, to pause and to contemplate, in order to decide where my next journey would take me. I poured myself a glass of fine red wine, opened the book, and started to read. I do not think I had ever taken the time to read it for enjoyment. This was a new experience.

As I read through the table of contents, I realized that this was a portfolio of stories, an historical document, an example of an arts-informed inquiry, a thesis, a body of work, a postmodern text, a self portrait of the artist at age forty, an allegory, and an embodiment of a teacher. The book (the fact that it is as yet unpublished is immaterial to me — it is, in every sense, a book) was a highly ornate document, very rich in visual material. It was multivocal and multilayered, an aesthetically pleasing thing.

Before I settled down to read, I thumbed through the multi-coloured pages and recognized that the organization of the chapters was disjointed and, at times, quite fragmented. This was deliberate and, since this is a postmodern text, the reader has the opportunity to access the text in a non-linear way. One could read the commentary and the theory, or choose to look at only the visual elements, or simply read the memoir. Either way the reader would have a sense of the research. It also encourages the reader to ponder these unsettling devices — just as I was now doing.

What I remembered most about the research journey was how organized I had to be with all the information I collected. I spent the first two years immersed in reading copious amounts of information and reviewing it in writing. It was my way of submerging myself in the theoretical frameworks that were out there. From these understandings, and the information I had gathered myself, I collected mountains of paper. The problem for me then was: What I am going to do with it all? So I reread everything in order to get a sense of the texture of the data and key into the sensory and performance qualities of the narratives. I also tried to perceive and understand that elusive phenomena: the nature of the experiences being recounted. All of this subjective stuff was where I went first. As I looked through the art works I lingered on the visual portraits I created of myself and my family. It was during the process of transcribing, editing, and reading the stories of my parents and myself that I was compelled to create them. I chose to do this using lino-block prints. I enjoyed the graphic nature of the prints and the ability to manipulate the many copies of the prints in highly individual ways. This technique compelled me to represent and interpret the same subject (and image) in several different ways.

The visual portrait enabled me to get inside each character, to use the words they gave me in conjunction with my observations of them, to create a "likeness" that is my interpretation of a self.

I find this difficult to do in writing. Image making slows down consciousness and writing can sometimes be too noisy in my head. By creating these images I was able to explore the characters in respectful and conscious ways. For me image making is more contemplative, than writing because I pause and reflect upon the participants and the information they have chosen to share during the actual act of creation. I felt that I had to do the portraits, first, before any of the other art forms and it was a suitable artistic starting point. The portraits, in fact, inspired the rest of the art making processes and products.

Taking another sip of nectar, I turned to the narrative passages. I recalled that, after I had "interviewed" my family members (and myself), I crafted the transcripts into first person narrative accounts. I struggled with how to portray the narratives of my family in ways that transcended the "written word only" approach. I did not want a gimmick; I wanted an experience more faithfully portrayed.

After a lot of thinking, sketching, talking, and writing, I decided to present the narratives as "Illuminated Manuscripts" or visual diaries. I used artifacts, documents, related imagery, and photographs in order to create yet another "portrait" — that of the monologue as well as the person who had performed it. The visual information on the page worked with the "verbal" facts to provide the reader with more information about the stories and their writers.

The decorative elements frame and augment the diary-style narratives. They complement the writing and provide an immediate, rich, and visual essence to the information presented. As I read through the illuminations again, I enjoyed revisiting the family photographs, letters, documents, and other personal historical visual information included. As I scrutinized them I realized that it is impossible to capture and portray direct experience but I felt that I had taken the reader on a journey close to it.

After reading through the manuscripts I went to the paintings. They were inspired by the themes that emerged from the narratives and from the conceptual scaffolds. They appear in the text in places that relate to theory, themes, and analyses. I had worked from the written material, as well as from my personal experiences, in a very complicated and reflexive process.

Doing the paintings, as well as the finished paintings themselves, clarified my thoughts about the data (by the spontaneous process of writing talking to image talking to writing).

After I had my fill of the visual I turned again to the beginning of the book. I smiled as I remembered that the creative writing and the poetry snuck up on me when I was not looking. The death of my grandmother (a complex, somewhat vicious, and extraordinary woman) was the catalyst for that epiphanic moment. It created a tsunami that had to be released and the emotions were so raw and so tumultuous they had to be liberated somehow. So, I started to write and could not stop.

This instinctive compulsion was a completely subjective experience. I remember that it was almost like the final stages of labour — you do not consciously realize that you want to push but your body takes over and you do it anyway. The writing was like this — it had an existence and character all of its own. At the time I had no idea what to do with it, thinking that I might be able to publish the story commercially in some form after I had completed my degree. It just had to come out of me, immediately.

After showing the story to some colleagues, and just after one of my family members withdrew from the study, it occurred to me that I should use this burgeoning memoir as another part of this ever evolving and expanding inquiry. Until that point, I had not considered using other arts forms and was intent on concentrating only on the visual. I felt that I was a visual artist, not a writer, and it had never occurred to me to embrace writing. Once I acknowledged that this too was part of myself, the words came out in a rush. Writing this way was challenging and daunting because I was such a novice — but it seemed to come effortlessly.

I went to Hungary with my parents. I recorded the events of this journey through photography, diary writing, and sketches in my art book. I collected artifacts and souvenirs. The experience of going to the country of my heritage with my parents was personally compelling. It was indeed life changing. When I returned home I decided that I could not present my family's stories in quite the same way. They were such unique experiences. They needed to be treated distinctively. The emotions were so intense that poems fell out of me as if a tap had been turned on. I was not, nor had I ever been, a poet but in the months after we returned my poetry writing was prolific.

The images that followed were not as satisfying. It was almost as if my grasp of the English language, my second language, was the medium that mattered most in this instance. The visual, with which I am so utterly comfortable, failed me somewhat. This was intensely ironic and quite bewildering. I, therefore, made the decision to let the creative urges be fulfilled (as if I ever had any choice in the matter). I had total faith in the artistic processes by this stage and believed that the artistic journey would guide the research journey. I was not disappointed. Once again my intuition and imagination lead me to the next leg of the journey. It was with my writing that I wandered into new and, for me, uncharted territories.

When I had almost finished the creative processes the dilemma of how to present all that I had produced was a considerable one. I knew that I did not want the original paintings and artworks to be assessed in isolation because they were integral to all the other texts I had created. The literature reviews, commentary, and theory were disrupted, enhanced, and related to the arts forms. It was true that the visual art needed to be able to stand alone as art but it was their function, as the products and tools of the research, that was the prime reason for their existence. It was at this time, when I had completed enough of the works to be able to contemplate these issues, that I discovered digital photography.

I do not believe in accidents or coincidences. And, in this case, the fates had led me to a curious place. Several of my Grade 12 students were intent on creating their final body of work for external assessment using digitally manipulated imagery. My students became my teachers. The barriers between student and teacher blurred as we worked on their projects. They shared their processes with me and I shared my analytical advice. My role became one of a critical friend — theirs of teacher. It was one of the most satisfying teaching and learning experiences in my life, the end result of which was that I developed the skills of digital image manipulation.

This was indeed a fortuitous development. It meant that the artwork could be photographed, manipulated, and presented in neat A4 format, suitable for presentation in a book. This also meant that my vision of creating an object d'art, that was also an object of research, would be realized.

The art works were therefore placed in the text in the appropriate places, so they fit almost seamlessly. They were now in a format that was easy to "read" and even though they were reproductions (with all the attendant issues) they were also interpretations of interpretations. This process added yet another layer to the information being presented. The book was now, indeed, an artistic and research portfolio.

I sat back from the table and stretched. My drink was finished, my eyes were gritty, and I realized it was now the early hours of the next morning. Nevertheless, feeling mentally stimulated, I took a few more moments to reflect upon the research journey.

My vigorous traveling companions had been the subjective partners of chance and serendipity, intuition, and imagination.

For balance, there was also hard work, discipline, and a vigilant self awareness. And yes, an "objective" posture was sometimes necessary so that I did not descend into solipsism. I had tried to portray the experiences so trustingly shared with me in authentic and respectful ways.

"Where to next?" I wondered silently as I wandered through the house, turning off all the lights. There were so many controversial issues to explore about the methods I had used. I knew that it would attract criticism from within the educational and artistic communities regarding the nature of art and the nature of research and these were debates that I wanted to be a part of. Rather than feeling as though my work was complete, I realized that I was at another border, and my next journey was only just beginning. It was these thoughts that filled my sleepy head as I climbed into bed. As my husband snored peacefully beside me, I realized that this was only a prelude.

There was so much more to learn.

Bibliography

Barone, T. E. (2001). *Touching eternity: The enduring outcomes of teaching.* New York, NY: Teachers College Press.

Barone, T., & Eisner, E. (1997). Arts-based educational research. In R. M. Jaeger (Ed.) *Complementary methods for research in education* (2nd Edition, pp. 73-99). Washington, DC: American Educational Research Association.

Bresler, L., & Davidson, J. (1995). Arts and knowledge: A discussion. *Educational Theory, 45*(1), 63-70.

Cutcher, A. (2004). *The Hungarian in Australia: A portfolio of belonging.* Unpublished doctoral thesis, University of Sydney, Sydney, Australia.

Diamond, C. T. P., & Mullen C. A. (Eds.). (1999). *The postmodern educator: Arts-based inquiries and teacher development.* New York, NY: Peter Lang.

Eisner, E. (1991). *The enlightened eye: Qualitative inquiry and the enhancement of educational practice.* New York, NY: Macmillan.

Finley, S., & Knowles, J. G. (1995). Researcher as artist / Artist as researcher. *Qualitative Inquiry, 1*(1), 110-142.

McNiff, S. (1998a). *Art based research.* London, UK: Jessica Kingsley.

McNiff, S. (1998b). *Trust the process: An artist's guide to letting go.* Boston, MA: Shambala.

Phillips, D. C. (1995). Art as research, Research as art. *Educational Theory, 45*(1), 71-84.

About the Author

ALEXANDRA CUTCHER is Head of Creative Arts, Banora Point High School, Far North Coast of New South Wales (NSW), Australia. She works part-time at Southern Cross University, Tweed Heads, Northern NSW and is a practicing artist. Her doctoral dissertation was awarded the NSW Institute for Educational Research's Award for Excellence in Educational Research. She lives a blissful life with her prince charming, their two duchesses, and a neurotic cat.

Alexandra's doctoral dissertation is entitled *The Hungarian in Australia: A Portfolio of Belonging.* It examines notions of belonging and alienation through the lens of the experiences of one post-war Hungarian migrant family in Australia. It is a postmodern research text, with multiple points of entry, that utilises the arts-based research methods of painting, printmaking, digital forms, creative writing, narrative, and poetry.

4. Performing Impossibility: Decolonizing Representation

by LYNN FELS, WARREN LINDS, AND KADI PURRU

> *Your dissertation speaks to performing the possible,*
> *what about performing the impossible?*
> — Ted Aoki, 1999

welcoming

As theatre / drama educators and emerging scholars we struggled to find ways to present our practices and lived experience of research. During the writing of our theses (Fels, 1999; Linds, 2001; Purru, 2003) we continuously confronted these questions:

- How do we identify, analyze, and document the complexities of theatre / drama education experiences performed in elusive spaces in-between presence and absence?
- What language might we use to perform our understanding on the page so that other researchers, educators, and scholars might be informed?
- How might performance as methodology, inquiry, and writing welcome new ways of knowing into the academy?

This is an exploration of rewriting the challenges of our theses struggles through a renewed journey. Our shared performative writing illuminates and frustrates as our E-mails flit between Vancouver, Burnaby, Regina, and Montreal. Three-way telephone conversations unravel stories, focus desires, expose raw nerves. We dare each other to a mentorship of working together that extends beyond our initial apprehensive steps as graduate students to this full textual embrace of remembering our thesis texts in concert, in dis/harmony, with hope and per/mission.

prologue: Rhapsciple rebels

> *Nor may they [rhapsodes] imitate the neighing*
> *of horses, the bellowing of bulls, the murmur of rivers*
> *and roll of the ocean, thunder, and all that sort of thing?*
> — Plato, *Republic, Book III*

ACADEMIURGE *(Academic Demiurge).*
A Platonic character, the deity and public magistrate who fashions the academic world.
     RHAPSCIPLE *(Rhapsodic Disciple)*
A rhapsodic character, a graduate student simultaneously passionate and in despair as she seeks recognition in the academic world.

39

RHAPSCIPLE: I am…alone on the stage. Under spot-
lights. I cannot see my audience, but I feel their expectations.
ACADEMIURG: Begin! What are you waiting for?
RHAPSCIPLE: I can't…. I don't know what to say.
ACADEMIURGE: Please, stop fooling around, how can you not
know what to say? We have taught you the Script and you have
rehearsed it conspicuously.
RHAPSCIPLE: I don't have the Script - I threw it away!
ACADEMIURGE: What??!!!
RHAPSCIPLE: *(mumbles)* I didn't like it, nothing
worked, it sounded obsolete…. I confess! *(throws herself
onto the knees)* I have lost faith in the Script!
ACADEMIURGE: *(in angry disbelief)* Are you crazy? You risk
your work of so many years, you abandon all our accepted princi-
ples and canons? Are you aware of what you have done? Don't you
want the applause of your honourable audience? Your actions will
have consequences…
RHAPSCIPLE: I cannot continue reciting the lines of the
Script anymore. Life has changed, I have changed…
ACADEMIURGE: Are you saying that you are abandoning the
Script?!
RHAPSCIPLE: *(with uncertainty)* I…i…i…want to per-
form…to be true… to…my own performance…
ACADEMIURGE: *(skeptically)* Good luck! Ha-ha-ha-haaaaaaaaa!

Although performative writing is gradually becoming recognized in the academy (Pelias, 2005; Pollock, 1998), particularly in
arts-based educational research and performance studies, it
remains a contested area. There are pained expressions and throats
anxiously cleared when new scholars write their theses against the
grain of conventional academic writing. Resistance plays out
among thesis supervisor, committee members, institution, and
graduate student. Ultimately, with permission, the practitioner /

researcher / graduate student decides how to perform his or her thesis through a process of inquiry and writing. Through encountering resistance, release, doubt, anticipated failure, and recognition of the impossible, new possibilities of engagement and learning open.

LYNN
I wanted to write a thesis that embodies integrity, presence, and resonance. I did not want to explain what happened…. I wanted to textually perform moments of learning that emerged from my performative work with my students.
WARREN
I wanted my written work to transform, reflect on, be consistent with, and deepen my understanding of the dramatic process I engaged in with others.
KADI
I dwell at the border between nations, "races", cultures, languages, disciplines, epistemologies, discourses, and wor(l)ds. As an im/migrant inquirer, I searched for a language conveying the tensions between settling in and being on the move, between home and away, between belonging and not belonging. My thesis engages "border writing", an attempt to decolonize dominant academic b/orders.
KADI WARREN LYNN
Our narrative is an invitation for scholars to shrug off the standard practice of the five chaptered thesis and to invite the reimagining of theses as narrative, autobiographical, performative texts of possibility and inquiry.
What learning emerges when form is challenged?
What happens to content?
 Think of a caged bird suddenly released…
 all that space, so many possibilities…
 do we dare to take flight?

reading: a back straight against the wall
(One day Lynn gives Warren her thesis proposal to read....)
I am used to skimming texts — sitting at the breakfast table, on
the bus, at the beach, or wherever. But this text asks me to pay
attention to it. I am sitting on the carpet of my father's townhouse
trying to read her proposal. Eventually I realize that I need to have
my back straight against a wall and engage my full body with this
text. Here is another way of writing that requires another way of
reading, a text that asks me to become part of a performance:

> *Let the moments speak their presence.*
> *And yet, they are elusive, like the wind that briefly sets clothes*
> *on a line*
> *   to dancing.*
> *Butterflies pinned, they lose their potential for flight.*
> *Phelan's suspension bridge momentarily*
> *announces presence and then abandons us*
> *with capricious indifference.*
> *We dance freeflight in remembered space, and*
> *recognize absence.*
> *Illumination is desperate, slipping in and out of view.*
> *And I am left with fragments of possibility.*
> *I suspect I am writing yet another version of breath-becoming*
> *knowing that is performative inquiry*
> *   pause*
> *   between this moment*
> *   of opening and closing*
> *opening*
> *   butterfly in flight.*

What language performs our knowing, our learning on the page?
Brings others into the performance? Languages the unlanguage-
able?

Performing Impossibility

how does one write breath?
capture elusive moments of transformation?
what language performs the impossible?

listening: windworn messenger
Lynn is stopped; the writing of her thesis eludes her. Six months pass. On the first day of the seventh month she attends a presentation by Quebec scholar, Jacques Daignault.

In his hands, between his toes, under his armpits, he carries notes. Notes spilling a haphazard path to the podium, notes in his pockets, his trouser cuffs, his socks, behind his ears, under his collar. Like a feather-tattered seagull windworn from travelling across an expanse of sky, he leans windworn against the podium, as if surprised to find himself momentarily grounded in the windless room where we sit, notebooks in hand.

He gestures at his papered vestments.

welcome words welcome characters welcome body emotion feelings welcome intertextuality welcome grace welcome the unknown

try to say nothing
listen
our text speaks
our text sounds our presence

welcome

She sits in the front row, wiping tears from her cheeks. She recognizes the landscape. With relief, she gathers the notes that drift to the ground, lost feathers of an unknown angel who wrestles Knowledge. She is not alone. This too is possible. The challenge of writing a thesis becomes one of writing a performative text that listens, interplays between absence and presence, and welcomes with grace the not yet known.

writing: bull in the pen
(Warren structures his thesis in the form of a drama workshop)
I need to describe a warm-up exercise. I recall experiencing *Bull in the Pen* (Sistren Theatre, 1987) which calls on participants to identify key social issues or "isms" that hem them in. As I write about this exercise, my fingers, shifting across time and space from present to past and back again, type.

Bull in the Pen come out   *Bull in the Pen come out*
A circle of people, hands linked, tightened, slowly circling. Surrounding one lonely person looking for a way out.

Bull in the Pen come out!

All of us **in** around the circle shout
                    Bull in the Pen come out!

                    What kind of Pen is this?
This bull, this person, feelings welling up inside, what is imprisoning me?
Bull in the Pen Bull in the Pen
        come out   *come out*
                Bull in the Pen
                                come out come out
What kind of Pen is this?
                    racism,
                    pain,
                    fear
                        (whatever comes forth).

KADI   un/belonging in English language and in this text
                             im/possibility of decolonizing writing.

KADI un/belonging in English language and in this text
im/possibility of decolonizing writing.
LYNN resistance
forbidden spaces.

In the Pen I try to marshal up my energy
Tears welling up in my eyes.
Now, and
Returning to a hurt on a playground, O those long years ago
I feel the energy
        to break the circle
                        to break free
      B u l l i n t h e P e n !
Are you Out?
      Are We?

performing: through form and destruction of form?
WARREN
At the end of a year of writing a thesis designed to bring the reader into the drama process, my co-supervisor said to me, "What do you think of what you have written?" This stopped me in my tracks.
KADI
Performative writing pays attention to form. Can form override the message, the substance of the text? Is this one of the dangers of performative text? What did your supervisor say was missing in your text?
WARREN
My interactive text was fine; the form was fine but, where, she asked, was Warren, drama facilitator, the person writing this thesis? Absent!
LYNN
Warren, your research project was facilitated through your pres-

ence! How could you, the facilitator / researcher / writer fail to
make a cameo appearance?
WARREN
Well, it did get me thinking because my immediate response was,
"But which me?" I wrote in response:

> Explorer, Mentor, Interrogator,
> Animateur, Provocateur,
> Difficultator,
> Instructor, Friend, Expert,
> Guide,
> Presenter, Planner, Sideline-
> Coaching or just along for the
> Ride?

LYNN
How does the identity and presence of the researcher interrupt,
influence, ignore, misconstrue, perform the text?
WARREN
That question took me into using masks to uncover more of my
work.
KADI
Masks? To masquerade…disguise. Why would you want to hide
your researching "self"?
WARREN
Masks didn't hide me. They became points of departure into
expressing different views of my "dynamic" self, distancing myself
from my practice yet exploring its familiarity. Why do you masquerade as Rhapsciple in our text?
KADI
I want to be in touch with my "true" feelings! Rhapsciple emerged
out of a moment of crisis. I abandoned three years of work in
comparative literature, transferred across disciplinary b/orders to
education where "alternative academic writing" was possible. My
feelings are those of an "outsider" in the culture of North

American scholarship. They are feelings of discontent and unbelonging which I cannot suppress even in conversations with my closest colleagues, friends like you. These feelings are not only rooted in my im/migrant condition they are also embedded in my home culture. My Estonian cultural memory is deeply wounded from more than seven hundred years of subjugation by German, Russian, and other European colonizing powers.

LYNN

Masks speak to the researcher / writer / performer who is not masquerading as an objective observer, but engaging as a living breathing snarling impulsive desiring performing poetic scholar.

KADI

Plato treated poets badly and threw them out from his Republic because he said, their creation "indulges the irrational nature" and "impairs the reason" (p. 36). He divorces "poetry" from "knowledge and truth" and submits non-rational impulses of life to the control of rational order. Isn't it time to bring rhapsodic poets-performers back to Academy? Rhapsciple, researcher-performer, subverts the logo-centric thinking dominating Western scholarship.

WARREN

Each different perspective co-mingled, contrasted, and added to the other, yet all of the masks are "me"! In writing *through* the masks, I responded to my supervisor's question and, simultaneously, extended and deepened the analysis of my text. Not only that, the masks created a performing text of multiple voices, multiple perspectives, interrupting the conventional thesis form.

LYNN

Sometimes we can get so caught up in the form that we forget its ethical complications. Think about performative writing in academia in terms of an etymological deciphering of per/form/ance: "through form and through the destruction of form" (Fels, 1998) we come to "action". It's the tension and interruption of form that matters as we seek new understanding. I think this interruption

47

has startled the academy.

KADI

Writing as a form of representation is also a way of knowing. That's why form is an important issue ideologically and epistemologically. Writing performatively allows me to search for ways to disrupt and decolonize the Western way of knowing and representing "other" wor(l)ds.

WARREN

Language, that is, writing, is not representing a world "out there" but, rather, is "an ongoing bringing forth of a world" (Maturana & Varela, 1992, p. 11). This emergence involves a disruption, through the action of writing *and* through reimagining forms of our taken-for-granted textual worlds. Writing brings us into contact with those thoughts, feelings, and intuitions we don't know we have. It is transformative because, as expression and exploration, writing brings us to an understanding that is beyond the writing (Merleau-Ponty, 1973).

KADI

Sounds perfect but here we are, still, in our Plato's cave, in a Western academic space of writing, attempting to deconstruct dominant academic forms through performance. How can we leave this cave? How can we undo the shadows of Platonic Forms that lurk even in the notion of per*form*ance? Do you think writing performative text is, in itself, a decolonizing action?

LYNN WARREN KADI

Striding confidently into unknown territory our first response is a giddy feeling of release, quickly followed by doubt, fear, and a desire to return to what was once known. It would be so easy to turn back, to return to the cave, blind to the light of possibility outside. Impossibility lies just one step beyond. Once taken, the desire to step outside the known form becomes irresistible.

epilogue: Rhapsciple surrenders
Eerie white deep cold hot cave. Ice and boiling water. Emptiness.
Enclosure.
Here is a place where I cower in a dream.

I can't climb back — the cave-slopes are steep and hard to grasp,
they slip away under my fingers. I can't swim — the water scalds
my skin. There is no place to secure my position — I take a step,
the snow melts and the ground disappears under my feet.
I have to acknowledge that I am here.
Entrapped in the stop point of ecstatic escape.
Enclosed in a place of no exit.
Loss of hope.
*Avoid*ance.
Death.
I am (in) a space of impossibility.
No possibility to continue with the "old" journey.
I surrender.

WHITENESS OF PAGE
EMPTINESS OF COMPUTER SCREEN
What are the possibilities of impossibility?

References
Aoki, T. (1999, March). *Question asked during doctoral defence of Lynn Fels*. University of British Columbia, Vancouver, BC.
Daignault, J. (1995, January). *Mixed autobiography or the acousmatic modality*. Paper presented at the Faculty of Education, University of British Columbia, Vancouver, BC.
Fels, L. (1998). In the wind, clothes dance on a line. *Journal of Curriculum Theory, 14*(1), 27-36.
Fels, L. (1999). *in the wind clothes dance on a line: performative inquiry as a research methodology*. Unpublished doctoral thesis,

University of British Columbia, Vancouver, BC, Canada.

Linds, W. (2001). *A journey in metaxis: Been, being, becoming, imag(in)ing drama facilitation.* Unpublished doctoral thesis, University of British Columbia, Vancouver, BC, Canada.

Maturana, H. R., & Varela, F. J. (1992). *The tree of knowledge: The biological roots of human understanding.* Boston, MA: Shambhala.

Merleau-Ponty, M. (1973). *The prose of the world* (Claude Lefort, Ed. & John O'Neill, Trans.). Evanston, IL: Northwestern University Press.

Pelias, R. J. (2005). Performative writing as scholarship: An apology, an argument, an anecdote. *Cultural Studies, Critical Methodologies. 5*(4), 415-424.

Plato. (n.d. / 1992). Republic. In Adams, H. (Ed.), *Critical theory since Plato* (pp. 18-38). Orlando, FL: Harcourt Brace Jovanovich College Publishers.

Pollock, D. (1998). Performing writing. In P. Phelan & J. Lane (Eds.), *The ends of performance* (pp. 73-103). New York, NY: New York University Press.

Purru, K. (2003). *Acknowledging home(s) and belonging(s): Border writing.* Unpublished doctoral thesis, University of British Columbia, Vancouver, BC, Canada.

Sistren Theatre (1987, June). *Bull in the pen.* Workshop activity, Regina, SK.

About the Authors
LYNN FELS is Assistant Professor of Education at Simon Fraser University. Her academic interests are located in performative inquiry as a research methodology, performative writing, and cross-curricular investigations in teacher education. Lynn Fels and George Belliveau's book *Exploring Curriculum: Performative Inquiry, Role Drama and Learning* was recently published by Pacific Education Press, Vancouver, B.C.

Lynn's doctoral thesis, *in the wind clothes dance on a line: performative inquiry as a research methodology,* conceptualizes performance as an action / site of learning and research. Through her experiences as a drama educator and readings of complexity theory and performance studies, Lynn articulates a research methodology that recognizes the learning and research possible through dramatic explorations. The thesis employs performative writing to illustrate the elusive moments of learning that "dance on the edge of chaos".

WARREN LINDS is an educator and community activist trained in methods of "Theatre of the Oppressed". He has worked in popular theatre and community education for the past 25 years. He is Assistant Professor in the Department of Applied Human Science at Concordia University, Montreal. Warren works with the Saskatchewan Association for Multicultural Education in the use of theatre techniques in developing leaders in anti-racist education in secondary and elementary schools.

Warren's doctoral thesis, *A Journey in Metaxis: Been, Being, Becoming, Imag(in)ing Drama Facilitation* explores the facilitation of drama workshops through an adaptation of "Theatre of the Oppressed", as he worked with high school students, teachers, and others in the community. He explored how knowing and meaning emerge through theatre and in the interplay between his life and work. Writing about this process enables the interpretation, interrogation and transformation of how one becomes facilitator, (re)writing / performing presence.

KADI PURRU was born in Tartu, Estonia. She studied theatre in St. Petersburg, Russia and taught theatre at the University of Valle, Cali, Colombia. Since 1991 she has lived in Vancouver. She is a Program Associate in Integrated Studies at Athabasca University. For her, an academic space is also a creative space to explore con-

51

tact-zones between cultures, languages, identities, and disciplines. Her academic work co-emerges with her community theatre work.

Kadi's doctoral thesis, *Acknowledging Home(s) and Belonging(s): Border Writing*, is a "homeward" journey through the discursive landscapes of nation, ethnicity, diaspora, and "race". An ethno-autographic inquiry, her research includes conversations with theorists, colleagues from different disciplinary backgrounds, and members of the Colombian and Estonian communities to which she belongs. Kadi constructs these conversations as borderzone art where a "third space" emerges. As an im/migrant inquiry the thesis intends to create an-other culture of scholarship.

5. Defying Templates to Honour Raging Grannies

by CAROLE ROY

My doctoral thesis, *The Raging Grannies: Meddlesome Crones, Humour, Daring, and Education* (Roy, 2003), is now quietly and serenely on the shelf but memories of its journey to light flood back. While seeking a form fitting the content I learned to live with a creative tension between uncertainty and excitement. Designing the thesis format was a challenge that led to an insight-ful process. Initially I could not envision how to translate the deeply fascinating and multidimensional women I worked with onto the flatness of a page. The form evolved through engagement with the material, countless reading and rereading, and through decisions big and small. Seemingly unrelated creative activities like painting, mask-making, and gardening were also significant, although invisible, parts of the thesis journey. The process required tolerance of ambiguity, doubt, and tension, as well as determination, passion, and the presence of others who, at times, seemed to know me better than I knew myself. It is a privilege to look back on that journey.

I have never taken design or art classes, yet, made a point to challenge myself throughout graduate school by creating unique documents and presentations, be it creating books with handmade paper and collage, or masks. These projects were my reward for producing the assignments. Yet, after years of seeking creative representations, I assumed that the final thesis would have to conform to "the" template, my only compromise to academic requirements. Thankfully, my supervisor encouraged me to think outside the usual format and stay true to myself and to the material. In search of form, I spent an eternity immersed in the vast world of fonts, lines, and borders, blindly searching for a path in the dark. What exactly was I looking for? I felt overwhelmed but had come too far to abandon the project so I struggled through. There were moments when it was difficult to believe it would ever take shape, partly due to the huge size of the document. I quickly rejected the standard 8.5 x 11 inch portrait page format for lack of visual space to work with and, after much reflection, also rejected the 11 x 17 inch format. While the latter provided the visual space I needed, I was concerned that it would be too much like a scrapbook and may be perceived as less serious or meaningful scholarship. I settled on the 11 x 14 inch landscape page format as it allowed sufficient visual space and permitted me to weave analysis, photographs, songs, and individual profiles of all women interviewed into a seamless text, not a series of groupings of similar elements.

Two conversations were particularly significant in the process of coming up with the unconventional thesis format. A crucial moment came with a mounting sense of crisis: What was I really trying to do? Independent by nature, it took a while to seek help. One morning I woke up thinking of an old friend who had studied graphic design and who lived half an hour drive away. Our one-hour visit turned out to be time well spent. I came with questions and puzzlement and quickly learned that I was intuitively using some simple design principles of contrast and alignment. I learned that visual cues communicate ideas to the reader through patterns. In my thesis representation music notes, for example, signal songs, a purple band indicates a short profile of an individual woman. I learned of three types of fonts appropriate for large documents, otherwise, the strain on the eyes can make readers angry without realizing why. Armed with the assurance that my questions were part of the process I could tolerate uncertainty and enjoy weaving 46 interviews, 36 profiles of individual women interviewed, 101 photographs, and 76 songs within the text. When my graphic design friend suggested that I leave wide margins, I voiced my concern over the length of my work and told her how I had to squeeze as much as possible in the least amount of pages otherwise I might have to cut, an exercise I did not relish. She then told me the story of her learning to write as a child.

Proud of her bold large letters she came home one day after the teacher said she had to write very small so as not to waste paper. Her mother replied that she should take all the space she needed and should not concern herself with making small letters as there was enough space in life to accommodate her. I had tears in my eyes. "Take all the space you need, it is your space, you are writing something important and you can take all the space you need," she said. She touched on a fundamental struggle with form and the thesis in general, that of un-apologetically claiming my space, on paper and in life as the Grannies in my research do.

Equally important was an earlier conversation with my thesis supervisor. As I lived 5,000 kilometres from the university, we had limited contact and distance increased my independent tendency. In the conversation following my first draft she told me of a dream she had in which I had found a publisher. While I did not take it literally, I believed that her dream meant that, somehow, I would make it through. At the time I felt a lifetime away from completion or publishing. This gave me a sense that it was only a matter of time. I would not have trusted it as much if it had been my dream. The other message from her dream was that I was on her mind and in spite of distance, silence and intermittent contact, the connection was alive. It was a measure of her wisdom to find such an intuitive way to communicate her presence so that I would trust: a dream. It echoed earlier experiences when my mother dreamt of me and knew how I was doing. Intuition has been an important aspect of my life, and it was meaningful that my thesis supervisor could be attuned to my need to such a degree that she perceived how I would best trust her message. That she never seemed worried and always seemed to assume that I would get it done was encouraging and soul fortifying. Within four months of this conversation I submitted my thesis and within seven months I had a publisher. One year later I was on a book tour. My work is in bookstores (Roy, 2004).

Only now, as I think about the process, do I realize how my choice of format reflects deeply held values. Over the years I found that over-abundance tends to diminish the value of each component and I did not want to group all photographs, or all profiles of individuals, or all the songs together in one part of the thesis. One constant orientation in my life has been a search for and enjoyment of diversity which is reflected in the design of the thesis by integrating these various elements together. Highlighting individuals and not losing sight of them while focusing on a group also reflects my view that we are both autonomous and interdependent. The words of my thesis supervisor regarding authenticity and congruence between form and content are taking on new meanings. Maybe a thesis is never totally complete as the learning goes far beyond the oral examination.

References

Roy, C. (2003). *The raging grannies: Meddlesome crones, humour, daring, and education*. Unpublished doctoral thesis, University of Toronto, Toronto, ON, Canada.

Roy, C. (2004). *The raging grannies: Wild hats, cheeky songs, and witty actions for a better world*. Montreal, QC: Black Rose Books.

About the Author

CAROLE ROY is Assistant Professor of Adult Education, Saint Francis Xavier University, Antigonish, Nova Scotia. She earned a PhD in Adult Education from the Ontario Institute for Studies in Education, University of Toronto. Her doctoral thesis was published in 2004 and received the Amelia Bloomer Award of the American Library Association in 2005. She is interested in social justice, creativity, women's collective resistance, and the contributions of older women activists.

Gathering the unique, at times moving, at times indignant, voices of the Raging Grannies across Canada, *The Raging Grannies: Meddlesome Crones, Humour, Daring, and Education* analyzes their unconventional approach to social responsibility and protests. From tears to laughter the Grannies share their motivations, their outrage at ecological destruction, unnecessary suffering inflicted by war, as well as their hope for the future by taking a stand — often unpredictable and brilliant by its humour.

6. Imaginative Energy:
Artistic and Autobiographical Dreams

by RENEE NORMAN

Rushing to Printing Services on one of those dark and rainy Vancouver days, I hurried to pick up my bound doctoral thesis. I had carefully arranged the copy: facing pages, double-sided writing.... But what was this? I stood there damp and dripping, flipping through pages that the helpful staff had carefully rearranged so they flowed in a normal manner. And so I took apart my words, turning the pages for rebinding, leaving small square window-holes raining down both sides of the text. Window-holes that seemed open to change and possibility, representative of a text that leaves room for more to come, in the white

spaces that always look empty but are ready at any moment, borrow-
ing from Hélène Cixous, "to burst into letters" (Cixous 1991, p. 44).

I completed *House of Mirrors: Performing Autobiograph(icall)y in
Language / Education*, in May, 1999. It is a hybrid text, and an
interdisciplinary one, housed in the Department of Language and
Literacy Education at the University of British Columbia (UBC)
but crossing over to other areas, particularly the Creative Writing
Department. The thesis is structured as a textual House of Mirrors
which examines autobiography in / as re-search and pedagogy
through performance and reflection, interweaving the strands of
my own poetic and narrative writing, other women's writings, and
autobiographical, feminist, and pedagogical theory in intertextual
ways.

Thinking retrospectively about the process of conceptualizing,
writing, re-writing, and justifying such a research text, I am
reminded of the philosophy of British drama educator Dorothy
Heathcote (1978). The struggle is the learning process. In working
differently in the academy and doing different work, there is a
sense that we are all feeling our way to a degree (pun intended).

It is not easy to work against the grain. The usual tensions get
tenser and new ones add sparks. Responses at times vary wildly. To
have a vision and hold to it, with / in these tensions, with / in this
wildness, is to maintain a sense of agency, and the conviction that
we each bring a wealth of prior lived experience and qualifications
to the process. Simply writing / being in a different step in the
hierarchy does not lessen who we are or what we have to offer.
The struggle is the learning process.

Dancing a Poem
i danced with children
in a carpeted classroom
the pain set aside for once

thoughts about imminent war
and stiff hips
trampled by playful steps
a winding changing throng
of circles
colleagues
and musicians
mothers
and lovers

this is education
at its finest
not foundation skills assessment
or political posturing
or meeting expectations for grade level
but joy
in its pure form
and passion
that fuels paintings and heartfelt words
dreams and poems
I knew I was working in an unorthodox way in re-search and writing when:
one of my committee members said: your academic writing is weak;
it took longer to write the abstract than it took to write the whole text;
I described my doctoral work to a lawyer / writer with whom I once worked at *The Vancouver Sun* and he said: "At UBC?"

I knew I was working differently when:
following a very tense committee meeting, I took my revisions to my supervisor, and he calmly said, "But it's still a House of Mirrors," and I said, "YES!";

one of the committee members wondered if I should include conclusions in what I called the exit, and I knew I did not have any.

I knew I was working against the grain when:
the chair at my oral examination handed me back the exam copy of my thesis and he had circled in red pen every single I and We in an autobiographical text;
the same chair wrote in the same red ink in the margin: "So why should we award you the highest degree for research?"

I knew I was writing in a different step when:
another doctoral student told me at the Xerox machine that in her doctoral seminar they had looked at my Table of Contents and compared it to the usual chapter arrangement.

How did I come to write a textual and performative thesis grounded in the literary arts?

I have been involved with the arts since I was a child: piano lessons, creative drama classes, speech arts…. The symphony, plays, choirs…. My middle-class parents knew at a deep level that the arts were important for their children, and they made sure to provide experiences that I still remember: Walking through imaginary woods as *Teddy Bears' Picnic* played, the dark shadows of trees not-really-there as real to me as the staccato notes that led the way…. When I began teaching, incorporating music and drama into my program seemed as natural as chalk on a chalkboard, and I have never wavered from my belief in the value of the arts in education.

So it seemed both possible and important to embark upon arts-based research when I returned to graduate school after the youngest of my three daughters turned two, first through a master's thesis and then a doctoral thesis.

Of course, back when I started, I did not yet know such work was called arts-based research. Those of us who wanted to work differently in academe chose what I called a creative approach. It was only when I started attending national and international conferences that I realized this approach had a name, not to mention several burgeoning and encouraging advocacy groups.

What I recall most is the overwhelming desire as a graduate student to do something meaningful to me, and in keeping with a newfound penchant for creative writing, breaking years of silence as a student, a teacher, a mother....

Painting with Your Tongue
what does it mean
when you see green and say orange?

that you're colour blind
that the synapses in your pop server
are not connected
that you were distracted by a fruit salad
that it was a Freudian peel
that your mind
was on the traffic in the right-hand lane
that there is too much green anyway
that as a poet you took poetic license
that you can't drive, talk, and chew colour
at the same time
that anyway orange
is just a redder shade of green
that you were painting with your tongue
you were talking with crayola
viewing the world through orange-coloured glasses
that you are losing your mind
losing your vision
losing words

losing green
trying to get everyone to take notice
that orange doesn't get its due
and after all, who decided green is green
and at least you realized what you'd said
at the red light
when you stopped screaming

Would such words circling in my head and eventually entered on
paper make possible the dreams that I held dear?

I wanted to write a thesis and a thesis that was creative, personal, meaningful. I wanted to focus on the importance of women's
lives and to do this by experimenting with text and research: A
text that wrote, constructed, and re-constructed the journey I am
still travelling; a research that recognized and revolutionized the
"I"s.

At the same time that more people took to arts-based representations in their theses it became more and more necessary to
defend such work. I have already referred to the challenging questions aggressively posed by the chair of my oral examination. I
answered all of these questions (and more), indeed receiving the
highest degree with little trouble, plus an award (The Distinguished Thesis Award from the Canadian Association for Curriculum
Studies) and eventually a book contract (Norman, 2001). But with
all this came another degree, the degree of suspicion such work
arouses in the academy — perhaps evident in the fact that I have
occasionally come close to a tenure track position but lost out to
candidates with more traditional research. And yet, I am still convinced that such research is not only worthwhile but is a vital way
of knowing and representing. I am convinced that it is through
arts-based research that questions that can be asked would otherwise never be acknowledged. I am convinced that such research represents knowledge and imagination in ways that help us "reshuf-

fle the composition of our world". Such research "generates an imaginative energy that emboldens us to venture down new paths" (Wyman 2004, p. 110).

How was my thesis developed as an artful form?

I considered autobiography autobiographically. So I read selected autobiographical writing by women as well as autobiography theory, writing autobiographically, and relating all of this to language and literacy education practice. I approached this work through an intertextual combination of these strands, using creative and postmodern writing strategies. I drew upon the zones of feminist thought, poststructuralism, literary criticism, and the hermeneutics of narrative and poetic interpretive inquiry moving between the spaces among them.

re-nee in the poem's pores
the poem
a breathing space: Cixous' *souffle*
trace the
mythico-poetico-theoretico
take a
       breath
in between the lines
être:
       to BrEathe
re-breathing the space
re-producing the re-adings
to live is to write
naître:
re-born through writing: *re-nee*
re-inscribing the theory
re-forming the poem
exhaling short gasps between airless words

deepening the gift: *le souffle*
a hot wind blowing on the neck
of my respiratory voice
      "renee"
invoking
sibilant puffs of air
      (renee)
bREathing the silences
that drift by
like cottonwood in spring
asthmatic matter
collected on the white page
      — renee —
an inhalator
the poem's pores opened
EXPLODING fire & air
re-flecting earth & water

suck the lips of muted mouths
until they bleed theory
shrieking words & silences
dripping the poem

   I envisioned my thesis as both conceptual and performative. How was autobiography re-configured when I considered the literature on the subject and my own experiences as an autobiographer and poet? How was autobiography performed by myself as a woman and a teacher and how might it be performed pedagogically in schools? How did the performance of my autobiographies relate to / change / deconstruct my re-visioning of what others have offered?

   But what was I to do with all the pieces of my thesis? How

would I present it? hang it all together? and yet still intentionally blur the boundaries between the creative and the academic, between the artistic and the scholarly in ways that interrogated and complicated what we do in the academy, in writing and research?

I had already seized upon Ted Aoki's (1994) theories about a discourse that was hybrid and metonymic and moved in the in-between. Della Pollack's (1998) work about performative writing also underscored the performative aspect of what I was hoping to accomplish. Writing turns. "After-texts, after turning itself inside out, writing turns again only to discover the pleasure and power of turning, of making not sense of meaning per-se but making writing perform…shaping, shifting, testing language" (p. 75).

As I examined my selves in all my many subject positions — teacher, writer, mother, among other roles — in the context of many living and textual others, I performed what I had written and, in so doing, turned the writing once again. Autobiographical writing can be turned over and over, looking back at itself reflexively. For example, I have written about an event in my life through poems, a scene, and an article published in a newspaper. Thus the event is both evoked and displaced. The form I choose changes the way the event is viewed, too. Even the same poem placed in different contexts, a turning over of sorts, causes us to re-read and re-think the writing.

But I was desperately seeking a structure. As so often happens in the arts, it was through an artistic experience that the structure for my thesis came to be. I was visiting a friend and, when she took a phone call, I sat at her piano and began sightreading *The Phantom of the Opera* music resting against the stand. Absorbed in this ornate music, and perhaps thinking of metaphors to do with appearance and image, I began to consider all the mirrors that were contained in my work.

I thought of all the mirrors I encountered in my reading and, surprisingly to me, in my own writing. Mirrors that could house the writing and reflect and refract what we think we see / find in writing autobiographically, both what is there and what is not there. The leitmotif of the mirror could connect and complicate the writing. André Gide's *mise-en-abyme* (Dällenbach, 1989), the mirror-within-a-mirror-within-a-mirror, would reflect exponential possibilities of meaning.

And the mirror, which is symbolic of the autobiographical I, is not only metaphoric but metonymic. Often the self (part of the selves) looking in the mirror is / are but a part of some imagined, reflected whole. The mirror reflects what is located near or opposite it, a contiguous association that is metonymic.

This led me to a textual House of Mirrors, which seemed to me a wonderful structure for writing that could be reflected and refracted back, that could be flipped and turned and turned again. I even positioned some of the writing so it was doubled, one side mirroring the other so that the writing, the meanings, turned. I also played graphically with framed pages that acted as paper mirrors that reflected back my musings.

My dreams of completing an arts-based thesis became reality, full of that "imaginative energy". Yann Martel (2001), in the Author's Note to *Life of Pi*, writes of how we must not "sacrifice our imagination on the altar of crude reality" in order not to "end up believing in nothing and having worthless dreams" (p. xi). With innovative and artistic work, our imaginations and our dreams live on.

References

Aoki, T. (1994). *Journalizing as writing /re-writing: Recovering and constituting /re-constituting meanings of lived experiences.* Unpublished manuscript, Canadian International College, North Vancouver, BC.

Cixous, H. (1991). *"Coming to writing" and other essays* (D. Jenson, Ed., & S. Cornell, D. Jenson, A. Liddle, & S. Sellers, Trans.). Cambridge, MA: Harvard University Press.

Dällenbach, L. (1989). *The mirror in the text* (J. Whiteley with E. Hughes, Trans.). Chicago, IL: University of Chicago Press.

Heathcote, D. (1978). Of these seeds becoming: Drama in education. In R. Baird Shuman (Ed.), *Educational drama for today's schools* (pp. 1-40). Metuchen, NJ: Scarecrow Press.

Martel, Y. (2001). *Life of Pi*. Toronto, ON: Vintage Canada.

Norman, R. (1995). *Writing and rewriting feminist and irreverent texts: Poetry, narrative, and life*. Unpublished master's thesis, University of British Columbia, Vancouver, BC, Canada.

Norman, R. (1999). *House of mirrors: Performing* autobiograph-*(icall)y in language / education*, Unpublished doctoral thesis, University of British Columbia, Vancouver, BC, Canada.

Norman, R. (2001). *House of mirrors: Performing autobiograph-(icall)y in language / education*. New York, NY: Peter Lang Inc.

Pollack, D. (1998). Performing writing. In P. Phelan, & J. Lane, (Eds.), *The ends of performance* (pp. 73-103). New York, NY: New York University Press.

Wyman, M. (2004). *The defiant imagination*. Vancouver, BC: Douglas & McIntyre.

About the Author

RENNE NORMAN is a teacher, poet and writer. Her doctoral thesis received the Distinguished Dissertation Award, Canadian Association for Curriculum Studies. Her poetry and stories have appeared in literary and academic journals and newspapers. Renee has taught courses at University of British Columbia and Saint Francis Xavier University. She teaches in a Fine Arts program in the Vancouver School District. Her interests include mothers and daughters, lifewriting, and arts education.

*House of Mirrors: Performing Autobiograph(icall)y in Language /
Education*, Renee's doctoral thesis, is a textual House of Mirrors. It
examines autobiography in / as re-search through performance and
reflection. It is presented through poetry, narrative, and theoro-
poetic ruminations on the literature and theory. Renee considers
the themes of writing, mothering, teaching by examining her self /
selves as writer, m(other), teacher, scholar, Jew, in the context of
textual and living others.

7. Jane and Pat Think and Do: A Basal Reader Story

by JANE BASKWILL AND PAT THOMPSON

Living Image (a poem in two voices)

Living Image

Shape shifter,

An Other-ness,

A strangeness with which to
become familiar,

Jane and Pat Think and Do

The mask breathes a life history of experiences into be-ing,
Imprinted upon their faces,
> *Faces that live without living,*

A life force that proclaims the presence of be-ing,
> *A shell that conceals and protects,*

Images emerge from inside,
Surprising,
> *Startling,*

Each mask mirrors a moment in time in the life of its creator,
> *(Re)-sculpted by fashion, design
> and social artifice,*

The many mental masks worn
Blend past experiences, current events and future dreams
> *Moving the wearer into Its
> domain,*

Towards discovery,
> *Struggling to shape features in
> ways remembered,*

A mirror that reveals and makes vulnerable,
> *As invisible as a child*

Masks come alive and speak for themselves.

This is Jane
   Making the decision to undertake a doctorate at the age of 50 was a huge one, in itself, let alone deciding to do it as a distance program offered by the University of South Australia. Once having

made the decision, however, the research began in a relatively conventional manner and a supervisor, whom I had never met, was brought on board.

I decided to interview women elementary school principals in Nova Scotia to ask the question "Is there room for the 'girls' in the 'boys' club?" In addition, as my reading progressed, I became very interested in research methodology and arts-informed approaches. My supervisor was not keen on this and E-mail, our sole method of communication, became tension filled. Nevertheless, 15 interviews were completed and I began to think about how to analyze and (re)present them. I was concerned about the vulnerability of the participants and maintaining their anonymity. As I started to experiment with aesthetic responses to my corpus of data, I created a *Mask of Administration* moulded from my own face using plaster of Paris bandaging material. It symbolized the participants' camouflaged identities in the research. They had to remain

Figure 1. Jane Baskwill, 2003. *The mask of the administrator.*

"faceless" so that my use of their words would not harm them. As the mask-as-metaphor took form I pursued the *art* of the mask and its power to visually (re)present the affective knowledge gathered during the interview process. As I listened to the audio recordings of the interviews visual images became clearer. I continued to create eight masks after the *Mask of Administration*, one for each of the women I worked with. Through the masks I was better able to explore the emotions of our relationships the forces, the pushes and pulls, and the participants themselves, in an otherwise faceless context. The masks were visual reminders for me that there was no absolute Truth.

My excitement with the arts-informed work was later dampened by my frustration with what I felt was my supervisor's lack of enthusiasm and outright misreading of what I had hoped to do. She focused solely on a few critical research incidents I had sent her and was determined to shape these into a scholarly dissertation — ignoring the mask-making altogether. My inability to articulate the murky design I was formulating and my supervisor's unwillingness to consider my art-making as either data or representation,

Figure 2. Jane Baskwill, 2003. *Eight masks*.

contributed to a rift that developed in response to a particular E-mail containing, I felt, caustic feedback. My enthusiastic beginning reached a discouraging impasse.

This is Pat

Jane was my first doctoral student. I was relatively confident about what constituted doctoral research and reasoned that supervision was a pedagogical relationship to which I could bring a repertoire of understandings and practices from which to build.

One of the added complications in the supervision relationship was that caused by distance. Most of our communication was to be by E-mail with the occasional visit. Pedagogical relationships are constructed from in-depth interpersonal understandings established in interactions which are more than simply verbal and much more than words on a page. This was not possible for us. We had to deal with more distantiated and impersonal means of negotiating "super-vision" — the disciplining gaze of the academy which I now personified.

A further complication was directly related to working with art forms where judgment about quality is based in scholarly-practical-professional trajectories with which only some educators are familiar. Jane was already a published author and I decided to leave the aesthetic evaluative work to her. If she had not been an accomplished writer, however, a different decision might have eventuated. I was able to avoid questions such as "Does arts-informed research have to be *good art*?" — a topic which continues to excite much debate.

Jane and Pat Meet —
Pat Helps Jane

Meeting Pat was a great comfort and relief. I felt immediately we had made an important connection. Pat was a former school administrator who would bring this experience to her understanding of my work and would also bring her knowledge of arts-informed methods. She shared her use of these in her own recent doctoral dissertation work. The most telling action on her part was when I brought out one of my masks for "show-and-tell". She asked me if she could photograph it. I was confident I had finally found someone who understood — or who was at least open to this work. I was buoyed by her response and energized by this newfound camaraderie and, yet, a bit overwhelmed by the questions Pat raised. At this point I immersed myself in making more masks, writing poetry, creating poetic transcriptions and a play representing my data analysis. Little did I realize the enormity of the task ahead or understand the full magnitude of the issues yet to be dealt with.

The most difficult part of doing a dissertation by distance is the communication. Although we had the one face-to-face meeting I did not have much information about my new supervisor to help me interpret her feedback. She was always positive but challenged me to think beyond the present. Pat sent articles she authored along with more readings. I would have been happy to have been left to my art but Pat had a knack of pulling my work back to the difficult theorization I would rather have avoided by saying repeatedly: "So, what *are* the theoretical underpinnings of your research?" Sometimes it was difficult to fathom just what the issue was with my wording / theorizing. I commented to another student in the program that I wished Pat would just tell me outright exactly what she wanted me to do. I found myself wrestling with the nuances of language / meaning trying to make it fit theoretical "rules". Meanings became multiple and murky. In addition, I also had to get used to the lingo — of the "field", of the "genre", and of Pat's Aussie slang (*Para* what? Beside? Beyond? Incorrect? Similar to? What am I supposed to think about this?).

Jane Writes and Writes and Writes —
Pat Worries

I was worried about the conservatism of the university in considering alternative dissertation forms. At the same time as beginning the conversation in the relevant Research Committee (something I did not tell Jane about), I also asked Jane to undertake a more conventional thematized data analysis while continuing to work with arts-informed analysis. I felt that although this was "doubling up" on analysis, it would reassure any university researcher / examiner that Jane was conversant with a wide range of qualitative methods. In E-mail conversation and face-to-face meetings we agreed that the final dissertation, whatever it was, would have to do double the work expected of a traditional doctoral degree. It would not only have to explain itself as feminist qualitative research that used standard data analytic techniques but also argue the case for arts-informed analysis and representation. Neither of us had any idea what this might look like. I did not know how far I, as a new faculty member, albeit a senior one, could push the rules. We both knew that what we were doing was without precedent in the university. While most doctoral candidates and their supervisors have many examples of completed dissertation texts to compare, we had none. We must, it seemed, invent the genre. It felt to me like a frightening but exhilarating journey into a high stakes unknown.

As Jane worked energetically to write stories, poems and make masks I became increasingly nervous. I did not want, however, to load Jane up with my concerns about potential examiners and the possibility that the university would just simply refuse to accept this work as research. This was my job to resolve.

While Jane wrote I met with key people in the university research administration to present the case for a different dissertation. Fortunately the university also had an art school and knew about research as artifacts. Because Jane was committed to the idea that all researchers should leave an "audit trail" — an explicit record of the conception of the project, the production and analysis of data, and the development of the aesthetic representations of findings — there was not going be the difficulty of arguing simply for the artifact: It was to be an artifact accompanied by its archive of production. I put the case to key research managers within the university that this would be research as an artifact and would also explicitly explain itself. It was a case I made over and over.

Look, Pat. Look at This!

There came a time in the research process when I came to a grinding halt. It seemed as if the dissertation would never be finished. The problem was finding a way to complete the dissertation that was not only in keeping with my convictions but that would also be "acceptable" to the evaluators and the university. It was at this critical juncture that Pat and I had another face-to-face in Halifax.

I had brought yet another draft with me. This time cleverly, I thought, it was laid out in the form of a *Director's Notebook*. It seemed like a perfect way to represent the research and all of its art-full components, one of which was the play script *Live Performance* (Baskwill, 2001). In the play I portrayed school bureaucracy and some of the individuals within it through humour and satire. I also blended the various forms of data analysis used, thus maintaining the participants' anonymity while using their actual words. The play was an intricate scripting of the numerous connections I had made during data analysis. The *Director's Notebook*, I felt, would enable me to show how various parts of the research process intersected with the script. I accomplished this by displaying the script in the centre of the page with columns to the left and right that contained the connections I had made to literature, poetic transcriptions, and contextual information. It had taken me a great deal of time and effort to format it in this way. I thought I had finally solved the problem of how to write up the research. This was a format that captured the multiple meanings, possibilities, and voices that were so much a part of the research process. Pat, however, was not so sure. I could hardly believe she was still concerned. Would there be no end to her questions?

Over the course of our lengthy meeting in Halifax, Pat summarized the situation by presenting me with three possible directions in which the research might go. I left the meeting deflated, depressed, and fearing I was just not up to completing the dissertation. As I drove the two hours back home, however, I played Pat's words over repeatedly in my mind. Two critical ideas became important catalysts that got me through this rough patch. The first was Pat's simple observation: "Too bad you can't stage the play." The second was one I embraced throughout the remainder of the research and even posted above my office computer: "This is *your* research."

Play, Jane, Play!

I continued to be worried about the research. It seemed little...somehow...something...somewhat unfinished. I could not put my finger on the cause of my unease. I was not confident that an examiner would consider it sufficient.

Jane meanwhile wrestled with how to format the play and its audit trail. Fortuitously, a face-to-face meeting made it possible for us to discuss what each of us saw as the problems. I offered Jane some alternative approaches to the dissertation. Among them I suggested: Why not sandwich the play in between more conventional writings about how it was produced and how the research participants responded to it? It seemed to me that if the research had evolved in thinking about how arts-informed research could best represent the everyday work of women principals, then getting feedback on the play was necessary.

I also became increasingly aware that the issue for Jane was about taking control of the research and staking her claim as a scholar. While she needed to use me for advice about university requirements, she was at the point where she had to stop doing "learner-researcher" mode and take on the scholar identity she had worked for.

Jane took up an idle comment I made about getting her play produced. She decided that the play would be performed and that the responses of the actors and audience would become the final stage of the research. This was a brave decision, I thought, and one that would round off the research. I was very pleased to get the video of the performance and watched it straight away. I must admit to some relief that not only was the play performed well it was also well received. I now felt quite confident that I could find the examiners and get the results that we needed.

Good Work Jane!

It was perhaps more a matter of serendipity that the play was performed. As it happened I mentioned Pat's comment to a colleague and expressed frustration over trying to find actors and a venue. I told her that I thought it would be "really neat" to have it performed by women principals and even better if there could be an audience of women principals. She said she knew just the venue and was sure she could find a director and actors from other principal colleagues. From there it seemed to take on a life of its own: video taping of the performance, live audience feedback, a cast party, and conference presentations.

I could see that Sachs' (2000) notion of the "activist professional" applied very much to my work as I had certainly been doing my bit in that regard. I came to understand that being a feminist, as well as an activist, in the conservative masculinist education system in Nova Scotia was important work to me as principal / leader / researcher / author / woman. From the feedback I received in

79

response to the play *Live Performance* (Baskwill, 2003), I was able to realize the important potential of this activist feminist educational leadership work. Most importantly I had been able to do research in such a way as to make a unique contribution to educational administration scholarship while adhering to my beliefs about how such knowledge could be ethically co-constructed.

After what seemed like an endless string of edits, along with a somewhat hectic time trying to actually have the dissertation bound (metric A4 paper, the standard in Australia, is not easy to come by in Nova Scotia, Canada. In the end it had to be shipped to Australia for binding!), my work was finally finished. The dissertation now contains a bound volume documenting the process and a matching sleeve containing the video of the performance and a CD Rom of artifacts.

Good Work Pat!

I spent a lot of time editing with Jane. I wanted to make sure that the first and third sections had some of the characteristics of academic writing. To Jane's frustration I insisted on signposting sentences — in this section I will…as flags to the examiners that Jane could not only do ordinary research writing but more as well. I fretted over how far this should go. I gave Jane's text to a colleague and asked her for her views. The answer was something of a relief, affirming my sense that there was sufficient in the text to now pass.

I was still concerned about one section of the dissertation but decided that there was no way that Jane could do any more, nor was it necessary that the text be perfect before being examined. Like Jane I also had to say that the dissertation had reached a point where enough was enough. What happened from then on was simply textual finessing, tying up loose ends, making sure that the argument was clear and as well supported as possible. A lot more fine editing went on before the final version was ready.

As it turned out the university had no difficulty with the unusual format of the dissertation. Perhaps this was because I had personally explained to the Director of Research the case for the dissertation. The university had been prepared to accept something that was different but sufficiently the same to fit into its definitions of acceptable contemporary research practice. The governing regulations at the university, however, have not been changed since, despite other students submitting work consisting of videos and paintings. These are acceptable "other" to the conventional dissertation "norm".

We chose the external examiners carefully from a very short list. One was a respected arts-informed research practitioner, the other a well known feminist researcher who I felt would respond well to the dissertation despite its non traditional approach. I was confident that the two examiners would treat the dissertation well.

This indeed was the case. Jane performed well. There was sufficient conventional research writing and analysis to satisfy the university requirements and sufficient scholartistry to satisfy Jane.

The End — Jane and Pat Speak with One Voice

One of the examiners commented, perhaps with some irritation / sadness, that it was a pity that scholartistry was deemed insufficient in its own right. We, however, had not been prepared to take this risk and were also not entirely in agreement with this view. In combining scholartistry and more conventional textual and methodological work, Jane demonstrated that she was expert in a number of research forms, not just one. She is also now able to advise other research students in a range of qualitative research approaches. And, we continue to ask ourselves what would have made this doctoral research — as opposed to a play developed out of interviews, a conventional mode of theatrical work — if the archive of the research had not been presented?

References

Baskwill, J. (2001). Performing our research and our work: Women principals on stage. In L. Neilsen, A. L. Cole, & J. G. Knowles (Eds.), *The art of writing inquiry* (pp. 132-158). Halifax, NS & Toronto, ON: Backalong Books & Centre for Arts-informed Inquiry.

Baskwill, J. (2003). *Women principals and their work: Is there room for the "girls" in the "boys" club?"* Unpublished doctoral disserta tion, University of South Australia, Adelaide, SA, Australia.

Sachs, J. (2000). The activist professional. *Journal of Educational Change, 1*(1), 77-95.

About the Authors

JANE BASKWILL is Assistant Professor, Faculty of Education, Mount Saint Vincent University, Nova Scotia. She is interested in arts-informed research methodology/ies especially as applied to gender and issues of power and control in the field of Educational Administration. She is researching family literacy and the literacy practices of fathers and male caregivers in relation to young children. Jane is also a playwright and a children's picture book author.

In *Women Principals and their Work: Is There Room for the "Girls' in the "Boys'" Club?* Jane describes the development of a process for "doing" educational research that speaks to feminist ethical issues around research and provides an alternative research methodology for exploring issues in educational administration. Using theater as metaphor and organizing construct she engages the reader / audience with the multiple ways in which the data was analyzed, re-presented, and shared.

PAT THOMPSON is Professor of Education and Director of Research in the School of Education, University of Nottingham, England. Her current research includes a national study of a school-based arts and creativity program, community arts programs for excluded young people, and everyday issues in school principal's work. Recent publications include *Helping Doctoral Students Write: Pedagogies for Supervision* (with Barbara Kamler, Routledge, 2006) and an edited collection, *Doing Visual Research with Young Children* (Routledge, 2008).

8. A Thought Per Day: Travelling Inside a Suitcase

by DARIA LOI

The art work opens up in its own way the Being of beings. This open-ing up, this de-concealing, i.e., the truth of beings, happens in the work. (Heidegger, 1971, p. 39)

Here are some scattered thoughts about my experiences during my arts-informed inquiry (Banks & Banks, 1998; Barone & Eisner, 1997; Eisner, 1997; Ellis & Bochner, 1996; Finley & Knowles, 1995; McNiff, 1998; Neilsen, Cole, & Knowles, 2001; Prosser, 1998; Watrin, 1999; Weber & Mitchell, 2004) which took the shape of a thesis-as-suitcase.[1] These scattered thoughts are congealed drops of my experiences in developing my doctoral thesis and do not serve in any way the purpose of explaining the content of my work. To know more about my thesis-as-suitcase, please refer to some of my publications[2] or, even better, enter the suitcase.[3] Although my background is in architecture and design my doctoral research was housed within a School of Management.

Thought #1 — A Neat Sound

Who would have imagined in 1998 that my doctoral degree would have become a suitcase? I was thinking while looking at a local manufacturer cutting cardboard for the main section of my thesis.

2004. *Crazy yet so obvious,* I was thinking. *Totally crazy,* I was told by some peers. Yet obvious — I could not imagine different ways of operating. While listening to the guillotine's neat sound

Figure 1. Daria Loi, 2004. *A Neat Sound.* Digital photograph.

on that black and grey cardboard, I was thinking about how my stumbling across art-informed inquiry changed my ways of looking at myself as a researcher and design practitioner. Finally, I was part of a community: supported, validated, empowered.

Thoughts of how I previously tried to fit my work into given parameters — a bound paper report — and in doing so I castrated what I intended to say. Thoughts of how the "discovery" of arts-informed inquiry allowed me not only to express my ideas in a form that was consistent with such ideas but also to re-engage with a part of me that had been asleep for long time as I was busy writing articles, chapters, papers. Using art and design to express and discover allow me to be myself as a practitioner within academic contexts.

I did not know about the existence of a tradition fostering, supporting, and validating a marriage between academic requirements and artistic inclinations. I did not know that I was allowed to discuss and share my research through an arts-informed doctoral thesis.

While the neat sound continues in the background, I think of how I started my thesis by developing ideas, speculations, theoretical concepts, and propositions to then *move* to their physical shape and representation. I think of how that *move* modified, in return, some of my initial ideas and propositions. A neat sound again — one side influenced the other in a constantly evolving loop.

Thought #2 — Question Marks

2001. Trying to explain to a committee about the shift in my inquiry. My incapacity to communicate my visions and their incapacity to understand what appears at odds with academic conventions. Thoughts of withdrawing and the support of critical friends[4] to go through a maybe typical doctoral degree crisis. Moving to a new disciplinary home for my research[5] — from design to management — and the beginning of a bothering question mark: *Why should I share my contribution to research by using an approach which is at odds with the nature of what I am discussing?*

My work is fundamentally an exploration of how to foster organizational spaces where collaborative activities can be undertaken. It is about collaborative practices, participation in design processes, and the active involvement of people. However, through my institution's regulations for doctoral theses I am required to articulate my work in a bound paper report — static, unparticipatory, detached, and ultimately closed ended. A question mark about the im/possibility of being consistent with my ideas starts occupying my head. *I cannot do this. I must be true to the knowledge I am about to share.* Then, a decision that changes everything: The thesis, as an artefact, will BE what the thesis discusses (collaboration platform), will ENABLE what the thesis promotes (collaborative practice), and will demonstrate IN ACTION what I have

Figure 2. Daria Loi, 2004. *Question Marks*, digital photograph.

developed (Playful Triggers, design tools to foster collaborative practices).

The notion of a thesis-as-suitcase then emerges, influenced by my need to reach a wide and diverse audience because "it seems foolish, at best, narcissistic and wholly self-absorbed, at worst, to spend months or years doing research that ends up not being read and not making a difference to anything but the author's career." (Richardson, 1997, p. 87)

My thesis-as-suitcase discusses ideas and portrays lived experiences in narrative and multisensorial manners, enabling a dialogue between researcher and reader, actively demonstrating issues discussed by the thesis, and respecting and mirroring the methods the research promotes. These were achieved using written content and non-textual elements that use metaphorical, tactile, audio, and visual means to express meaning. For instance, *illustration-objects* to show the reader how the tools discussed in the thesis look, feel and operate; *trigger-objects* to elicit readers' responses and create communication via interactive activities with both researcher and future readers; *CDs* to expand the thesis content by adding new appendix-like material; *found objects* included in anomalous contexts and linked with ambiguous material to foster curiosity and wondrous experiences; *game-like elements* with related tasks asking readers to play so they can reiterate issues discussed in the text; *sculptural elements* to amplify the thesis content and the experiences described in the text; *gifts to the reader* to generate a sense of bonding with the researcher and with future readers; *enabling-items* to assist readers in navigating through the thesis, and *ambiguous objects* that due to their ambiguity are left for readers to make sense.

Thought # 3 — Ticking Boxes
Back to the suitcase manufacturer. 2004. The thought of my first prototype and the reasons behind its construction feels like

the memories of someone I encountered in a movie. And, the irony of being asked to show a prototype of my suitcase because my written request to submit a doctoral thesis in an "alternative format" does not enable them to visualise what I intend to do.

2003. I enter a boardroom where the university's Higher Degree Committee is sitting around the table, waiting for my request, my reasons, my evidence, my vision. It is like ticking boxes. If the committee says yes, then a doctoral thesis can be submitted in an alternative format. If the number of words is the same as a "normal doctoral thesis" (90,000) then the thesis is a thesis. Ticking boxes. I start "the show" with my home-made prototype: They listen but do not seem to know what to do. What to tick. *Should this be a yes or a no?* They seem to wonder.

Conceptual artists lead us to question and leads us to question in the real, everyday world. The legacy of conceptual art is not a historical style but an ingrained habit of interrogation. It is in the

Figure 3. Daria Loi, 2004. *Ticking Boxes.* Digital photograph.

act of questioning that the subject, reader or viewer becomes himself or herself. Then, perhaps, we can determine whether our answer is "yes" or "no". Or perhaps, as in Tania Mouraud's 1978 project, when she stuck fifty-four identical posters on Paris billboards, it is "NI" — neither (Godfrey, 1998, p. 424).

In the end it is a yes with a BUT — the *but of accountability*. I am reminded that, if something goes wrong during the examination process, the responsibility is mine. The suitcase is ultimately a risk and I should be aware of the consequences. But I do not mind, I feel inside *this is right*, it is worth a risk. It is a decision between me and what tradition tells me I should be. I never liked ticking boxes.

Thought #4 — Lost in Translation

Dealing with the issue of translating. 2004. Translating my ways of seeing and doing to enable others to unfold ideas or to enable myself to go ahead (see thought #3). Translating my vision to help supervisors understand and support me. Translating my propositions to enable readers to access them. Translating for someone that cannot see.[6] Many things can be lost in translation and writing about experiences at times feels not enough. However, there are some reflections I can share.

One. Marry written texts and artefacts and be careful not to underestimate their relationships. It was challenging yet exciting to find ways to hyperlink the two within a non-virtual space, to help readers navigate content without compromising my message, to offer diverse ways to access ideas and empower readers rather than alienate them with one-way choices.

Two. Develop research within an interdisciplinary setting.... Many times I was asked to fit within one or another paradigm. *Should I? Can I? Where does my work fit in reality?* — asking questions while navigating the linguistic differences of the contexts I was operating within.

Three. Be part of a supportive community of practice. This

Figure 4. Daria Loi, 2004. *Lost in Translation?* Digital photograph.

type of work, when operating within institutions without a tradition in arts-informed inquiry, requires a higher dosage of energy, time, resistance, passion, and love. Rarely these are lonely operations. Dialogic inquiry (Cunningham, 1988) is a methodological way to operate that helped me.

Four. Deal with invasions. Some supervisors like one's work so much that they want to do it on one's behalf — conquer it. Instead of providing feedback to ensure the work is thorough and scholarly, they feel entitled to direct one's art. One supervisor[7] had the habit of asking me to modify my designs. She sounded excited about the opportunity to design my work on my behalf. Lacking any experience or training in art and design practice, she obviously felt entitled as my supervisor to influence my artistic directions, the physical "look and feel" of my work. Although such an enthusiasm can be filtered as flattering, I find such behaviours complex to reconcile. In these unfortunate circumstances a change of supervisor can be the only thing left to do. In my case the more I waited the more I was trapped by the feeling that experts were entitled to influence my artistic nature. It is not a *Nobel Prize but it is my thesis* I had to remind myself before changing that supervisor.

Five. Make things visible for my visually-impaired supervisor. What an experience for a designer, used to dealing with the visual world! Translating what I saw and made to a person that can touch and imagine. Renegotiating with myself what I thought I saw and made to then describe it. Knowing that those descriptions were my mere projections, not what another reader / viewer would see and describe. A truly formative process.

Thought #5 — Tricky Encounters

2003 and 2004. Days spent writing and nights spent printing, gluing, making, drawing, designing. As the vision of the work is clear, the propositions of the thesis evident and the contribution to the body of knowledge confirmed, my senior supervisor starts concentrating only on the written text — what is in words seems to be what really counts. A tricky encounter I could not anticipate. My arts-informed text is considered a progressive notion to cultivate and promote, yet not what constitutes the *real* thesis. A fissure between theory (who writes) and practice (who makes) starts emerging and suddenly there is no evident interest in addressing the relationships between text and non-text. *But isn't this space in-between a major aspect of this work? isn't this an arts-informed text? Shouldn't my suitcase have an internal consistency?* I often wondered in frustration. Cole and Knowles (2001) discuss a number of criteria that characterise scholartistic works, including the notion of holistic quality. *I must protect this aspect in my work*, I decide and to do so I find one compromise-solution: adopt two parallel approaches. I keep negotiating the written text with my supervisor while, on my own, I ensure the big picture (a marriage of textual and non-textual elements and the space between them) is coherent. Tricky encounters are great teachers — through this one I learn that those undertaking arts-informed inquiry understand all its facets *in practice* and are better suited to supervise arts-informed works.

Thought #6 — Experiencing and Reflecting

If I had to start again...2005. A part of the suitcase-journey is finished. I would not change anything of what I experienced, as each up and down made me what I am today and I like to believe I am a better practitioner now (*isn't this what a doctoral degree should ultimately be about?*). However, my learned lessons could help others find a comfortable platform where to develop *their own ways* of challenging traditional formats, generating, and dreaming of new ones.

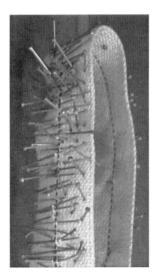

Figure 5. Daria Loi, 2004. *Tricky Encounters*. Digital photograph.

About Production

There are production issues, which might need upfront negotiation. *Funding* is necessary for materials, to develop exploratory and working prototypes and to manufacture the final pieces in multiple sets. *Extra time* might be necessary as, besides writing, data collection, and analysis there may be a lot of making, designing, building, and extra thinking / testing to structure the work so it is accessible. *Amount of required words*: when granted permission to develop my thesis in an alternative format, I was asked to produce the same amount of words as if it were a conventional doctoral thesis — 90,000 words. One of the comments that came back through my examination was that this was an inappropriate requirement due to the demonstrated amount of work associated

Figure 6. Daria Loi, 2004. *Experiencing and Reflecting.* Digital Photograph

with my arts-informed inquiry. Besides the irony of this situation, the number of words should be negotiated. *Balance between textual and non-textual elements*: How much can / should be said via non-textual means? *Copyright*[8] issues can substantially slow down one's work and they should be addressed as early as possible. Thesis copies: Aside from those required by the institution (three in my case), it could be a good idea to have two personal copies — one for filing and one for displaying / playing with.

About Accessibility

How a work is structured and how the reader is asked to relate to it are crucial. How much time and effort are readers required to properly access the work? How accessible is each component and how accessible should it be? What are the relationships among each section of the work?

About Freedom

How free should readers be when interacting with a work? Freedom can be embedded (or not) in a piece using structural strategies[9] designing the interactions among various elements, and through the life-span of the work.[10]

About Disciplinarity

The potentially diverse background of researcher, readers, and context of the research can represent an issue depending on how readers are asked to access the work, on what kind of disciplinary assumptions underpin the work, and on the ways in which readers will access it.

About Institutions

How open to arts-informed inquiry and supportive is the institution hosting the research? One might have to ask for permission to undertake an arts-informed thesis or could discover s/he is accountable if something goes wrong during the examination process. A supportive institution helps. However, if there is no such luxury but the work is worth believing in: persevere.

About Supervision

The development of an arts-informed text implies an amplification of what normally occurs when developing a traditional thesis as the work requires higher levels of risk-taking, creative awareness, sensitivity and skills, and a shared understanding of how the work might be shaped in practice. In regards to this, I often reflected on these questions: Do my supervisors have art and / or design capabilities? Are they aware of what arts-informed inquiry requires? Are they experienced in supervising such works? Can they ensure their taste and / or personal artistic orientations will not over influence my work? What is the risk level associated with supervising my thesis and can my supervisors provide consistent support within such a context? Will my supervisors *understand and support* my vision during the entire candidature? Can my supervisors and I ensure we share similar understandings around my work during my candidature?

About Examination

Depending on one's institutional context many questions can be asked with regards to examination. In my case, as I was not allowed to know who my examiners were,[11] I often asked myself: Are my examiners open to alternative thesis formats? Are they capable of accessing such formats? Do they have experience in examining theses articulated in alternative ways? And, are they in a position to access, relate to, and handle non-textual theses?

About Dissemination

I believe in the power of sharing one's work to make one's ideas significant and useful. To be honest, I personally found complex finding a balance between my vision and my capacity to disseminate it properly within academic and non-academic circles.

Surely, I can publish my work via conventional paths (conferences, journals, books), but the truth is that many aspects of my arts-informed text are lost in a process of translation between the actual work (a 13 kg medium sized cardboard suitcase carrying an enormous amount of artefacts and text and their relationships) and the space in which I have to fit it. I have not solved this riddle yet.

In the meantime, I travel with my suitcase to those who are curious enough. However, this path has a number of limitations due to the size of the work, the number of elements readers are asked to connect with, the time that each element requires to be unfolded and deeply appreciated, and the engagement required by the relationships between various elements.

As one of my examiners suggested, due to the *time-consuming nature associated with fully accessing the work*, my suitcase may receive *dubious access from academics* (there is simply not enough time in academia!) and it could be better suited *as a means of promoting collaborative design than communicating concepts and theories with scholars*. I tend to agree mostly with such an observation and I am currently exploring different ways of using my suitcase to promote collaborative practices.

Thought # 7 — Back to the Beginning

Of course, anomalous formats and arts-informed inquiry are not novel. However, most institutions seem not to be clear on their full potential nor equipped to facilitate them properly and postgraduate research is impacted due to a lack in the competencies necessary to supervise such activities.

In a previous publication (Loi, 2004) I suggested that a new generation of supervisors will emerge as the volume of completed arts-informed theses increases. I strongly believe that these people,

Figure 7. Daria Loi, 2004. *Back to the Beginning.* Digital photograph.

having experienced *on their skin* the process of developing their inquiry within arts-informed paradigms, will likely offer more suitable capabilities to those intending to undertake arts-informed research at postgraduate levels. While this trend becomes a consolidated reality, "supervisors and their relationships with postgraduate students intending to produce such works will require greater levels of engagement, patience, risk-taking, coordination, flexibility, and openness" (Loi, 2004).

Through my experience with the suitcase I found that there is a higher level of pressure associated with producing these works yet a higher level of pleasure and challenging engagement. I learned to pay more attention to the supervisory process as I often had to operate as a reassuring entity, foster dynamic supervision loops, translate my vision into a language that was accessible to my supervisors, and establish shared understandings with them.

Graduate students will, in cases such as mine, be likely to spend extra time in helping supervisors learn how to supervise them and in teaching themselves how to be supervised, how to be active participants within the supervisory process.

The Eighth Day Day — Final Thoughts

   End of 2005. I am about to participate to the official ceremony where I will be given the "piece of paper" that states I hold a Doctor of Philosophy. Looking back, I see experiences I would never have imagined or dreamed of in 1998 when I started. Looking back I see an incredible journey which helped shape the person I am today. Learned lessons (Thought #7), obstacles and decisions (Thought #2), tricky encounters (Thought #5), institutional requests (Thought #3), experiences which cannot be totally shared and should be lived to be totally appreciated (Thought #4), memories and discoveries (Thought #1), and questions to ask (Thought #6) all contributed to my final piece and my ongoing practice. I would not change one second of the time I spent travelling with my suitcase, regardless of challenges, doubts, and hiccups.

Figure 8. Daria Loi, 2005. *Final Thoughts*. Digital photograph.

How should I end these scattered thoughts of mine? If you are considering engaging in arts-informed inquiry I like to visualize you ending this reading with the reassurance that it will be an exciting, wondrous, challenging, and playful journey. It surely was for me. I now see you turning this last page with a smile, ready to travel.

In setting out…the traveller immediately confronts the problem of the map, an organization of the land according to a certain sense of space, and an evaluation of what is important. I travelled everywhere with maps, no one of which was ever entirely accurate. They were a projection of a wish that the space could be this well-organized. You cannot blame the maps, of course; nor can you travel without them…but I would be wary. Even a good map, one with the lines and symbols of a handwritten geography on it…masquerades as an authority. What we hold in our hands are but approximations of what is out there. Neatly folded simulacra (Lopez 1989, pp. 279-280 in Walck, 1996).

Notes
1. This project was undertaken at Royal Melbourne Institute of Technology (RMIT) University, Melbourne, Australia, where doctoral candidates can choose among two distinct options: Doctoral degree by Project (which outcome is a project coupled with an exegesis) and doctoral degree by Research Thesis (which outcome is a 90,000 words bound paper report). The work I discuss in this chapter belongs to the second category.
2. Loi, 2004, 2005, in press — available for download at http://www.darialoi.com
3. One copy of the suitcase is available at the Centre for Arts-informed Research at the University of Toronto and another at RMIT University in Melbourne, Australia.
4. In particular, I would like to thank Dr. Peter Burrows and Dr. Dominique Hes.

5. Due to government funding, at RMIT, doctoral research is normally housed in the department where the senior supervisor is employed. As my "communication" problems implied the need to change my senior supervisor and the department that was housing my research did not have any supervisory capability to support my work, I was forced to seek a new senior supervisor in another department and, then, move my research to such a place. Consequently, I started my doctoral program within the School of Architecture and Design to then developed and finished it in School of Management at the same university.

6. My senior supervisor is blind.

7. During my candidature I changed supervisors a few times.

8. Of images, videos, and other non-textual elements one might adopt or include.

9. For instance, one can provide various access-options to readers (as I did in my suitcase) or none. If you opt for the second option, I suggest you consider very carefully how such a decision can impact your examination process.

10. A bound book can last for a long time, while a thesis, which includes a range of artifacts, can potentially be torn and damaged more easily. Aging could be a key feature of one's work (my suitcase system is an example of this) or an issue to address.

11. In my institution the senior supervisor is in charge of selecting two examiners who do not know the work and do not know the candidate. A copy of the thesis is forwarded to each examiner who has a certain amount of time to review the work and then return a detailed report and related recommendation.

References

Banks, S. P., & Banks, A. (1998). *Fiction and social research: By ice or fire*. Walnut Creek, CA: AltaMira Press.

Barone, T., & Eisner, E. (1997). Arts-based educational research. In R. Jaeger (Ed.), *Complementary methods for research in educa-*

tion (2nd edition, pp. 73-99). Washington, DC: American Educational Research Association.

Cole, A. L., & Knowles, J. G. (2001). *Lives in context: The art of life history research*. Walnut Creek, CA: AltaMira Press.

Cunningham, I. (1988). Interactive holistic research: researching self-managed learning. In P. Reason (Ed.), *Human inquiry in action: Developments in new paradigm research* (pp. 163-181). London, UK: Sage Publications.

Eisner, E. W. (1997). The promise and perils of alternative forms of data representation. *Educational Researcher, 26*(6), 4-10.

Ellis, C., & Bochner, A. P. (1996). *Composing ethnography: Alternative forms of qualitative writing*. Walnut Creek, CA: AltaMira Press.

Finley, S., & Knowles, J. G. (1995). Researcher as artist / artist as researcher. *Qualitative Inquiry, 1*(1), 110-142.

Godfrey, T. (1998). *Conceptual art*. London, UK: Phaidon Press Limited.

Heidegger, M. (1971). *Poetry, language, thought* (A. Hofstadter, Trans.). New York, NY: Harper & Row.

Loi, D. (2004). A suitcase as a PhD…? Exploring the potential of travelling containers to articulate the multiple facets of a research thesis. Working Papers in Art and Design, 3, *The Role of the Artefact in Art and Design Research*. Available at http://www.herts.ac.uk/artdes1/research/papers/wpades/vol3/dlfull.html.

Loi, D. (2005). *Lavoretti per bimbi: Playful triggers as keys to foster collaborative practices and workspaces where people learn, wonder and play*. Unpublished doctoral thesis, Royal Melbourne Institute of Technology, Melbourne, Victoria, Australia.

Loi, D. (2005, April). *Open the suitcase: Readers as active partici pants*. Paper presented at the Include 2005, International Conference on Inclusive Design, Royal College of Art, London, UK.

Loi, D. (in press). Can this suitcase be a PhD thesis? Author, read
ers, academia, multisensorial writing, and the story of an anomalous thesis format. In J. Booth (Ed.), *I, we, it, they: Finding
voice in creative research*. Altona, Melbourne: Common Ground
Publishing.

McNiff, S. (1998). *Art-based research*. Philadelphia, PA: Jessica
Kingsley.

Neilsen, L., Cole, A. L., & Knowles, J. G. (Eds.). (2001). *The art
of writing inquiry*. Halifax, NS & Toronto, ON: Backalong
Books & Centre for Arts-informed Research.

Prosser, J. (Ed.). (1998). *Image-based research: A sourcebook for
qualitative researchers*. London, UK: Falmer Press.

Richardson, L. W. (1997). *Fields of play: Constructing an academic
life*. New Brunswick, NJ: Rutgers University Press.

Walck, C. L. (1996). Organizations as places: A metaphor for
change. *Journal of Organizational Change Management, 9*(6),
26-40.

Watrin, R. (1999). Art as research. *Canadian Review of Art
Education, 26*(2), 92-100.

Weber, S., & Mitchell, C. (2004). Visual artistic modes of representation for self-study. In J. Loughran, M. Hamilton, V.
LaBoskey, & T. Russel (Eds.), *International handbook of self-
study of teaching and teacher education practices*. Dordrecht,
Netherlands: Kluwer Press.

About the Author
DARIA LOI, PhD, is Research Scientist in the User Experience
Group at Intel Corporation. In the past she has worked as an
architect, designer, journalist, lecturer, and Senior Research Fellow.
Daria has run workshops and presented her work in Europe,
Australia, Canada, and the United States. Her practice revolves
around: Participatory Design, Practice-Based and Arts-Informed
Inquiry, Playful Triggers, Human Computer Interaction, post-dis-

ciplinarity, collaborative environments / practices, constructivist learning / teaching, Product-Service Systems, and Management Consulting (see, http://www.darialoi.com).

Daria's doctoral thesis, *Lavoretti per Bimbi*, is a collaborative platform, which involves readers / viewers in active relationships and co-authorship engagements. Participants are invited to enter the space delimited by a cardboard suitcase to explore, modify, play, touch, smell, listen, keep, place, and read on multimodal levels a range of "texts" — written pieces (postcards, letters, booklets, pamphlets, cards) and artifacts (illustration-objects, trigger-objects, CDs, found objects, game-like elements, sculptural elements, gifts to the visitors / viewers, enabling-items and ambiguous objects).

Method, Theory, and Process

9. Into Artfulness:
Being Grounded but Not Bounded

by PAULINE SAMESHIMA AND J. GARY KNOWLES

In this chapter we share some aspects of the mentorship and development of Pauline's doctoral thesis, *Seeing Red: A Pedagogy of Parallax* (Sameshima, 2006, 2007; see also Sameshima, Chapter 12 in this volume). Through this sharing we seek to incite thoughts on the complexities, complications and conversations of creating arts-informed work that is transformational in process and possibilities.

Seeking to provoke and open process imaginings further we intentionally situate the reader in an ungrounded space between the past and the present. This text emerges from current reflections on a telephone conversation between Pauline and Gary that took place two years before Pauline completed her thesis. At that point in time *Seeing Red* was, simply, a faintly flashing possibility. Also, in hopes of describing core arts-informed research processes — and as arts-informed research practitioners conscious of reader accessibility and communicability — we share elements of the transcribed telephone conversation. We organize the chapter in sections associated with researcher process, intentions, and authority.

Researcher Process
Pauline: What is arts-informed inquiry?

Gary: The researcher who employs arts-informed inquiry is grounded in a traditional social science research orientation. That means that the researcher has a solid grounding in a qualitative research method and has a sound knowledge of the processes associated with it. And, then, the researcher allows herself to become inspired by the arts — broadly defined — or an art form, or a particular artwork, or an artist. What invariably needs to occur is that the researcher be inspired to work differently. The researcher (who has the authority or assumes the authority) is not bound by rigid research protocols but knows that what makes sound, qualitative research is that which is mindfully and artfully developed. The researcher's ideas are enhanced by creative possibilities derived from the working knowledge of an artist, understandings of an art form, or artwork (perhaps uncovered by happenstance and its immediate application being obvious).

So the researcher becomes inspired by an artist, an art form, an artwork, or a circumstance and uses that inspiration to shape her inquiry (and, eventually, its representation). It could be through the use of photography, or visual art making, poetry, drama, or film or any other art form. It is by understanding the possibilities

108

of the processes that artists use that arts-informed research can begin. So the researcher finds ways to involve the artistic enterprise in her inquiry and works at developing a fairly unique process, a method of gathering and making sense of information that is compatible with and greatly enhances the possibilities of representation (or telling the research story). So the art form, or the art, influences process. I emphasize this understanding of artistic process (as employed in its myriad forms) because it is very central.

In order to communicate to others (perhaps broadly) what the researcher understands through the research process she draws on the inspirational art forms or artwork or artist and develops a way, or ways, to represent (or to show or tell) the researched-based understandings to the "world". So a key consideration is communication. It is important to present one's work in a way that is befitting the study and the topic, as well as the purposes and people involved and the processes employed. More important is the need to be serious about communicating one's research in ways that honour both the work and the audience. So the researcher needs to think about purpose and audience. While the thesis or research is informed by the arts it must ultimately address intellectual or other issues which make a contribution to a particular knowledge base. Further, what is "said" (or shown or performed) must be communicated in such a way that it offers possibilities for making a difference in people's lives (Cole & Knowles, 2001, 2008; Knowles & Cole, 2002, 2008).

Pauline: You mention that one must have a strong qualitative research background. To be involved in arts-informed inquiry don't you need to have an eye or some background in the arts to do the work?

Gary: A sound knowledge and comfort with one of the qualitative researching traditions is the fundamental starting point — as is a willingness to be inspired by the arts. If you do not have a background in the arts, you may develop a working knowledge. You may take courses in, for example, creative writing, or photography, or printmaking, or playwriting, depending on your inclinations, or you might work alongside an artist-mentor. You may have a strong interest in doing work informed by the arts but that does not mean that you must come to the researching process with all the skills associated with an art or art form. Of course, all the better if you have a grounding in an arts practice. It is not, however, about being an artist with a capital A.

Arts-informed research is not about having the qualifications of an artist before you can begin. It is about having the qualities that enable one to be innovative in an inquiry that rests in the arts. It is about being open to highly creative ways of being a researcher and practicing the craft of researching. It is about being inspired by the arts and about using the arts as a way of working and communicating. It is also knowing when you can access or tap into the knowledge or judgment or practice of a more experienced "artist" guide.

Arts-informed research needs to be highly presentable (to selected audiences according to the work's purpose) and be recognizable and have the authority of an art form. However, it is not the art form that is judged first; it is the quality of the research, the possibilities for influence. Ideally, in a perfect world, both are equal. It depends on the creativity energies and competencies of the individual doing the research.

Pauline's Reflection

Seeing Red contains 17 art pieces. Throughout the writing of the thesis I created artworks in various media as part of my learning. Art making initiated the written texts which accompany the visual art pieces in the thesis / book. It was often through art making that I came to understand readings and ideas. Ideas were also shaped by conversations with guests at various art exhibitions during this time. I remember well one particular exhibit at the

University of British Columbia's Alma Mata Society's gallery. It was an exhibition of some of the gallery's permanent collection with a few student works subversively hidden among the "great" works. This show was exciting because it represented a boundary crossing between educational research and renowned Canadian fine art.

Researcher Intention
Pauline: When providing space for thesis writers to find their own locations how do you find the balance between the tensions associated with guidance and support? How do you guide something for which there is no path to follow?

Gary: So much depends upon the strength of the relationship between supervisor and thesis researcher. I try to put my efforts into helping people imagine what their completed thesis might be like. Of course, this is assuming that they have a point of interest, a concept, or a preliminary mapping out of the direction of their work. I am not talking about the sometimes challenging task of helping a new researcher settle on a focus for her work. I am attentive to process and want to work closely with the researcher throughout but I am also interested in provoking inspiration for how the researcher might see the finished work. For me, having a vision of what the completed work may be like is very important. New researchers have to see that their work has a place and can be shared — and they need a purpose for doing that. I am not very good at talking about how I support thesis writers but I do try to have a deep mindfulness about the tasks of researching and the qualities and strengths that the new researcher brings to the task. I try to be open to change. I try to be open to surprise. I try to give appropriate feedback. Such feedback is not always possible (especially when it is obvious that a new researcher has to learn by trial and error) but I do try, although my guidance is fairly loose, as some would say.

111

Pauline's Reflection

In terms of mentorship, loose is a very good way to put it. In writing *Seeing Red*, I felt well supported by my committee Gary and Rita Irwin, and my co-supervisors, Anthony Clarke and Carl Leggo. I frequently spoke with them during their mentorship about my vision and intention but the text and how I envisioned completing it — based on my own authority to fulfill what I hoped to achieve — were completely up to me. I was "given" authority to be artful by my mentors and the research itself gained authority because the parts I gathered were grounded and supported by research and were attentively considered. To illustrate the idea of research gaining authority through process I share my experience of being introduced to and observing the process of Gordon Smith's art-making.

Gordon Smith is a well established, Vancouver-based, visual artist. At our first meeting Gordon showed me his studio, spoke about his work and the work of artists he admires and the works of those who influence him. He showed me in-progress pieces, photographs from which the works began and how he planned to morph his visions into the completed paintings. Gordon's work reflects a beauty that is full. The integrity, authority, and authenticity of the work are visible in the final product. These traits cannot be denied, hidden, or masqueraded. Through the multilayered "thickness" of the work's transparency (the artist being merged with the work's processes) I hear the resonance of the art calling. Roland Barthes (1981) calls this *punctum* — a cupid's arrow that shoots from the work and hits the heart even when you do not know what you feel or understand what you see. Punctum is created through a love for the work that honours the process and searches for a guiding quality that is in and beyond. This is the vision that Gary spoke about. Gordon's work has a fullness that is broad and quiet and wise that is not hasty or impulsive but grows and develops, gently unfolding. The work looks both simple and deeply complicated.

Pauline: You spoke about how you want arts-informed work to be transformative.

Gary: The work needs to transformative in the sense that it makes a difference, a dramatic influence on the person, or family, or community, or neighbourhood, or for whatever phenomenon is being studied. It must count for something. It must mean something. It must be something that has greater value than merely satisfying the researcher's interests. The potential for arts-informed work to inspire listeners, readers, and observers (that is, the various or singular audiences) is great. Arts-related works allow for hearts and minds and spirits to be engaged, to be moved.

Researcher Authority
Pauline: How do you justify or legitimate arts-informed research when people question it?

Gary: Let us say, for example, that your underlying research orientation is life history. The research method is grounded in sound, qualitative life history research so there is no need to justify that. You may have a feminist perspective, or a critical theorist perspective or whatever theoretical perspective that supports your research. Then you have an arts-informed perspective that adds another dimension or multiple dimensions to the core method and theoretical orientation. You have to be grounded in an intellectually sound research orientation. Once you have committed to that, it is about taking on the responsibility and authority to step outside of the box and think creatively about how you can gather the kinds of information that you need for your particular project, analyze that information, and develop creative representations of it (that is, all the while being informed by the arts). It is about not imposing boundaries on yourself but knowing where the intellectual boundaries might be.

Pauline: What do you mean by knowing where the boundaries might be?

Gary: It is having a certain savvy about the researching process. You develop different types of conversations and engage artfully in the process of gathering information so you become inspired and think outside of the traditional researching frameworks. In the case of arts-informed, life history work you think about it by maintaining an a awareness of the multiple (multi-sensory) ways to understand peoples' lives in context; you think about creative ways in which you can understand those lives by engaging in art-work, employing an art form or connecting to it, or through the inspiration of an artist or artwork. And you think about the creative possibilities of representing lives — making them come alive to an audience. You know you are stepping outside the box, crossing boundaries, when you actually do it.

Pauline's Reflection

Authority liberates the researcher to trust the process, to allow the research to unfold. In writing *Seeing Red* I focused on Heidegger and Rugg's view of the "meditative moment", "giving of oneself to concentration, a quiet waiting...for significant meaning to emerge and be known" (Rosario, 1988, p. 346). *Seeing Red* contains only about a third of the writings I created as data. I wrote intentionally about certain topics and, at other times, I wrote to record reflections on coursework and readings. Over time significant issues and foci emerged. From there I laid out the chapters and noted where and when I wanted a particular theme to surface. This organizational process is similar to the writing of this chapter. The questions did not have a significant order at the time of the conversation. They reflected issues I was wondering about. In writing this chapter the questions are clustered into three groups in an attempt to draw out pedagogical meaning.

Pauline: At the University of British Columbia there is a growing group of a/r/tographers, which seeks multilectical views and understandings among the constructs of being artists, researchers, and teachers (Irwin, 2004). From your vantage point, how does arts-informed inquiry differ from a/r/tography?

Gary: While I cannot speak for a/r/tographers this is how I see the differences. A/r/tography emphasizes the relationships between art making, researching and teaching while also emphasizing notions and practices of collaboration. As an arts-informed researcher I am not necessarily interested in teaching although, obviously, I am but considerations of teaching are not at the forefront of arts-informed inquiry. And I am not necessarily interested in collaborative work although I often collaborate and some of the best arts-informed research involves collaboration. Collaboration may be part of arts-informed inquiry but it is not something that is an essential element. Rather, it would be something that grows naturally out of the particular project.

In addition, I am not necessarily interested in emphasizing the art and the art making, per se. The art in arts-informed research, however, is always present. A/r/tographers express a central preoccupation with being artists and researchers and teachers, emphasizing the art making so that identifying oneself as being an artist is an important element. I, on the other hand, do not see the need for a researcher to consider herself an artist in order to do arts-informed research — although doing so, and having all the inherent skills, techniques, and knowledges associated with being an artist may well greatly enhance the work.

If the arts-informed researcher needs to develop facility with a particular art form in preparation for doing inquiry work then that is what they have to do (not an uncommon circumstance). And this may be an involved and evolving preoccupation. For me, the essential qualities for an arts-informed researcher include a particular artfulness in process and an artfulness in representation. That is, to have a willingness to be creative and be grounded in traditions but not be bounded by them. And there must be a commitment to making the work accessible to the audiences beyond academe. The differences between these two approaches are subtle yet quite profound in their own ways.

Pauline: Arts-informed research seems to be a pretty sophisticated method.

Gary: It is a method that is grounded in layers of possibilities. First the inspiration, then the grounding in a qualitative method (the order of awareness being interchangeable), then various theoretical overlays, followed by an overlay related to the arts (that is the arts-informed part). It is not necessarily sophisticated but it can be. You need to bring together all your powers and experiences to do this. Don't just think about researching as an intellectual scholarly endeavour. Think of it as an artistic and artful endeavour. Think of it as a relational endeavour. Think of it as an endeavour imbued with the responsibilities of developing convincing representations that may influence the public or whomever the audience may be.

Pauline's Reflection

Coming to an understanding of a/r/tography and arts-informed research and how they could each shape my work was a difficult process. I did not understand the differences between the two and I learned that I needed to take authority of my own meaning making. I understood arts-informed research as having three parts: to be provoked by something artful, which sparks the research; to gather the data in an innovative way; and to represent the research in such a way that it ignites further inquiry (or action). This cycle guided my research process. Within that process I was / am an a/r/tographer. I am an artist, researcher, and teacher.

I also find the need to clarify what I mean by the word "artist". People often assume I refer to *artist* as the profession of one who makes and sells visual art. The "a" in a/r/tography can refer to one who is a visual artist, dancer, poet, musician, and so on but, more often, for me the letter "a" refers to one who seeks to develop an artistry in teaching. This means that I gather ideas and work with collaborators from other fields and disciplines. As a researcher, I critically and artfully draw these people and ideas together to form something pedagogically new. Thus the "a" refers to the artfulness and creativity needed to develop the art of research and the art of teaching. So, for *Seeing Red* arts-informed research was the overall guiding process while a/r/tography guided me within that process. It is important to remember that arts-informed research is not specifically connected to the field of education while a/r/tography currently is. It is quite possible that as notions of a/r/tography develop, the "t" can expand itself from the classroom teacher to teachers of any skill or subject.

Pauline: Tell me about your conscious and unconscious pedagogy.

Gary: I am not sure what to say about it. I am not sure I can tell you. They are in part tacit understandings after all. My pedagogy is such that I try to honour the adult learner. I try to pose questions that are intellectually stimulating while offering creative implications. The primacy of experience is paramount. That is, experience is highly informative and has equal footing with the intellectual, the theoretical. I try to draw responses from new researchers so that they may honour their experiences and their innermost interests in their inquiry (see, Knowles, 2001). More importantly, I try to help people honour their convictions and assert themselves, assume responsibility, and take charge. It is about new researchers not backing down from their vision of possibilities, about not being subservient (particularly to a supervisor or another intellectual) but honouring their vision through creative connections with the arts. It is not about being differential but about claiming authority as a new scholar, an emerging scholar, a scholartist.

Conversation Closing
Pauline's Reflection

Looking back at the building blocks in the development of *Seeing Red*, I am drawn to two significant facets: Trust in the authority of time and process and incredible, privileged mentorship. *Seeing Red* deals with issues of truth. Truth is connected to time — questions and answers unfold. Worthy arts-informed work takes time to craft — not slow time but consistent, full, rich, and artfully connected time. I lived and breathed this work. And I breathed it with my mentors who did not hold my hand and guide me each step of the way but encouraged my authority to surface within the research process. Collectively they continually refocused me on my research intention. I created my own learning and from my mentors, I drew deeply from their stories, from their own works, and from the ways they live. This continual negotiation and renegotiation of self in relation to those close to us and those who shape our worlds challenges us to ask deep epistemological questions and to continually live our lives through a bildungsroman — a developmental journeying challenging conformity — and to research in ways that are grounded but not bounded.

References

Barthes, R. (1981). *Camera lucida: Reflections on photography* (R. Howard, Trans.). New York, NY: Hill & Wang.

Cole, A. L., & Knowles, J. G. (2001). Qualities of Inquiry. In L. Neilsen, A. L. Cole, & J. G. Knowles. Eds.), *The art of writing inquiry* (pp. 211-219). Halifax, NS & Toronto, ON: Backalong

Books & Centre for Arts-Informed Research.

Cole, A. L., & Knowles, J. G. (2008). Arts-informed research. In J. G. Knowles & A. L. Cole (Eds.), *Handbook of the arts in qualitative research: Perspectives, methodologies, examples, and issues* (pp. 55-70). Thousand Oaks, CA: Sage.

Irwin, R. L. (2004). a/r/tography: A metonymic métissage. In R. L. Irwin & A. de Cosson (Eds.), *A/r/tography: Rendering self through arts-based living inquiry* (pp. 27-38). Vancouver, BC: Pacific Educational Press.

Knowles, J. G. (2001). Wondering place, wondering pedagogy. In L. Neilsen, A. L Cole, & J. G. Knowles. (Eds.), *The art of writing inquiry* (pp. 89-99). Halifax, NS & Toronto, ON: Backalong Books & Centre for Arts-Informed Research.

Knowles, J. G., & Cole, A. L. (2002). Transforming research: Possibilities for arts- informed scholarship? In E. O'Sullivan, M. O'Conner, & A. Morrell (Eds.), *Expanding the boundaries of transformative learning* (pp. 199-214). New York, NY: Palgrave.

Knowles, J. G., & Cole, A. L. (Eds.). (2008). *Handbook of the arts in qualitative research: Perspectives, methodologies, examples, and issues*. Thousand Oaks, CA: Sage.

Rosario, J. (1988). Harold Rugg on how we came to know: A view of his aesthetics. In W. Pinar (Ed.), *Contemporary curriculum discourses* (pp. 343-358). Scottsdale, AZ: Gorsuch Scarisbrick.

Sameshima, P. (2006). *Seeing red: A pedagogy of parallax.* Unpublished doctoral thesis, University of British Columbia, Vancouver, BC.

Sameshima, P. (2007). *Seeing red — A pedagogy of parallax: An epistolary bildungsroman on artful scholarly inquiry.* Youngstown, NY: Cambria Press.

About the Authors

PAULINE SAMESHIMA is an Assistant Professor at Washington State University. Her creative writing, research, and art-making center on curriculum studies, teacher education, art education, educational leadership, and system organization. She is particularly interested in life-history, arts-informed research, a/r/tography, artful scholastic inquiry, and alternative forms of knowledge production.

Seeing Red: A Pedagogy of Parallax, Pauline's thesis, was published by Cambria Press and recognized with awards in curriculum studies, teacher education, and arts-based research. The work is made up of sent and unsent letters, poems, and art from a graduate student to the advisor she is in love with. The book is a mystery and love story which shares the process of thinking and living a/r/tographically while completing an arts-informed thesis.

J. GARY KNOWLES is Professor of Education and Co-director of the Centre for Arts-informed Research, Ontario Institute for Studies in Education of the University of Toronto. He teaches and writes about research methodologies, particularly life history and arts-informed research. Thus far in his career Gary has supervised 40 doctoral theses with half of them being arts-informed work. He is co-editor, with Ardra L. Cole, of the *Handbook of the Arts in Qualitative Research: Perspectives, Methodologies, Examples, & Issues* (Sage Publishing, 2008).

10. Researching Queer:
Showing, Telling, and Theorizing

by ANDRÉ P. GRACE AND KRISTOPHER WELLS

In this chapter we explore researching and producing a thesis as a reflexive, dialogic, and dynamic engagement involving *the supervisor and the graduate student*. In the spirit of Renato Rosaldo's (1989) research methodology aimed at producing insightfully nuanced and authentic research, we consider the supervisor and the graduate student as the researched as we position our researcher selves as cultural workers and scholartists. In relation to the thesis journey, this textured research involved continuously deliberating issues of researcher positionality and vested interests,

121

and how our dispositions — attitudes, values, and beliefs — and our contextual and relational locatedness in the world affect them. This discussion was vital. We see researching queer as an ethical and political commitment to be transgressive and transformative as we accept our social and cultural responsibilities in research as a situated scholarly and artistic practice.

Since queer is an historically fugitive category in the academy, our work is never easy. Researching queer has personal and political consequences that can hurt the researcher, especially in conservative university cultures where queer — the term we use to name and represent the spectrum of sex, sexual, and gender differences that mark humankind — still remains a moral and political relationship of power that is not broadly accepted, widely accommodated, nor unequivocally affirmed (Grace, Hill, Johnson, & Lewis, 2004; Grace & Wells, 2004).

Beginning the Thesis Journey:
Who Are We?

As supervisor (André) and graduate student (Kris) we began the thesis journey by exploring the dispositions, contexts, and relationships that shaped us individually and now mould us in new ways as the supervisor-graduate student relationship emerged. In keeping with key tenets of post-structuralism, which has been integral to the emergence of queer theory as a discourse focused on the fluid, multifaceted, and disenfranchised queer subject, we are each multiple and complex subjects whose identities are caught up in the identities of others (Grace & Hill, 2004). This belief infuses our reflexive, dialogic approach to researching queer, helping us to mediate the shifting research landscape, its tabooed terrain, and the uncharted territory that shaped this thesis journey. Sharing our narrative vignettes was integral to this open and unfixed approach. It informs our political and pedagogical task of researching queer to understand the dynamics of relationships, the ethics of respecting ourselves and our research participants, and the space and place of a queer research engagement that challenges the parameters of heteronormative assumptions.

André

I remember the first day I met Kris. He arrived at my office with many questions and the kind of persistence and insistence that marks a queer on fire. Kris knew what he wanted to study: queer students' lives and the mixture of hurt, tragedy, resistance, and resilience that variously marks them. He wanted to explore how queer students are caught up in an ongoing struggle for space and place in heteronormative schools which is part of a larger struggle for personhood and full citizenship in Canada. Having experienced institutionalized homophobia in schools, both as a student and a teacher, Kris wove caution with determination as he sought a university setting where his research would be accepted, accommodated, and affirmed.

As a new professor I wanted and needed to provide the kind of academic and cultural space and place that Kris desired. After spending 15 years as a closeted gay teacher in heterosexualizing Catholic schools, I had also searched for what was just and fair when I began doctoral studies at Dalhousie University, Halifax. Being closeted made me sick and tired. I needed to change that, so I was out, visible, and vocal from the beginning. I brought up queer issues in my coursework as well as in my teaching. Researching queer became a lived ambition during my doctoral studies. When I interviewed for my current position at the University of Alberta I kept my queer research and cultural work front and center. I wanted them to hire all of me, including the queer me.

The professorship provided me with an opportunity, which I consider a mission, to make a welcoming and collegial space and place for queer students and their research projects. In this milieu, queer researchers can be, become, and belong as they explore the spectrum of sex, sexual, and gender differences. They can engage in the cultural and political task of confronting the ignorance and fear that feed heterosexism and homophobia, all of which can engender violence. Kris is such a transgressive researcher and cultural worker.

Kris

The first time I met André was in the autumn of 1999 shortly after he arrived. I left teaching and five long years of hiding in the school closet. I was tired of living a double life. I longed to be an authentic teacher but the costs of homophobia were too high. I left the painful memories behind and wondered if I would ever return to the classroom (Wells, 2003a). After a year away from teaching I worked with queer youth in my local community. I felt valued and alive. In this informal learning setting, I found that I could be the proud and openly gay teacher that I had always wanted to be. I listened to the youth describe their school experiences (often characterized by narratives of exclusion, abuse, and harassment). Their narratives gave me a mission. In the spirit of Paulo Freire's (1998) notion of teachers as cultural workers I accepted my ethical obligation to do something to help make schools safer and more caring places.

With renewed energies I made appointments to visit with professors in the Faculty of Education. I told them about the kind of queer research that I wanted to do. Some were decidedly cautious and seemingly unreceptive. They highlighted what they perceived as the problems of doing queer research at a university in a politically and religiously conservative province. Door after door appeared closed. Then someone suggested a new professor. Later, when I knocked on his door, André was waiting to see me. He affirmed my proposed research and said the words I had been waiting to hear, "As far as I'm concerned, you can start tomorrow."

André and Kris

As we reflected on these and other vignettes we gained a sense of one another that helped us think through the issues of researching queer in order to transgress its status as a fugitive research culture. We came to see *showing, telling, and theorizing* as vital elements in our queer research engagement. As well, the narrative vignettes provided a springboard for discussing arts-informed research methods that might enhance the thesis journey. We were intrigued by Denzin and Lincoln's (2000) notion of qualitative research as an interpretive practice of "making sense of one's findings [that is] both artistic and political" (p. 23) affirming the researcher as scholartist. In making sense of our findings, however, we also wanted to affirm the integral role of theorizing in our reflexive, dialogic approach to researching queer. To keep theorizing as the guiding heart of our research strategy, we developed a transgressive research methodology that explored what Freire (1998) calls "the word and the world" in cultural and political ways that invigorate the thesis journey as an intellectual, artistic, and interpretive endeavor.

Researching Tabooed Terrain:
Finding a Way
Kris

My thesis, *Understanding Difference Differently: Sex-and-Gender OUTlaws in Alberta Schools* (Wells, 2003b), involves four queer young adults (17-22 years old). Drawing on queer theory and post-structural discourse I worked with André to develop an arts-informed research methodology, framed by multi-perspective theorizing, that kept queer subjectivities and positionalities at the centre. Specifically, I investigated how formal secondary and post-secondary educational environments socially, culturally, politically, and pedagogically construct (and thus marginalize) queer youth as sex, sexual, and gender OUTlaws.

125

In deliberations with André I explored a variety of arts-informed research methods that helped me to develop and employ a multifaceted research design, which included open-ended conversational interviews, narrative vignettes, found poetry, and visual narrative (photographic) techniques. Because of my experiences as a queer teacher, I also wanted to interweave my narrative vignettes throughout the thesis so I could create a multilayered text that constituted queer knowledge building as a political, pedagogical, and personal act. In articulating this research process, I emphasized the importance and value of integrating intellectually rigorous showing, telling, and theorizing with creativity in research methodology. This approach gives scholartistry sustenance and vitality.

André

I helped Kris develop an extensive bibliography that explored both multi-perspective theorizing, narrative, and visual inquiry as multifaceted ways to build knowledge of self and others in the intersection of the personal and the political. As Kris and I shared positional narratives and our interpretations of the literature we considered the importance of situating narrative within theory. We used theory as a lens to see our stories differently or in more complex ways. In this engagement narrative inquiry has an epistemic function, enabling access to social and cultural forms of knowledge from different subjectivities and positionalities (Enslin, Pendlebury, & Tjattas, 2001), where experience is problematized. As Pitt and Britzman (2003, p. 759) ask, "Where does one situate the event that is experience? In the past that is narrated or in the presence of interpretation?"

Conducting Textured and Multifaceted Research Inquiry:
Following Through
Kris

My thesis involved a polyphonic and multifaceted research strategy that enabled me to investigate and provide a textured account of the complex lives of the queer youth research participants and my own. This strategy challenged me to focus on the crystallization of experience. It moved me beyond a traditional emphasis on triangulation and the "fixing" or "securing" of research data (Richardson, 1998).

Following Richardson's premise, in the photographic inquiry component of my arts-informed research methodology, I provided research participants with disposable cameras to take pictures. I asked them to take photographs representing various aspects of their queer lives and formal and non-formal educational experiences. The participants used initial guiding themes as starting points from which they began to investigate and re-present their own uniquely situated educational experiences and identities.

Prior to beginning their photographic work, I carefully reviewed ethical considerations and responsibilities with each youth. As sex, sexual, and gender OUTlaws, queer persons often have to hide their queerness — being and acting queer — in order to maintain their safety, anonymity, and confidentiality. Knowing that these photographs would be utilized in my thesis (a public document) I asked the participants to take pictures of images, symbols, and objects, not of themselves.

In conversations about the images, the participants explored the images, symbols, and objects captured in their photographic representations. Importantly, as an integral part of this relational inquiry, the youth were given the opportunity to remove photographs that made them feel uncomfortable. I asked the youth to hold and touch their photographs as they talked about what they had created. I wanted to encourage them to develop a physical and emotional intimacy with their visual narratives. Moreover, I wanted the participants to become the story makers and storytellers of their own images and experiences.

In many ways these photographs composed a series of lived and historical biographies. These visual biographies — which in accordance with Pink (2001) construct a visual grammar — portray very intimate, emotional, and personal experiences and provided increasing folds, depth, and richness to the research process. It is in this texturing of the research process that showing, telling, and theorizing converge as research participants make meaning and sense of their experiences.

Creating these visual narratives was not always an easy task. While Alex — this and other names of participants are pseudonyms — took over 70 photographs, Jordana described how it took her over a year to take one role of film. There were times, during the course of the project, when she felt as though she could not take a picture. Kevin and Jamie opted not to take photographs at all. Instead they took the research in a new and revealing direction by creating collages of their experiences. The visual narratives which follow capture aspects of this reflexive, dialogic research engagement.

At one point Jordana, 19 years old, used the metaphor of a flower responding to light and darkness to reflect on issues of visibility versus hiding her lesbianism. She recounted,

I took pictures of a flower. One picture is of it in the morning when the flower is open and alive as it tries to adapt to the day. The other picture is at night when the flower is closed and adapting to the darkness. I just thought it was beautiful. It's red and red is my favorite colour. The flower is trying to adapt to day and night like we all do.... When you need energy you always open yourself up and you feel free and safe. When you are closed you feel kind of dark and scared. Everything is constantly changing and you have to learn how to adapt.... I'm like the open flower now. There is so much more that I am going to learn and be open to share, just like the flower. She is open to beauty, but also drawing energy from the sun. That's how I feel. I'm the red.

In another discussion Alex, 18 years old, used a photograph to reflect on his childhood experience on the school playground where he first confronted difference. He reflected,

This is where it all begins. This is where you find out who you are. You begin to develop your identity as a person.... On the playground I was the different one. I was Chinese. I've devel oped an identity that I'm different than everyone else.
I'm fine with that. I guess I found out that I create controversy wherever I go.

Both Jordana and Alex have unique stories but, at the same time, they contribute to a collective story marked not only by experiences of trauma and pain but also by moments of hope and resilience. These visual narratives ask the viewer to bear witness to the youth narratives, not with sentimentality or pity, but with the deliberate intention of sitting with, lingering, and revisiting these stories and images as a means of countering the fears and silences that exist in the daily experiences of queer youth in Alberta schools and communities.

By embracing arts-informed research methodologies I wove together a text that was both intensely personal and political. I wanted to move my readers beyond the written and visual texts and into the lived experiences of the participants. In the intertexts, between my thesis chapters, I explored my own story of what it meant to engage in scholartistry. I wanted readers to know of my lived experiences.

Figure 1. Jordana, 2003. *Flower Open*. Kodak disposable camera. 10 cm x 15 cm.

Figure 2. Jordana, 2003. *Flower Closed*. Kodak disposable camera. 10 cm x 15 cm.

Figure 3. Alex, 2003. *Playground*. Kodak disposable camera. 10 cm x 15 cm.

André

This new generation of queers heartens me. I love their increasing visibility, and focus on educating the larger community, and advocating for its queer constituents. Like this new generation I want people to really see the queer me, to really see all of me as whole, sufficient, caring, giving, involved. I want to be taken as I am, to be taken seriously. Some days I still get sick and tired but I recover more quickly now knowing that it's getting a little better every day.

André and Kris

Having experienced and embraced this thesis journey with all of its intellectual, experiential, and emotive elements, we can now look back on a reflexive and dialogic queer research experience that not only investigated other queer lives but also helped us to study our lives as queer-invested researchers and cultural workers. This experience situated the research as deeply personal and political cultural work aimed at moving queer forward in individual, social, cultural, and political contexts. The research took us beyond feeling fugitive and worrying about the consequences of doing this work in the academy as we linked scholartistry to education and advocacy. We are left ambitious. We want to continue showing, telling, and theorizing in our scholartist research so we can inform cultural work for social change.

References

Denzin, N. K., & Lincoln, Y. S. (2000). Introduction: The discipline and practice of qualitative research. In N. K. Denzin & Y. S. Lincoln (Eds.), *Handbook of qualitative research* (2nd edition, pp. 1-28). Thousand Oaks, CA: Sage Publications.

Enslin, P., Pendlebury, S., & Tjattas, M. (2001). Political inclusion, democratic empowerment and lifelong learning. In D. Aspin, J. Chapman, M. Hatton, & Y. Sawano (Eds.), *International handbook of lifelong learning* (pp. 61-78). Dordecht, The Netherlands: Kluwer Academic Publishers BV.

Freire, P. (1998). *Teachers as cultural workers: Letters to those who dare teach* (D. Macedo, D. Koike, & A. Oliveira, Trans.). Boulder, CO: Westview Press.

Grace, A. P., & Hill, R. J. (2004). Positioning Queer in adult education: Intervening in politics and praxis in North America. *Studies in the Education of Adults, 36*(2), 167-189.

Grace, A. P., Hill, R. J., Johnson, C. W., & Lewis, J. B. (2004). In other words: Queer voices / dissident subjectivities impelling social change. *International Journal of Qualitative Studies in Education, 17*(3), 301-323.

Grace, A. P., & Wells, K. (2004). Engaging sex-and-gender differences: Educational and cultural change initiatives in Alberta. In

J. McNinch & M. Cronin (Eds.), *I could not speak my heart: Education and social justice for gay and lesbian youth* (pp. 289-307). Regina, SK: Canadian Plains Research Centre, University of Regina.

Pink, S. (2001). *Visual ethnography: Images, media, and representation in research*. Thousand Oaks, CA: Sage Publications.

Pitt, A., & Britzman, D. (2003). Speculations on qualities of difficult knowledge in teaching and learning: An experiment in psychoanalytic research. *International Journal of Qualitative Studies in Education, 16*(6), 755-776.

Richardson, L. (1998). Writing: A method of inquiry. In N. K. Denzin & Y. S. Lincoln (Eds.), *Collecting and interpreting qualitative materials* (pp. 345-371). Thousand Oaks, CA: Sage Publications.

Rosaldo, R. (1989). *Culture and truth*. Boston, MA: Beacon Press.

Wells, K. (2003a). Where is the hope? In Canadian Teachers' Federation (CTF) & Elementary Teachers' Federation of Ontario (ETFO) (Eds.), *Seeing the rainbow: Teachers talk about bisexual, gay, lesbian, transgender, and two-spirited issues* (pp. 68-70). Ottawa, ON: CTF & ETFO.

Wells, K. (2003b). *Understanding difference differently: Sex-and-gender OUTlaws in Alberta schools*. Unpublished Master's thesis, University of Alberta, Edmonton, AB, Canada.

About the Authors

ANDRÉ P. GRACE is a professor who works in educational policy studies and inclusive education at the University of Alberta. He initiated AGAPE, an action group in the Faculty of Education that focuses on sex, sexual, and gender differences in education and culture. He is currently conducting a national study of welfare-and-work issues for lesbian, gay, bisexual, trans-identified, queer (LGBTQ) teachers in Canadian schools, funded by The Social Sciences and Humanities Research Council of Canada.

KRISTOPHER WELLS is a Killam Scholar and a Social Sciences and Humanities Research Council of Canada Graduate Scholar in the Department of Educational Policy Studies, Faculty of Education, University of Alberta. His research, teaching, and service work focus on creating safe, caring, and inclusive schools and communities for lesbian, gay, bisexual, trans-identified, queer (LGBTQ) students and teachers. Kris is also a facilitator for *Youth Understanding Youth*, a social / support group for LGBTQ youth in Edmonton.

Kristopher's Master's degree thesis is entitled, *Understanding Difference Differently: Sex-and-Gender OUTlaws in Alberta Schools.* He employed a multifaceted research design that included open-ended interviews, narrative vignettes, found poetry, and visual narrative (photographic) techniques. Working with four queer youth he investigated how formal secondary and postsecondary educational environments construct queer youth as sex, sexual, and gender OUTlaws. He also examined how youth create spaces and languages of resistance in non-formal learning contexts.

11. Created Worlds and Crumbled Universes

by MORNA MCDERMOTT

Looking Back
Is it that I can't recall or that I won't recall
When is memory selective?
There is no linear tracing of breadcrumbs I can follow back to find
the way through the maze that I travelled.
Like collage itself, my recollections are patched together
Moving, like a worn out and watercoloured slide show
Less like a movie
that succinctly links together plot, character, and setting

Setting was plot, and characters were...fluid
Shattered and sparkling. (Personal Journal, August 2005)

   In this chapter I explore the ways that thinking and being collide, explode, and emerge, like the birth of a star, to create an arts-informed research study. But, more than that, this chapter has become my confessional. I want to tell a story I have never told out loud, publicly, and openly. Like the process of doing my dissertation work itself, the reflection on my work, the telling of it here, is a "dangerous thing". The idea of doing a "dangerous thing" for me was inspired by the words of Charles Bukowski. He suggests in the film *Tales of Ordinary Madness* (1999) that "to do a dangerous thing with style is...art." Style is a way of doing something, and so it was an emergent "style" that gave form to my dissertation theory, shaped by breadcrumbs of desire emerging from passionate moments. After all, I wanted it to feel dangerous. I wanted the artistic act to be passionate. We act passionately when we act dangerously.
   My motto is: *When in doubt write honestly. Tear it open, let it bleed.* In order to tear it open in this chapter I collage together words and images that span across years and locations. I want to "map" or re-trace my steps in the journey to performing an arts-informed dissertation. The collaged "passion pieces" included here are both academic and personal. They serve as breadcrumbs I use so as not get lost along the way. Being honest, I am afraid to go back and I do not know how to move forward. In arts-informed inquiry, as in the experience of living, the end is always the beginning. Like Uroboros, the mythical snake eating its own tail, we emerge, transform, spiral, dance, and continue.

Collaging a Framework
   I believe that life events past, present, and future produce a kaleidoscopic lens through which we construct, disrupt, define,

and embody notions of "self", "reality", and "truth". These concepts are collaged together, overlapping, layering, blurring, and rupturing linear notions of time and space. Susan Finley (1998), exploring her own research process, reflects that "[her] research text is intended as a forum, a place for multiple voices to articulate their experiences, to define their situations" (p. 5). Such situations are shaped not only by our professional lives but also by "personal space of home, church, and other social entities, as well as in the life long course of the personal history of the individual" (p. 5).

For years prior to writing my dissertation I kept journals in which I copied, drew, or cut-and-pasted words, especially from the *Sunday New York Times,* that struck me as interesting even though at times my posting seemed random. But as I journalled I imagined other ways of thinking and, perhaps, for creating a research study. I found myself "playing with" possible modes of representation, using images and words, and challenging traditional ways of knowing.

At the time I did not realize that I was constructing the layers of my dissertation process. The journey itself emerged, much

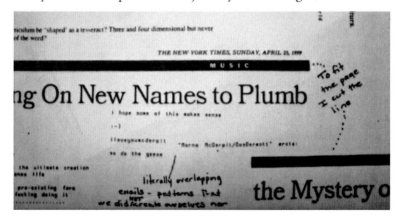

Figure 1. Morna McDermott, 1999. *New York Times Collage.* Mixed media on paper. 20.32 x 25.4 cm.

through chance, serendipity, and creative nonlinear connections that forged unexpected meanings. What I realize now is that the "roots" (or is it rhizomes?) of my dissertation journey began long before I knew it. As Springgay (2004), drawing on Deleuze and Guatarri (1987), remarks:

> Arts-based educational research un/folds possibilities of engaging with research that is open and full of excess. It embodies a powerful linkage between signs, reminding us at the same time that there is no uniformity to patterns of suggestions, there is no point of origin, there are only rhizomatic spaces or folds. (p. 13)

The three guiding principals of the theoretical framework of my dissertation, *collaboration, emergence, and transformation —* were born from my own lived experiences. The central focus of my research involved having preservice teachers create collages to represent how they constructed their identities as teachers. Collaging one's experiences illustrates the elements of *collaboration, emergence, and transformation,* leading to alternative ways of knowing and seeing self and the world. These three elements seemingly had nothing to do with the research itself — unless. of course, you believe in the power of synchronicity.

An arts-informed inquiry process requires complete immersion of the whole being: knowledges, feelings, memories, hopes, and fears. Rather than maintaining a stance of so-called objectivity "it is learning which engages the passions and imagination in which [to quote Dewey] the individual 'does not remain a cold spectator'" (Davis, 1997, p. 287). When we "do" inquiry with a passion spines tingle, hearts race and, immersed in the moment, senses are heightened.

I also found myself immersed in examples of post-modern arts-based scholars including Slattery (1995, 1999); jagodinski (1992,

1997); Finley (1998); Mullen and Diamond (1999), and Butler-Kisber and Davis (1999), to name a few. According to Mullen and Diamond (1999), in aesthetic forms of research "data are not so much collected, as meanings shared and reconstructed" (p. 2). When seen from a postmodern perspective language is fragmented "pieces" of multiply constructed meanings (collages?). Rather than being fixed and finite, language and meaning making constructed in "pieces" leave spaces open for alternative discourses. Every theory, paper, poem, or essay I read, crept its way into my views of self and the world. My academic experiences began to forge cracks in the world I had known and led me to leave that life. I did not just "know" such artistic and postmodern theories, I was living them. They were me.

> *Caution — Objects in the Rear View May Be Closer than they Appear*
> It's 2 AM and I'm still awake, writing a song
> If I get it all down on paper, it's no longer
> inside of me, threatening the life it belongs to
> And I feel like I'm naked in front of the crowd
> 'Cause these words are my diary, screaming out loud
> And I know that you'll use them, however you want to
> (Nalick, 2005, n.p.)

The theoretical foundation for the dissertation was grounded in "passions" — passion for a particular person, as well as for life, for art, for teaching, and the desire for "meaning".

> To: Toby
> writing in fits cause don't wanna get disconnected
> thinking of how we began collage
> it began us actually
> when everything around me began to collide and rupture

constant synchronicity which showed me wonder
you showed me wonder
i remember saying "i am seeing vampires everywhere!"
first Email...how true.
(Email, December 3, 1999)

Looking back now I wonder to what extent my scholarly work was really emotional work. Scholarly creations are not merely born out of intellectual practices, and the lines between personal and private often blur, shaping "our ability to engage the possibilities offered by our experience which constantly shapes and reshapes the work we do" (Robbins, in McNiff, 1998, p. 106). After all, Bukowski (1999) contends that even "loving can be an art".

To: Toby
hi cajun fishing boy
i said it before
there are two philosophical approaches to life
one begins with doubt
the other with wonder
i choose wonder
i choose us

you will continue to amaze me everyday of our life
i know that
i believe that
i SEE that.
(Email, July 28, 1999)

August, 2004. Subconscious thought [enter stage right]: *Maybe you don't have a coherent "style". Maybe the whole thing was a farce and you indeed are an imposter. If you write this chapter you will be discovered.*

The journey back appears more like a vast sea rather than a land-locked road defined by concrete pathways:

Waves of experience continuously shape the contours of mind and being, leaving remnants like sea glass and dissolving foam to hang scattered along the shoreline of my awareness. I selectively gather them in the palm of my hand to bring home and arrange them so that I may look to them and recall, to re-create and to know. (Personal Journal, March 14, 2000)

In that metaphoric sea, from the passage above, I saw endless memories of events and thoughts all that contributed to the dissertation journey. To understand why I chose collage and the process I underwent in creating the work is to understand how my scholarship was directly intertwined with a personal relationship during the time I began doctoral studies. I cannot reflect on one without exhuming the other. Both were born from bone and blood. Our life together for those few years was a collage. How could I envision my own writing and research through any other life-scape than the one I was living?

Collaboration: Beginning from the Bone

Art is a system of encounters, inter-subjectivities…. It advocates an intercorporeal relationality, a way of knowing (that is)…redolent with sensuous knowledge, full of ecstasy and excess. It speaks the language of images and words, smells and textures, sights and sounds…. It cultivates breath. (Springgay, 2004, p. 15)

When I began doctoral studies I felt like I was on fire, feeling alive in a way I had not for a very long time. And then, in Dewey and Eros fashion, I found the passion for knowledge became a passion for a person. *Or was it the other way around?*

We met at Bergamo, 1998. It was something about his eyes. Or was it the conference presentation he gave? Or both? A dangerous combination. After that first meeting Toby and I exchanged quotes, poems, images, sultry words of longing.

> To: Toby
> curriculum is:
> Passion pieces about people and places that were just moseying down the street one day, minding their own business, when suddenly and almost spontaneously they caught fire ending up by days end, somewhere altogether different from where they'd imagine they were setting out this morning. (Wescheler, 1999 quoted in Lord, p. 21)

> ...Made me think of dichotomy / synchronicity...both visual art terms in making reference to meaning.... how we compose our realities...that somewhere between memory (the past) and dreams (the future) we create some kaleidoscope image of the present. (Email, July 29, 1999)

At first, the relationship was long distance. I was married at the time but that relationship was hanging on by bare threads. And here I was entering a new intellectual uncharted territory, a place, one of many, my husband and I did not share. Sometimes things are troubled not by what they are but by what they are not. By 1999, I left my marriage to pursue a relationship with Toby, venturing into unknown landscapes.

Summer 1999. Toby and I have a fight (one of many). In an attempt to "make-up", Toby creates watercolour paintings and express mails them to me. In a moment inspired by my creative *daimon*, I rip up the watercolours, and paste them onto scraps of light wood board I have lying around and then add other images and words. These words are mostly copies of printed Email

Figure 2. Morna McDermott (with Toby Daspit), 1999. *Opus Contra Naturam.* Mixed media on wood panel. 30.48 x 91.44 cm.

exchanges between the two of us. Collage by this point had become not only a way of thinking, but of being.

Working on our first collaborative manuscript together (Daspit & McDermott, 2000) we write:

> By exhuming memories and blending them with passionate dialogue and aesthetic experiences, we intend to represent the process of our collaborative work, life, and love efforts to explore the multiple connections between self and theory. Such connections blur the boundaries between past and present, self and other, and theory and living. (p. 179)

Enter: Emergence

My memories are the inner labyrinth that forges a definitive outer form from the myriad of possibilities that swirl around each of us every second of every day, making order out of chaos.... Art is a way of living and seeing our lives (McDermott, 2003, p. 12). During the first year as a doctoral student I became more aware of the notion of "emergence", of how my thinking, my emotional life, my spiritual condition, and my academic mind converged on one another. I saw things emerge from these small moments and felt alive at the prospect of what might reveal itself and inform my process. I was continuously seized with the urge to write. I discovered what synchronicity was all about because I found it everywhere. *Isn't this so true when one is in love?* A full moon would inspire me to find a poem and Email it to Toby. Or driving down the road I would hear a song that would make me think of something relating to my academic world. The terms such as *emergence* and *collaboration*, which became guiding forces, were born out of these experiences. The element of chance made each day like the opening of an unexpected gift. Unlike scientifically driven methodologies that require clearly stated predictions and goals, my "style" found itself — a living process, which I did not shape but in which artist and medium were mutually shaping.

To: Toby
From letters to colors: reviewing the form and meaning of words. Inquiry is about seeing things from a new perspective, finding / discovering — to look at things as they are is to retell what's been said from a new perspective, making the familiar strange by seeing experience / language outside the monoscopic view. The "letter form" (as solid lines) dissolves and the liquid sense of colour in it emerges (becomes different inquiry here) — relating to something (not as an object) in different ways — involvement of self, with object, and the in-between, the exchange alters how we conceive of it — in flux, the immediate becomes multilayered mercurial visions of memories, dreams, and senses and creates a new strange lens with which to per ceive the outside, the ordinary, the common…submerging the self, beneath the lines where boundaries are blurred and new patterns and meanings emerge with vital influence.

144

it sounds like the ravings of a madwoman i know
but that's what i wrote (at some point) hope it's useful.
(Email, July 28, 1999)

The Beginning of the End
November 12, 2005. *This is a first. I have never cried while writing a book chapter before. Some things always stay close to the bone I guess.*

> To: Toby
> alchemical theorizing…transformative living…us.
> This is where we started. Here — In this space
> We have brought each other to life and nearly put each other to death
> Here…. Created worlds and crumbled universes
> A space bigger than the whole universe and yet completely intangible
> Except when you're holding me…. The smallest things
> The result of this nebulous high tech anti space that made
> a whole new
> universe for us
> Created by us.
> (Email, December 15, 1999)

I realize now that I was not lost in the journey itself but, rather, lost in my attempts to retrace it.

August 25, 2005. *I am struggling to write this chapter. Why? I have no idea. The capacity to articulate "my process" seems impossible.* The theory and the living are always directly intertwined. We transform ourselves into agents of change through the application of artistic techniques and aesthetic analysis. We can allow for an approach to inquiry that "feels risky, dangerous, forbidden — for within it, we are able to imitate nothing but who we are" (Sumara, & Davis, 1998, p. 2). Is it any coincidence that Toby and I finally allow our relationship to self-destruct only three months after I successfully defend my dissertation? I do not know.

> To: Toby
> The smallest things
> Can be the largest
> The inverted gaze shattered into a million stars
> And here we look up trying to read them and what they
> all mean.
> (Email, December 19, 1999)

Uroboros: Transformations

November 15, 2005. I am driving home from work. I am thinking, as I have been doing almost obsessively, about how to revise this chapter — to say what needs to be said. I turn on National Public Radio and light up a cigarette. A reporter is interviewing Bruce Springsteen. I smile. This again is serendipity. One of the romantic connections Toby and I shared was our love for Springsteen's music and the role it played in our young lives. I am struck again by the role that emergence plays in doing arts-based inquiry. As artistic inquirers we need to always be aware and awake because the "answers" are unfolding each minute. And I found Springsteen's (2005) words in that interview speaking to the understanding that I was searching for. Springsteen was talking about how the artistic and the personal collide. He suggested that worlds between art and living can become blurred and that there need to be some boundaries at the "edge" because if we live life too much like our art, we might self-destruct. Prophetic hindsight.

So this is not the end. The ending has indeed returned to the beginning and to my premise that in doing arts-based inquiry the personal is the academic and the academic is personal. Unlike more scientific methods of inquiry, arts-informed inquirers live their process, they don't just "do it". Sitting in my car, listening to the interview, and thinking this through I am drawn to the third guiding principle of my dissertation research: *transformation*. I assert that transformation occurs when one is changed by engaging in the artistic / inquiry / life process. Specifically I argued that the preservice teachers I studied were transformed by the process of creating their collages. Like a collage, the pieces (or fragments) of our lives can be arranged and re-arranged. Now, looking back at my process and my life at the time, I am again re-arranging the pieces of what happened. Transformations in thinking and living — we are the subject, the data, the process, and the final opus of our own inquiry journey.

As a result, new "reve(al)lations" (Daspit & McDermott, 2000, p. 182) are also occurring. Time folds into itself, ruptures, and overlaps. Writing now, I am creating new layers. Maybe Springsteen was slightly off when he said we "self-destruct". Maybe what he meant is that certain aspects in our life, parts of our identity or relationships, may self-destruct but that art (and artistic living) is also what helps keep us going — not towards death but towards transformation into something else. This is what the art of inquiry (and inquiry as art) has taught me — how to live, burn, bleed, transform.

And, then, how to live again.

References

Bukowski, C. (Writer). (1999). *Tales of ordinary madness* [Video]. United States: Image Entertainment.

Daspit, T. & McDermott, M. (2000). Frameworks of blood and bone: An alchemy of performative mapping. In C. Bagley & M. Cancienne (Eds.), *Dancing the data* (pp. 177-190). New York, NY: Peter Lang.

Butler-Kisber, L., & Davis, D. (1999). *Arts-based representation in qualitative research: Collage as a contextualizing strategy.* Paper presented at American Educational Research Association Annual Meeting, Montreal, QC.

Davis, H. E. (1997). If art is good for the soul can education do without art? In S. Laird (Ed.), *Philosophy of education yearbook* (pp. 285-288). Champain, IL: Philosophy of Education Society.

Deleuze, G., & Guatarri, F. (1987). *A thousand plateaus: Capitalism and schizophrenia.* Minneapolis, MN: University of Minnesota.

Finley, S. (1998). *Teacher education faculty as researchers: Composing lives in context, a blend of form and content.* Unpublished doctoral dissertation, University of Michigan, Ann Arbor, MI.

jagodinski, j. (1992). Curriculum as felt through six layers of an aesthetically embodied skin: The arch writing on the body. In W. Pinar & B. Reynolds (Eds.), *Understanding curriculum as phenomenological and deconstructed text* (pp.159-183). New York, NY: Teachers College Press.

jagodinski, j. (1997). *Postmodern dilemmas: Outrageous essays in art and art education.* Mahwah, NJ: Lawrence Erlbaum.

Lord, M. (1999, April 25). *Crank Cases.* Sunday New York Times Book Review.

McDermott, M. (2001). *Flinging the piano of critical post-avant-garde arts-based inquiry: A study of four pre-service teachers' collaged representations of self and pedagogy.* Unpublished doctoral dissertation, University of Virginia, Charlottesville, VA.

McDermott, M. (2003). Spiral of the shell. *art-informed, 2(*1), Centre for Arts-informed Research. Retrieved November 2, 2005 from http://home.oise.utoronto.ca/ ~aresearch/newsletter.html.

McNiff, S. (1998). *Art-based research.* Philadelphia, PA: Jessica Kingsley.

Mullen, C. A., & Diamond, C. T. P. (1999). Prologue: An invitation to an in-quest. In C. T. P. Diamond & C. A. Mullen (Eds.), *The postmodern educator: Arts-based inquiries and teacher development* (pp. 1-11). New York, NY: Peter Lang.

Nalick, A. (2005). Breath (2 AM). *Wreck of the day* [Album]. Sony Records. Retrieved November 18, 2005 from http://www.soundtracklyrics.net/song-lyrics/lot-like-love/breathe-2-am.htm.

Slattery, P. (1999). Popular culture and higher education: Using aesthetics and seminars to reconceptualize curriculum. In T. Daspit & J. Weaver (Eds.), *Popular culture and critical pedagogy* (pp. 201-218). New York, NY: Garland.

Slattery, P. (1995). *Curriculum development in the postmodern era.* New York, NY: Garland.

Springgay, S. (2004). Inside the invisible: Arts-based educational research as excess. *Journal of Curriculum and Pedagogy, 1*(1), pp. 8-18.

Springsteen, B. (2005, November 15). Interview on *Fresh Air with Terry Gross*, WYPR Baltimore, MD (National Public Radio) Radio Station.

Sumara, L., & Davis, B. (1998). *Underpainting. Journal of Curriculum Theorizing, 14*(4), 1-5.

About the Author
MORNA MCDERMOTT is an Assistant Professor Department of Elementary Education, Towson University, Maryland. She received a PhD from the University of Virginia in 2001. Her scholarship and work with preservice teachers and practicing educators centres on relationships between critical aesthetics in education, arts-based inquiry, democracy, and social justice. Her recent publications include an article in *Education and Social Justice: Democracy and Education.*

Morna's doctoral dissertation is entitled *Flinging the Piano of*

Critical Post-avant-garde Arts-based Inquiry: A Study of Four pre-service Teachers' Collaged Representations of Self and Pedagogy. It examines how collage may be used to represent preservice teachers' knowledges and perceptions of themselves in relationship to teaching and learning. Her study also examines the implications of using collage as a form of data analysis and representation.

12. Navigating Marine Drive: Embarking on an Arts-informed Thesis

by Pauline Sameshima

Using the frame of Body Connections, Research, and Artistry, in this chapter I share my thought processes on embarking on an arts-informed thesis. This work was written from journal entries in 2004 and constituted part of my thesis proposal. The completed thesis was written as an epistolary bildungsroman — a book of letters describing a developmental journey of a graduate student in love with her mentor. The thesis was published by Cambria Press under the title of *Seeing Red* (Sameshima, 2006, 2007).

Marine Drive is one of the main transport arteries in

Vancouver, British Columbia. In the sea of darkness, on my way home from a late meeting, the dark February light is mingled with intermittent lines of moving red tail lights and distant yellow and white diffusions. I feel at sea — the road is swimming before me and the rain flashes on my windshield. Even though the radio is silent, the movement, hustle, and traffic sounds fill the air with a cacophonous urgency. For most, the travel time is a bother. But I remember that, in my learning journey, I want to breathe deeply and be at home in my vessel, to feel and relish my being in the learning moment in a hermeneutic way of living. The unwelcome noise, possible dangers, rough seas, ambiguity, constant vigilance, joy, beauty, laughter, excitement, and hope in learning are all part of the process. I accept the unanswerable questions. I am a teacher and researcher.

I look at the far off yellow and white lights and imagine they are guiding stars as I mindlessly move on Marine Drive to reach the Knight Street Bridge that will take me to Richmond where I live. I do not need a sextant. I have travelled this road, this same course, for many years. I follow this route because it is the only way onto the bridge from the east. I reflect on the way I learn — by mixing up metaphors of sea and stars and cars, by looking for connections, similarities, and relations. I think about the way I so easily follow the main roads, the roads that were built decades or even a century ago. I value numbers, history, and the experiences of others and have no choice but to catch the prevailing wind currents of Arendt's natality (1968), which Levinson (2001) explains, is tempered by belatedness:

> The world does not simply precede us, but effectively consti
> tutes us as particular kinds of people. This puts us in the diffi
> cult position of being simultaneously heirs to a particular hist
> ory and new to it, with the peculiar result that we experience
> ourselves as "belated" even though we are newcomers. (p. 13)

I do feel peculiar at times. I want to be guided by the stars not bound by gravity. I want to research in a way that resonates — always moving forward in a rhythm that allows for time to see deeply, render, and articulate connections. I do not want to follow the highway mindlessly. I want to go slow and reflect, cycling forward and back, looping and looping, and seeing anew.

Sometimes on the learning path I have no choice but to follow. In this particular mid-January Vancouver experienced record rain levels. When I reached the south end of Royal Oak and had to turn onto a flooded Marine Drive the water level rose midway over the tires of the cars ahead. I drove as close to the center of the road as possible. I had no choice but to continue. This is how I navigate my learning within established practices and organizational frames which delineate my research. I remain in the centre and imagine these narrow channels as rites of passage. I steer, sometimes fearful, other times on a crest of a wave, knowing that on the sea there are no roads and I direct my own learning in a movement forward, which takes me closer to the bridge that draws us, as a collective, closer to "home".

As a doctoral candidate, contemplating the pragmatics of the form my research and thesis will take, I question why an arts-informed thesis. I think about Strong, Silver, and Perini's (2001) description of rigour as complex, provocative, ambiguous, and emotionally challenging. I want to design a project that does all this. I want to do something different, carefully calculated, but creative. Nick Bantock's (2004, p. 1) words remind me that "what matters is the degree of poignant emotion evoked by the resultant piece of paper." But how do I begin? Bantock says, "the method of working that I propose tends to be 'chicken and eggish' — the finding directs the making and the making feeds the finding" (p. 2). So I just begin. I think I will write a novel.

Body Connection

> For the artist there is no more serious and, at the same time,
> more joyous task than to create, through art, a new aesthetic
> and, ultimately, a new way of being. (Karel Zeman in L.
> Zeman, 1992, n.p.)

The rhythm of my movement and learning is my body. It
breathes form into the thesis. I did not know this for the first two
years of graduate school. I learned but did not feel the learning or
let myself learn from the feeling. Lorri Neilsen (1998) says, "We
are learning that we are no longer mere creators of text, we are
texts ourselves.... Writing not only lets me know what I know,
writing leads me to what I need to learn" (pp. 10-11). I am a
writer, a poet, an artist, a musician, a dancer — a person living
within the arts. It is natural for me to do an arts-informed study. I
layer my arts with conceptual understandings and organizational
processes which seek to represent and reflect what I have come to
understand. Sometimes my arts echo each other; other times, they
open understanding to my unconscious knowing. My intent is
always integrated with the creatively informed process because my
living has become my research, my curriculum for deconstruction,
reconstruction, and transformation. "To research is to reveal the
autobiographical — the self or elements of the self" (Cole &
Knowles, 2001a, p. 45). To research well is to live transparently
and congruently as researcher and self and to find processes and
forms to authentically represent personal understanding.

My learning process is this journey on this body ship. Although
I have left port, I continue to be shaped by both the dock I have
left (my past experiences) and the ship I am travelling in (a
methodological form). I am steering toward a fusion of horizons
(Denzin, 1997, p. 36; Gadamer, 1989), postmodern ethnography,
a navigational chart filled with a text that is a parallax of discourses in which nothing is ever stable with a particular firm

154

representation (see Bakhtin, 1986). My role as researcher is to question, seek, and render. Denzin reminds that postmodern ethnography "values and privileges the authority and voice of the reader and thus changes the role and authority of the researcher as meaning maker and theorizer" (Cole & McIntyre, 2004).

As I use arts-informed inquiry to research and render understanding I consider the viewer who is also informed by the completed work. Is not all educational research ultimately intended for the public (to effect positive social change)? The art dynamically informs in its creation and again informs in its completion. Meaning making struggles between the creative arts' function as a verb and as a noun; however, I am reminded of the beauty of ambiguity. Nancy Mairs (1993) summarizes my thoughts:

> The endless replication of a single system for structuring beliefs and behaviors in relation to the whole complicated world…strikes me as a dangerous idea…. We're human, after all…safer to recognize our fallibility, generate a number of dif ferent imaginative patterns, and share them freely. (p. 8)

Cole and McIntyre (2004) challenge conventional models of research text which display fixed meaning created by the researcher. They introduce *contemplative texts,* research texts which "do not represent or illustrate experiences or events; rather, each engagement with a research text is a new meaningful interaction" (p. 12). This innovative perspective invites viewer engagement and creates multiple spaces for interpretation.

The dock (past experiences) is the place from where I, the researcher, embark. Ayers (1988) believes that teachers have a special responsibility for self-awareness, clarity, and integrity because they are in powerful positions to influence and guide the choices of others. Researchers, too, have these responsibilities and must acknowledge their own individual and collective understandings of sense-of-place and community (Knowles & Thomas, 2000; Relph, 1976; Von Maltzahn, 1994); philosophical and experiential self-formation (Polanyi, 1964; Stark, 2003); ecological identity (Knowles, 2004; Thomashow, 1995), and teacher-identity (Jardine, 1998; Palmer, 1998) which all culminate to materialize a dock or a configuration of subjectivities from which the researcher can then explore. I imagine the dock as the needlepoint of a compass firmly planted, allowing the pencil point to extend and draw with freedom.

I acknowledge "my past is always included in the present, implicated, inextricably present with the present" (Leggo, 2004, p. 22). My subjectivities create the details of my vessel and directly influence my voyage of learning. My "stories represent the meeting place of thoughts and experience (the internal landscape) and the events, objects, and character of surroundings (the external landscape)" (Knowles & Thomas, 2000, p. 6). Again, because the sea has no roads, it is important for me to continue to dialogically engage in seeking convergence of understanding with others who have travelled the sea. I do not seek a known route or follow ephemeral wakes. My authority in interpreting others' research, amalgamating my own ideas with theirs and developing new notions, further embraces and values multiplicity, ambiguity, and wonder. I continue to write new stories of understanding. Gary Knowles (1998, p. 8) suggests that teaching, living, and researching is an "on-going literary and poetic story" — a narrative event.

Gadamer (1989) speaks of transformation in terms of structure, not representation or alteration. Alteration implies that the original is still present, only changed. As I render my conscious understandings through song, visual arts, poetry or narrative writing, my initial constructs transform into a composite construction of new understanding brought to awareness — the subconscious made conscious through the creative rendering. I question the power and form of arts-informed research; the restriction and liberation

156

of articulating an arts-informed inquiry; how understandings arise from the rendered images; how my learning takes shape when I am living as researcher-as-artist and, tangentially, how viewers observe and create understanding from arts-informed inquiry with / without footnotes, explanations or prolepses. I cannot lay a path. I am on the sea. I can only share my journey. Is it enough to evoke — to share, to raise awareness, and to provoke query in the viewer?

Meet Me Tomorrow
I will paint
brush and pen
all night long
till golden dawn breaks
over the dew
and the grass
is freshly glistening
Then you'll know
I'll know too
what I know
what I am
inside come out

Research
   As a researcher I need to (re)search in complex, sophisticated, and holistic ways, seeking connections off charted courses. Eisner (1994) proposes a shifting of focus "from statistical reliability and validity to what he terms *referential adequacy* — experiencing an object or situation in a new or more adequate way — and *structural corroboration* — linking the parts to the cohesive whole" (in Slattery, Krasny & O'Malley, 2004, p. 10). In order to impart my understandings, I need to take my learning and express a wholesome rendering. To express a wholesome rendering, for me, is to

express through the body — through music, movement, art, poetry, narrative fiction, and non-fiction.

Representation and embodied expression through the creative arts involves the re-creation of knowledge or experience in an alternate form. The form can be *concrete*: three dimensional, direct overt physical action such as movement, drama, dance, or music making; *transformational*: indirect representation such as two-dimensional drawing, painting, or pictographic writing; or *symbolic / abstract*: representation which bears no direct resemblance to the concept represented such as talking, writing, and musical notation (British Columbia Ministry of Education, 2000).

> Somehow I too must find a way of making things; not plastic, written things, but realities that arise from the craft itself. Somehow I too must discover the smallest constituent element, the cell of my art, the tangible immaterial means of expressing everything. (Rilke, 1985, n.p.)

Barone and Eisner (1997) suggest that several aesthetic features inform arts-based learning:
- the use of contextual and vernacular forms of language;
- the use of expressive rhetorical devices (such as metaphor) to recreate experience;
- the capacity of the text to evoke alternate realities;
- the presence of heightened ambiguity;
- the promotion of empathy;
- the personal signature of the researcher or writer;
- the presence of aesthetic form.

I also explore connections to Cole and Knowles' (2001b, pp. 214-217) *Defining Elements of Arts-informed Research* which maintain that quality arts-informed research considers:
- intentionality, intellectual and moral purpose;
- researcher presence, reflexive self-accounting;

- methodological commitment, principled process, and procedural harmony;
- a holistic quality, internal consistency and coherence, and authenticity;
- communicability, issues of audience and the transformative potential of the work;
- accessibility, connecting with hearts, souls, and minds of readers;
- aesthetic form, honouring quality and appeal;
- knowledge claims, made with sufficient ambiguity and humility to allow for multiple interpretations;
- contributions, theoretical and transformative potential.

Like Cole & Knowles (2001b, p. 219), I prefer to use the term "arts-informed research" over "arts-based research" because the processes of my research are not about the arts, nor based within the arts. My understandings seek connections and revelation from the arts, in the doing, as well as in the interpretive reflexive viewing of my own work.

Artistry
Nick Bantock (2004) says:

The children of the latter portion of the twentieth century, bought the Emperor's New Clothes when it came to art philosophy. We've accepted a line of thought implying that aesthetics are purely a matter of individual taste and personal whim. Ironically, in so doing, we've laid ourselves open to be led by cheap fad…. There is a universal aesthetic, an internal visual balance mechanism that defines beauty and composition. This means that the opposite is also true — equality is admirable, but why kid ourselves that ugly doesn't exist. Awareness of balance and harmony is something that needs to be worked on and developed within us. (pp. 4-5)

I agree with Bantock yet wonder what a rarefied public under-standing of balance and harmony means. The distinction between researching artfully and using art to research should not be blurred. Eisner (2004) speaks of "artistry as an icon of excel-lence… and as a concept [providing] a vision of human possibili-ty" (in Henderson & Slattery, 2004, p. 15). Eisner echoes Herbert Read's claim that "the aim of education can be conceived of as the preparation of artists, namely, people who make things well" (p. 15). On the other hand, using art to research involves using cre-ative means to unveil new understandings. I have concerns about my artistic skill inhibiting the rendering of my intentions. Can my body perform inquiry work? Is deep understanding reserved for only the "professional artist"? I disagree. The researcher is always becoming; the artist within should attempt to honour the form.

I have been inventing myself through writing and art. I am capturing moments in my body and mind by articulating a way to control — as a way to bring meaning to the unexpressed and known in the body but unsaid through the head. The stories and responses I make determine the reality that takes shape in my mind, the place where I can exert control of retrieval. My art expresses the summary of my knowing. My line of vision is all I know. I see, write what I see, and see what I write — an ultimate-ly confining, limiting control over my own "truth", yet, the text is simultaneously liberating because it articulates and renders the unconscious — a true paradox of postmodernist thinking.

Opening the World
how do I learn to soar?
not taking step by step
but gathering information and
flying over the path
I turn to artful research to ideate
the periphery of understanding

draw the edge of imagination
where conceptualization is not limited to lexicon.
How can I describe what I understand
without a language — that which I myself do not know?
but with a brush, an instrument with no rules
with my body, and layered with words
I try to express
all that is yet confined to one alphabetic glossolalia
all that needs to be expressed
all that calls for representation
and interpretation.
Iterating the wordless
translating the unnamed noesis
understanding what we can't but need to
pushing to the unbound
dwelling and moving in rhythm and breath
letting the process teach
opening to ambiguity and
postmodern subjectivities
drafting on the power of others
on the crest of natality
I write and story myself understanding
incorporate both sides of the brain
as I type with both hands
integrating the hemispheres
opening the world.

> To meditative minds the ineffable is cryptic, inarticulate: dots,
> marks of secret meaning, scattered hints, to be gathered, deci
> phered and formed into evidence; while in moments of insight
> the ineffable is a metaphor in a forgotten mother tongue.
> (Abraham Heschel in Thomashaw, 1995, n.p.)

As I continue my journeys home on Marine Drive, I am cognizant that as I travel new roads of understanding, I must document my paths and celebrate all that is around me. There is no singular method of researching. The methods and form of research used must complement the inquiry just as the representation must honour the research and provoke the audience. As I inch along Marine Drive, on the road or in the water, I welcome the changing ambiguity of colours settling on my skin from the rain shadows on the windshield and welcome the complexity of leading and letting the research lead, open to the beauty of possibilities, mindful of careful observation, connection-making, and, again, accepting the unanswerable questions. I am a teacher and researcher.

References

Arendt, H. (1968). *Between past and future: Eight exercises in political thought.* New York, NY: Penguin Books.

Ayers, W. C. (1988). *Teaching and being: Connecting teachers' accounts of their lives with classroom practice.* Paper presented at the Annual meeting of the American Educational Research Association, New Orleans. LA.

Bakhtin, M. M. (1986). *Speech genres and other late essays.* Austin, TX: University of Texas Press.

Bantock, N. (2004). *Urgent 2nd class: Creating curious collage.* Vancouver, BC: Raincoast Books.

Barone, T., & Eisner, E. (1997). Arts-based educational research. In M. Jaeger (Ed.), *Complimentary methods for research in educa tion* (pp. 73-116). Washington, DC: American Educational Research Association.

British Columbia Ministry of Education. (2000). *Primary program: A framework for teaching.* Retrieved on August 10, 2007, from www.bced.gov.bc.ca/primary_program/ primary_prog.pdf

Cole, A. L., & Knowles. J. G. (2001a). *Lives in context: The art of life history research.* Walnut Creek, CA: Alta Mira Press.

Cole, A. L., & Knowles, J. G. (2001b). Qualities of Inquiry. In L. Neilsen, A. L. Cole, & J. G. Knowles (Eds.). *The art of writing inquiry* (pp. 211-219). Halifax, NS & Toronto, ON: Backalong Books & Centre for Arts-Informed Research.

Cole, A. L., & McIntyre, M. (2004). Research as aesthetic con templation: The role of the audience in research interpretation. *Educational Insights. 9*(1). Retrieved April 4, 2005 from http://www.ccfi.educ.ubc.ca/publication /insights/v09n01/arti cles/cole.htm

Denzin, N. K. (1997). *Interpretive ethnography: Ethnographic practices for the 21st century*. Thousand Oaks, CA: Sage Publications.

Eisner, E. (1994). *The educational imagination: On the design and evaluation of school programs* (3rd edition). New York, NY: Macmillan.

Eisner, E. (2004). Artistry and pedagogy in curriculum. *Journal of Curriculum and Pedagogy. 1*(1), 15-16.

Gadamer, H. (1989). *Truth and method, 2nd revised edition*, (D. Marshall & J. Weinsheimer, Trans.). New York, NY: Continuum Publishing. Original work published in 1960.

Henderson, J. G., & Slattery, P. (2004). Editors' introduction: The arts create synergy for curriculum and pedagogy. *Journal of Curriculum and Pedagogy. 1*(2), 1-8.

Jardine, D. W. (1998). *To dwell with a boundless heart: Essays in curriculum theory, hermeneutics, and ecological imagination*. New York, NY: Peter Lang.

Knowles, J. G. (1998, August). *The power of personal experience: Place, perspective, and pedagogy*. Paper presented at the American Educational Research Association, England.

Knowles, J. G. (2004, July / August). *Sense-of-place: Reflexive artful inquiry and ecological identity*. Education course: EDCI 508, section 951. University of British Columbia, Vancouver, BC.

Knowles, J. G., & Thomas, S. (2000, April). *In search of place within natural and professional contexts: Place, perspective, and pedagogy.* Paper presented at the American Educational Research Association Conference, New Orleans, LA.

Leggo, C. (2004). Tangled lines. In A. L. Cole, L. Neilsen, J. G. Knowles, & T. Luciani (Eds.), *Provoked by art: Theorizing arts-informed research* (pp. 18-35). Halifax, NS & Toronto, ON: Backalong Books & Centre for Arts-informed Research.

Levinson, N. (2001). The paradox of natality: Teaching in the midst of belatedness. In M. Gordon (Ed.), *Hannah Arendt and education: Renewing our common world* (pp. 11-36). Boulder, CO: Westview Press.

Mairs, N. (1993). *Ordinary time.* Boston, MA: Beacon Press.

Neilsen, L. (1998). *Knowing her place: Research literacies and feminist occasions.* San Francisco, CA & Big Tancook Island, NS: Caddo Gap Press & Backalong Books.

Palmer, P. J. (1998). *The courage to teach: Exploring the inner land scape of a teacher's life.* San Francisco, CA: Jossey-Bass.

Polanyi, M. (1964). *Personal knowledge.* New York, NY: Harper & Row.

Rilke, R. M. (1985). *Letters on Cézanne* (C. Rilke, Ed. & J. Agee, Trans.). New York, NY: Fromm International Publishing Corporation. Original work published in 1952.

Relph, E. (1976). *Place and placelessness.* Brondesbury Park, London, UK: Pion.

Sameshima, P. (2006). *Seeing red: A pedagogy of parallax.* Unpublished doctoral thesis, University of British Columbia, Vancouver, BC.

Sameshima, P. (2007). *Seeing red — A pedagogy of parallax: An epis-tolary bildungsroman on artful scholarly inquiry.* Youngstown, NY: Cambria Press.

Slattery, P., Krasny, A. K., & O'Malley, M. P. (2004, April). *Hermeneutics, aesthetics, and the quest for answerability: A dialogic possibility for reconceptualizing the interpretive process in cur-*

riculum studies. Paper presented at the American Association of Advancement of Curriculum Studies, Montreal, QC.

Stark, H. (2003). A fierce little tragedy: Thought, passion, and self-formation in the philosophy classroom. *Philosophy of Education, 147.* New York, NY: Rodopi.

Strong, R., Silver, H., & Perini, M. (2001). *Teaching what matters most: Standards and strategies for raising student achievement.* Alexandria, VA: ASCD.

Thomashow, M. (1995). *Ecological identity: Becoming a reflective environmentalist.* Cambridge, MA: The Massachusetts Institute of Technology Press.

Von Maltzahn, K. (1994). *Nature as landscape: Dwelling and understanding.* Montreal, QC & Kinston, ON: McGill & Queen's University Press.

Zeman, L. (1992). *Gilgamesh the king.* Toronto, ON: Tundra Books.

About the Author

PAULINE SAMESHIMA is an Assistant Professor at Washington State University. Her creative writing, research, and art-making center on curriculum studies, teacher education, art education, educational leadership, and system organization. She is particularly interested in life-history arts-informed research, a/r/tography, artful scholastic inquiry, and alternative forms of knowledge production.

Seeing Red: A Pedagogy of Parallax, Pauline's thesis, was published by Cambria Press and recognized with awards in Curriculum Studies, Teacher Education, and Arts-based Research. The work is made up of sent and unsent letters, poems, and art from a graduate student to the advisor she is in love with. The book is a mystery and love story which shares the process of thinking and living a/r/tographically while completing an art-informed thesis.

13. The Dance of Co-creation Continues

by Kathy (Aikatherine) Mantas and Solveiga Miezitis

This dialogue is a reflection on our, Kathy's and Solveiga's, co-creative process and relationship as we explored our creativity and the stories of our lives.

The beauty of playing together is meeting in the One....The work comes from neither one artist nor the other, even though our own idiosyncrasies and styles, the symptoms of our original natures, still exert their natural pull. Nor does the work come from a compromise or halfway point but from a third place that isn't necessarily like what either one of us would do indi vidually. What comes is a revelation to both of us. There is a third, totally new style that pulls on us. It is as though we have become a group organism that has its own nature and its own way of being, from a unique and unpredictable place. (Nachmanovitch, 1990, pp. 94-95)

If you had looked in on our process you would have seen us eating, talking, and painting. We co-created art-work for over one hundred hours from December, 2000 to May, 2001. We discovered that we were able to collaborate in the thesis process as much as in the co-creative process. Our trust and deep respect for one another made it possible for us to learn and move forward in our reflexive inquiry, creative self-expression, art, and lives. Together we were blessed by the muse and ventured into places where we would never have dared to tread alone. Now, we invite you to participate in a reflexive dialogue about our experience of co-creating visual art and making meaning of the forms that emerged in the context of Kathy's doctoral thesis.

Figure 1. Co-creators Olivia / Kathy and Dawn / Solveiga, 2001. *Two little Tricksters with Their Hands in the Cookie Jar.* Tempura paint on paper. 46.5 cm x 66 cm.

Method, Theory, and Process

Solveiga, why did you choose to participate in my doctoral inquiry?
I was very excited when I heard about your project. The idea of researching co-creation struck me as very novel and unusual. When I volunteered to participate as one of your three co-creators, I realized that I did not really understand the concept and I was not sure how it was going to work for me.

I saw you as a facilitator who would allow me to open up and explore my creative process. During the first meeting, however, I learned how tentative I felt about co-creating. I was uneasy about putting myself out on paper. If you had elicited my censor in any way then my inner critic would have taken charge. I discovered that I really was diffident at first, when trying to paint together, even with someone as open and non-threatening as you. I really did not anticipate being pulled into this co-creative and relational process with you....

Kathy, how did you feel about having me as a co-creator?
I sensed from the beginning that co-creating with you, Solveiga, would be different. Before our first meeting I waited in anticipation for you to arrive. I puttered around my little studio / study space, checked the art materials, covered the worktable in a plastic sheet, and made sure that the camera and tape recorder were loaded with batteries, film and a cassette. Then I headed downstairs, put the teapot on, and waited for your arrival. I remember how uncertain I felt. I was a student, struggling with my thesis, and you were an established professor.

I did, however, feel very comfortable in my role as one of the co-creators. Sometimes, I facilitated the process and other times you guided it. I felt that you had an intuitive sense of when to guide and when to walk beside me. You have been down the academic research path before and were always open to sharing personal experiences of your individual and unique inquiry process. You were committed and courageous enough to enter into a

168

vulnerable, at times messy, ambiguous, and absorbing process. You brought much richness to this inquiry and took ownership, to varying degrees, of the documentation of the process through photography and the audio-tape recording of some of our conversations.

Solveiga, I found the process both enchanting and humbling. I wanted for us to create a space for our authentic forms of expression to emerge. A lot of individual process and dialogue needed to occur, however, before the room in which we were creating felt safe enough. In the beginning we were tentative, creating in the same space and, essentially, making art on our own. The earlier art pieces that we made on our own — side by side — were very important. They provided a space that helped us get to know each other, start to dialogue, build trust and our relationship. We started with an initial conversation, paint and paper, but quickly moved into different media and forms. Although we struggled with the media, forms, images, and text, especially, we did not struggle with each other.

Solveiga, what about you, how did you experience the process?

The notion of letting go of our own control is significant in the co-creative process. It is an inner process that depends on when things are ready to come out and what will trigger what in our psyche. Strong emotions may erupt and there is always that uncertainty. This inner sense of movement depends on how safe the space is. Co-creation is not therapy. It is about exploring, creating, and dialoguing around where we can go with it. There is much more to it than art making. It is also a self-validating process that involves a lot of witnessing. It is the pleasure of having someone to play with, listen to us, and spend time on us. It is also to recognize and validate those risky moments when we feel vulnerable to the inner critic, to that accumulated history of being told that we are not doing it right. Being witnessed is a very satisfying experience in and of itself.

169

I agree that initially we struggled to find a space. What was created in the beginning was not terribly satisfying to me; we were not really working together. Instead we worked side by side. When we created images with pastels that was the first time I really felt that something beautiful could emerge. We gained trust in the process and were very excited. What emerged was something that I could never have created alone. As we progressed we made quantum leaps forward. The compositions became more complex and powerful and the colours more vivid and dynamic. We became more experimental, playful, and daring with materials. We engaged in storytelling and in exploring myths and metaphors.

Kathy, what surprised you about engaging in an arts-informed inquiry?

I did not know the direction the process would take but I enjoyed its mysterious unfolding. Things miraculously fell into place. When we tried to co-ordinate schedules we were always faced with the complexity of our lives. Through our research relationship we vicariously relived and experienced deaths, births, celebrations, illnesses, surgeries, job changes, home renovations, and other — both major and minor — life events. There was a lot going on during the entire co-creative process. Some days we literally went from laughter to tears, from a birthday party to visiting a dying relative in the hospital, and then back to co-creating. Through these shared experiences we built relationships. For me the relationships with you and the other co-creators carried the co-creative process, informed the inquiry, and encouraged me to keep going.

It is important to acknowledge the full experience of the co-creative process. It was very physical and it took a lot of time and energy to prepare a space, to be in the process for several hours and, later, to clean up. We were constantly lifting, carrying, cleaning, pushing and pulling, packing and unpacking clothes, art supplies, and our art. It was my responsibility, for the most part, to ensure that we had art supplies, a variety of media with which to explore and create, and a creative space. These preparatory hours and moments anticipated our meetings. These meetings, though under the umbrella of inquiry and for the purposes of the thesis, were always uplifting and invigorating and cascaded us further along in the process.

In between co-creations the studio space once again became a study space — a quiet space for writing, transcribing, reading, contemplating, and entertaining. Whenever a new co-creation was about to appear, I recreated the study / studio space by removing and putting away the art pieces made in the last session, and putting up the pieces appropriate to the current co-creation.

Solveiga, what did you learn through this process?
I discovered that co-creation is not just about art making and exploring creative possibilities. For us it became an opportunity to explore the meaning of relationship in sharing life stories and opening the space for imagination and freedom to play and have fun. We did not plan the paintings. It was not about competition, control, or individual achievement. The focus was not on the product. Sometimes there was a fleeting sense of loss when something that I had created disappeared when you engaged with the image. There is always a risk involved that we may lose something. But we have to accept that possibility to be rewarded by a surprising "Aha" as things come together in unexpected ways — like they did for us when the mermaid emerged.

We are immersed in the experience and have lost sense of time. In a state of flow our artwork becomes an expression of our unconscious energy streams; streams shape and reshape the image of the vision of the metaphor that is trying to find expression. As we continue to add to and transform the painting, we suddenly stop and scream "Eureka!"

171

We recognize the product of our creative encounter: It is a Mermaid! Look! Here is the tail. Look, if we put this other painting underneath it becomes the water with seaweeds at the bottom, the deep dark depths in which she is swimming. This painting, look if we turn it this way, with the little fish and colourful squiggles floating above her — shows the playful side of her existence.

Whose existence? What had we uncovered? Who was the mermaid? The metaphor began to unfold. How did it happen? Did the inner process drive the artful expression? Or did the co-creative process manifesting in two previous paintings become the engine that generated the mermaid image? The third image, the mermaid, pulled it all together.

The first image was a dark mucky seaweed scene that felt oppressive. Perhaps in response to that depressive energy we became playful and created whimsical figures and imaginary fish dancing in much lighter water. This more uplifting scene evoked exhilarating laughter and a sense of relief at having gotten out from under. And then, out of the blue, the Mermaid emerged! We had never spoken of mermaids before. The mythical metaphor caught us by surprise. It was a challenge to our imagination. The mermaid image became the metaphor that stimulated our narrative reflections. We reconnected it to bits and pieces of our previous conversations about our art, stories about our lives, women's lives and struggles, myths from the collective unconscious, and the feminine mystique of our existence. The mermaid metaphor and image helped us to integrate women's stories of oppression, submission, and empowerment as we reflected on the legacy of the Goddesses and the mythical embodiments of the multiple facets of women's psyches.

The stories led to moments of insight and integration as we elaborated on the metaphor and found connections to our own experiences. The metaphor allowed us to grieve our limitations and losses and envisage our creative possibilities as we dove back into the depths of the ocean. Many other powerful works emerged as we continued with our art making. Finally it was May, time to finish the data collecting phase of the project. There were so many images, too many. As we looked at them, other details began to emerge that led us back to the mermaid image. Recognizing pieces of the puzzle that could fit together gave expression to the intuitive process. We grabbed scissors and began to cut some of the paintings to create collages. These recreations of the mermaid were in complex shapes and multifaceted contexts and helped us bring to closure the intensive co-creative journey of one hundred hours over a six month period.

Kathy, how did your thesis process evolve?

I had several concerns about how to be in a research relationship, how to continue to nurture it throughout the entire process, and how to collect and later engage the data so that a new and unique form — one that resonated with me and was mindful of the data collected — would emerge. I was also nervous about including myself in my own research. Questions about my inquiry, myself, and the other co-researchers — if there were to be any — occupied my mind often.

In my own way, Solveiga, I always knew I would co-research. By researching together I did not take for granted your participation in the inquiry. I remained mindful of your unique process. In this kind of work everyone, the reader too, is asked to consider his / her own subjectivity. Co-researching and co-creating were my ways of exploring my subjectivity and moving away from detached ways of seeing and researching.

In the beginning I did not know how rich an experience co-creation would be and how much deeper and further along my process and inquiry would move because of our relationships. There were many times along the way when I thought about walk-

173

ing away from the thesis. If it was not for my commitment and sense of responsibility to the co-creators I might have left it unfinished. It was, indeed, my desire to honour your experiences, the long process, and my relationship with the co-creators that kept me going. Once someone begins this kind of journey it really is too late to turn back; nothing ever is the same again. Everything had changed and so had I.

Figure 2. Co-creators — Olivia / Kathy and Dawn / Solviega, 2003. *Untitled*. Tempura paints on canvas. 71.5 cm x 84 cm.

References

Mantas, A. (2004). *becoming AIR-BORNe: Women co-creating, expressing and in-forming our lives.* Unpublished doctoral thesis, University of Toronto, Toronto, ON, Canada.

Nachmanovitch, S. (1990). *Free play: Improvisation in life and art.* New York, NY: Penguin Putnam Inc.

About the Authors

KATHY (AIKATHERINE) MANTAS is a PhD graduate of the University of Toronto and an Assistant Professor of Education, Nipissing University, North Bay, Ontario. Kathy's research interests include teacher and adult education, arts education, arts-informed research, creativity in teaching and learning, and creativity and wellness. She is currently re-engaging aspects of her doctoral thesis, open to new possibilities and looking forward to more co-creating. Kathy's chapter *Meeting Mermaids: Co-creating images and process* in inquiry appears in *The Art of Visual Inquiry*, Volume 3 of the Arts-Informed Inquiry Series by Backalong Books and the Centre for Arts-Informed Research.

In Kathy's doctoral thesis, *becoming AIR-BORNe: Women Co-creating, Ex-pressing and In-forming Our Lives*, metaphors, words, and images meet to collectively tell about the paradox of being an educated woman. Her work is an arts-informed inquiry about creativity in women, co-creation, and creative processes. It asserts that knowing is rooted in relationship and the interconnectedness of life.

SOLVEIGA MIEZITIS is Professor Emeritus, Ontario Institute for Studies in Education, University of Toronto (OISE/UT). Her doctoral thesis is entitled, *An Exploratory Study of Divergent Production in Preschoolers* (1968). She continues to teach a course on *Creativity and Wellness: Learning to Thrive* at OISE/UT. Creativity has been a fascination of hers since age four, in Latvia, when her grandmother taught her to read.

14. Travels and Transformations: The River of Then and Now

by Anastasia Kamanos Gamelin

The journey to my thesis was an especially difficult one. As an immigrant, mother, writer, and academic I had lived with a sense of social disorientation and cultural dislocation. I had to overcome self-doubt, silence, lack of history, distrust of the future. I also had to overcome the sense of beginning from nothing, of starting from nowhere. To do this, I had to grope my way through gender, cultural, and social biases. This meant kicking addictions, examining open wounds, and facing imposters.... And, regardless of what I was told, academic writ ing was not like learning a new language for me. Rather, it was like learning to be a new person. I felt obliged to sing off key, to paint blindfolded, and to write with my hands tied behind my back. The difficulty lies in never being yourself. (Kamanos Gamelin, 2001, p. i)

The above quote from my doctoral thesis still reclaims my soul as I reread it. I would have thought that years after writing these lines, their truthfulness might have, like unpolished silver, lost their brilliance. After all, hadn't publishers regretfully assured me that the topic's lustre had tarnished, that the usefulness of the work had been reaped as far as the lecture hall. The thesis now sits on the floor of my office, bound and baled, like dry hay. I write this on a Friday. I am in Jeddah, Saudi Arabia, gazing out the window of my study that overlooks Medina Road. Brazenly, I have rolled up the blinds to let in the cloistered world. The Imam is particularly boisterous and loud this afternoon. His voice penetrates the closed window, swirling into the steam from my coffee. His words catch in the curls of the Greek music I am playing, curdling the dark, syrupy coffee I am stirring. The tingle of the spoon, the tangle of words, the tapping of tambourines.

As an artist in academe, an immigrant, and woman I have been trained to recognize paradox, to be what Whitehead (1993) calls a "living contradiction" (p. 17). One must possess this heightened awareness, this sense of place, of groundedness in order to teach, to live daily on the razor's edge of conformity and change. Here in Saudi Arabia, one must attend to each syllable, to translate each stride, to interpret each gesture.

I write of my life in Saudi Arabia here because it serves to illustrate how the experience of the thesis journey can infiltrate your being, change who you are, and transform what and how you know. "Really, Anastasia", said Ann, my thesis supervisor, one day, "should transformation be the purpose of a thesis?" I mulled over her question, turning her words around in my mouth like an unpitted cherry. Transformation, I realized, might not be the explicit purpose but it should, I suggested, be its reward.

Then: The Journey
Rewards, Re-words and Half-truths

My thesis experience compelled me to confront the artist and to face the complexities of being inside the academy while working to transform it. For the major part of the process I was caught in a struggle with the work and felt that, ultimately, only one of us could survive. After years in the academy I was weary at the idea that under the auspices of white-gowned, rubber-gloved, "objective" science I would have to claim to observe, analyze, examine and explain the world with little reference as to how that world became observable to me in the first place. My language would be stark, my data would be lean — none of the "thick" descriptions Geertz (1973) refers to or the "language of the arts" that Eisner (1991) proposes. In order to be successful I would conform and learn to write my knowing as a "well-socialized member of the culture", at what cost, however, to my voice, authority, integrity and agency?

Luckily, as hard as I tried, I could never get to that point of numbness. As a woman and artist, I was uncomfortable with the "piecemeal" approach to knowledge construction, feeling that it was not only unfulfilling but also produced half-truths. I needed instead to construct a form of persuasion that explored and defined the fullness of being, body, mind, emotion.

The concessions of Self in exchange for the doctoral degree were steep. Yet, I was enmeshed in the process and had invested so much in it. Caught in its undertow, it took from me all that I could yield, suckling ever more than I imagined I possessed, physically, spiritually, psychologically, and financially. I was crumbling, disintegrating against the grain of institutional misunderstandings.

I was not alone and found some hope in the words of other women who described their own thesis experience and "the damage it can do to women's mind and bodies" (Christian-Smith & Kellor, 1999, p. 229). To say nothing of our spirits. Audre Lorde (1981) reminds us that survival "is not an academic skill, it is learning how to take our differences and make them strengths. For the master's tools will never dismantle the master's house" (p. 99). I had read Lorde's infamous quote a thousand times over but it had never had as deep a meaning. Simultaneously, I both lost and found myself in the process, was turned inside out and upside down. The experience was, as Florence Howe (1991) put it, "like having your eyeballs peeled" (p. 23).

In my quest for meaning, I mapped the distinctive path of transition and transformation travelled in my academic experience. I discovered that much of my writing and knowing came from what Sternberger (1991) calls, the "stewpot of discontent" (p. 17). And keeping a lid on the conditions that shaped my knowledge was a constant struggle to re-fine and re-define ways of disguising this knowledge in academia. It meant struggling with the contradictory nature of being an academic and artist, of dismissing what has been central to my creative life. As Sternberger claims, "It isn't a matter of whether you can go home again. You just do. Language, the most ghostly kind of travel, hands out the tickets" (p. 134). My ticket came in the form of women's words. Lost in the "academic wilderness" I followed the path of bread crumbs left by the women who had walked the path before me.

My Travels with Alice

During the development of the thesis quiet moments of reading for simple pleasure were few and far between. Having sold my car I came to appreciate the long train rides into the city as a time to indulge in such a luxury. During these passages, from home to the university, I began reading Alice Walker's (1996), *The Same River*

Twice: Honouring the Difficult. Here, Walker chronicles her transition following the immense success of *The Color Purple* (1985), from the reclusive life of a poet and writer to one of public figure. Composed of journal entries, correspondence, essays, articles, and a screenplay the book, Walker considered, would be especially useful for women "as a record of a process" (1996, p. 33).

Back and forth, as I rode the tracks and read her book, in the early mornings and the silent evenings, the parallels of our creative, inner journeys surfaced despite the so different landscapes of our outer lives. How do the private and public mesh during times of intense creativity and stress? In what ways do they support or weaken each other?

At times I was overcome by the relief and joy in recognizing my own way of perceiving the world in Walker's. In passages where Walker (1996) describes moments when she could not "speak" I felt silenced; at times when attempts to "forget" failed her, my memory faltered, and the well of her "soul-deep exhaustion", I shared daily. I had been struggling with my writing, sidetracked by attempts to write in a voice that was not truly mine. I felt the split. It was as if I had to leave the artist in her seat the moment I got off the train.

The university was a lonely place. Caught between the constraints of time and the confines of the isolation I needed in order to create, I often spent days on end talking to no one but myself. But I was never truly alone. As Walker (1996) explains,

> Always with me was the inner twin; my true nature, my true self. It is timeless, free, compassionate, and in love with whatever is natural to me. This was the self that came in dreams, to be pursued in essays I was writing at the time. (p. 32)

I had secretly relied on my own "inner twin" for company since childhood but dared not bring her out publicly now. She had been called everything from naughty and funny to wild and loose. She was attracted to the oddest of people met under the strangest of circumstances. She had been labelled stubborn and silly, worthless and weird. But here I was reading in Walker's words a recognition of my authentic perceptions — not in terms of defects and inadequacies I had been accustomed to but, rather, in terms of uniqueness and abundance. Like Walker (1996), I also thought I was suited to "the wondrous quality of life to which I was apparently born attuned" (p. 33) but, unlike Walker, I had spent a lifetime trying to conceal rather than celebrate this. Walker explains the value of her own authenticity: "I know I am of most use to others and to myself by being this unique self. Nature, I have noticed, is not particularly devoted to copies, and human beings needn't be either" (p. 33).

I found in Walker's words a way home. I returned to my writing. My focus had shifted; the bedrock had moved. I began again; the same river twice.

Now: The Return Home
Accepting the Paradox of Creativity

The risk involved in being a writer is tremendous, particularly in the academy. I had tried so hard not to be a writer, not to let it show — to myself or to others. I had fought to disregard the wild rush of images and the heady feeling of euphoria when the images seemingly translated themselves into words. How not to be a writer? How to kick the addiction? At times the heat of an idea would be so overwhelming that I would literally push myself away from the table, lest the warmth of it be so luring as to draw me into its flame. I resisted as best I could.

Linda Schierse Leonard (1990) suggests that perhaps the journey of the creative person and the addict are similar. She explains that while writing she had oftentimes experienced the terror, anxiety, and desperation that accompanies the creative process as well as the "moments of mystical fervor" (p. 3). She writes that the connection between addiction and creativity is buried in the original etymological roots. Originally, the word addiction had a spiritual meaning — dedication to the gods — stemming etymologically from *addicere*: to say. Thus, inherent in the spiritual meaning of addiction is the sense of dedication and determination to bear witness, to live within the tension of paradox and contradiction, in the intensity of the creative fires. Understanding the pull of creativity calmed my fears, allowed me to recognize that the only way to explain the world to myself and to others was by maintaining my integrity and honouring my authentic Self.

Transforming Self

A person of integrity is concerned with substance rather than appearance; facades crumble. Like Trinh T. Minh-ha's (1989) image of a butterfly pinned to a board I had felt trapped in an academic name game where "classification entails death" (p. 48). Clipping the voice of the writer from my texts was like plucking my tongue. I was speechless. I needed the artist to draw, to give shape, to name the fullness of my experience in order for it to become seen, known, heard, understood, in order for it to appear whole before my very own as well as others eyes. Zeidenstein (1989) explains that writing "is one of the few experiences that matches the intensity of life. Almost everything else seems partial, or not able to *contain* the feelings aroused, as Stanley Kunitz wrote, by living and dying at the same time" (p. 81).

Indeed, there is the sentence that you save and then there is the one that saves you.

Why Do It?

Cameron (1992) argues that "an artist in order to function fully, must be both vulnerable and resilient. Turned in on itself, creativity becomes both consolation and a source of isolation." (p. 11) Certainly writing allowed my private self to survive. And feminist theory enabled the initial stages of change that helped me to close the gap, heal the wound between my public and private writing lives. I soon learned that separating who I was from how and what I wrote was demeaning. In the past writing had meant foregoing important nuances in meanings, transforming the colours and depth of experiences. It meant shrinking the scope of my knowing to a kernel from a cob. My confidence as a writer was faint and fragile. I bent with each gust of wind, each word of critique or questioning. I mistrusted and stood in disbelief at my thesis supervisor's suggestion that entitlement was not something I would be rewarded with. Instead, it was something I would have to appropriate for myself. That, Metzger (1992) explains "is the beginning; to know that we have a right to the creative and to follow it where it leads"(p. 31). This is something we know when we are young but forget as we age. Certainly, the concept of this was contrary to my understanding of the world from my position of class, education, and background. In academe, you do not create your own life, you must create the one they give you.

Transforming Academe

Lillian Robinson (1994) says that immigrants move into the temple of culture and dare to rearrange the altar. As an innovative text and process, my work was an example of this realignment. Indeed, narrating this kind of renovation and renewal remains important. For by revealing the relationship between the author, the work, and her circumstances we re-accentuate the connections between art and life and break the silence of the cultural realities of gender, class, and creative destinies. Martin (2000) too makes the important point that "to be ignorant of how educated women of this and earlier times solved the dilemma of living contradictions is to be condemned to reinvent our lives and our work from one moment to the next" (p. 145).

Robinson's and Martin's words are a reminder of my obligation as an academic, woman, writer, of the social contract between the academy and women like myself. Women whose life circumstances are such that they rarely experience conditions which nurture their art or work, conditions of financial and spiritual leisure, and physical space, energy, and power to create alternatives to mainstream ways of knowing and being. Indeed, if women like myself are to join in the knowledge-making enterprise we must reveal the weave of the text, name the stitches used in its conception. It is in this spirit and with such conviction that I write here. It is, as Alice Walker (1996) reminds us, the process that needs to be documented. And though the doctoral thesis process itself was almost disabling, the lessons I have learned from it are what have helped me move ahead and have strengthened my writer's spine.

However, like my immigrant heart, the work of the thesis itself has not yet found a port. It remains at sea, caught in the ebb and flow of acceptance and rejection, in the perception of what "counts" and what does not "count" as knowledge.

To Begin Again the Same River Twice
Chambers (1994) suggests that we might regard movement not as an awkward interval between fixed points of departure and arrival but as a mode of being in the world. The question would be, then, not how to arrive but how to move, how to identify convergent and divergent movement, and the challenge would be how to notate such events, how to give them historical and social value. And so, the importance of documenting thesis journeys remains in its movement geographically, psychologically, ontologically. Mapping the terrain of women's educational experience remains crucial to the project of transforming academe.

Ironically, the very contradictions which the thesis journey fostered served to heighten my own awareness of my identity as a writer. And, though I had struggled to contain the writer, she did break free. It was inevitable. From Caroline Forché, I learned that "what keeps you from your work becomes your work" (in Sternberger, 1991, p. 233). Indeed, for years what took me away from my work was the inherited belief that as a female artist and writer I could not possibly speak in a language that best revealed my knowledge. However, in maintaining my integrity in the thesis process I learned that vulnerability is the "place", the stance, from which I write and teach (Kamanos Gamelin, 2005). As anthropologist, Ruth Behar (1996) explains, "when you write vulnerably, others respond vulnerably…. [T]o write vulnerably is like a Pandora's Box. Who can say what will come flying out?" (p. 77).

Gloria Steinem (in Martin, 2000) notes that "academic acceptance too often demands the rejection of authenticity — one's own, other people's and sometimes whole chunks of human experience" (p. x). Indeed, all women do not think, talk, and write alike. Our visions are multiple; our creative forms varied. Our history, knowing and experiences collide, contrast, and jostle for recognition. And along with the scientists, historians and traditional female scholars, we need to begin to recognize and acknowledge these alternative ways of women's knowing, being, doing. This cannot be accomplished by replicating what is already in the mainstream academic picture but by recognizing the importance of what has been left out (Kamanos Gamelin, 2000).

It is to begin again, the same river twice.

References

Behar, R. (1996). *The vulnerable observer: Anthropology that breaks your heart.* Boston, MA: Beacon Press.

Cameron, J. (1992). *The artist's way.* New York, NY: G. P. Putnam's Sons.

Chambers, I. (1994). *Migrancy, culture, identity.* New York, NY: Routledge.

Christian-Smith, L., & Kellor, K. (Eds.). (1999). *Women of the academy: Everyday knowledge and uncommon truths.* Oxford,

UK: Westview Press.

Eisner, E. (1991). *The enlightened eye: Qualitative research and the enhancement of educational experience.* New York, NY: MacMillan.

Geertz, C. (1973). *The interpretation of culture.* New York, NY: Basic Books.

Howe, F. (Ed.). (1991). *Traditions and talents of women.* Urbana, IL: University of Illinois Press.

Kamanos Gamelin, A. (2000). The Canadian quilt: Image of us in small squares. *Atlantis: A Women's Studies Journal, 24*(2). 147-153.

Kamanos Gamelin, A. (2001). *Home and away: The female artist in academia.* Unpublished doctoral thesis, McGill University, Montreal, QC, Canada.

Kamanos Gamelin, A. (2005). The sand diaries: Visions, vulnerability and self-study. In C. Mitchell & S. Weber (Eds.), *Just who do we think we are? Methodologies for autobiography and self-study in teaching* (pp. 183-192). New York, NY: Routledge Falmer

Leonard, L. (1990). *Witness to the fire: Creativity and the veil of addiction.* Boston, MA: Shambhala.

Lorde, A. (1981). The master's tools will never dismantle the master's house. In C. Morrage & G. Anzaldua (Eds.), *The bridge called my back: Writings by radical women of color* (pp. 99-103). Watertown, MA: Persephone Press.

Martin, R. J. (2000). *Coming of age in the academy: Rekindling women's hopes and reforming the academy.* New York, NY: Routledge.

Metzger, D. (1992). *Writing for your life.* San Francisco, CA: Harper Publishing.

Robinson, L. (1994). Writing & arithmetic: The lessons silence has taught us. In Hedges, E., & Fishkin, S. (Eds.), *Listening to silences: New essays in feminist criticism* (pp. 23-48). New York,

NY: Oxford University Press.

Sternberger, J. (Ed.). (1991). *The writer on her work* (Vol. 1). New York, NY: W.W. Norton.

Trinh-Minh Ha T. (1989). *Woman, native, other: Writing postcoloniality and feminism.* Bloomington, IN: Indiana University Press.

Walker, A. (1985). *The color purple.* New York, NY: Simon & Schuster Publishing.

Walker, A. (1996). *The same river twice: Honoring the difficult.* New York, NY: Scribner.

Whitehead, J. (1993). *The growth of educational knowledge: Creating your own living educational theories.* Dartmouth, UK: Hyde Publications.

Zeidenstein, S. (Ed.). (1989). *A wider giving: Women writing after a long silence.* Goshen, CT: Chicory Blue Press.

About the Author
ANASTASIA KAMANOS GAMELIN received her PhD from McGill University, Montreal, QC. She is a professor, Faculty of Education, Effat College, Saudi Arabia's first institution of higher learning for women, and Adjunct Professor, Liberal Arts Program, Union University. She holds a postdoctoral research fellowship from GREAPE (Research in Ethnicity & Pluralism in Education) at the University of Montreal's Centre for Ethnic Studies. Anastasia recently accepted a position as Program Leader with the Royal University for Women in Bahrain.

Anastasia's doctoral thesis *Home and Away: The Female Artist in Academia* examines the conflicts, contradictions, and paradoxes inherent in the lives of those women who, as artists and academics, seek to connect their personal and professional lives in their work. This performative text explores how creativity and the pursuit of self-knowledge relate to the lives of female artists and academics and arises from a study of her own experience as woman, writer, and academic.

15. Disrupting Character Development: On Not Knowing Who We Are

by Elizabeth de Freitas

Anomalous thinking teases the border between the known and the unknown and creates a third imagined space where contingency and potentiality thrive (Ellsworth, 2005). Fiction, according to Wolfgang Iser (2000), "subsidizes the unknowable" and creates a space for speculation. This chapter explores the process of fiction writing as a form of scholarship that works the ruins of post-foundational research. It traces my development as an arts-informed scholar during my doctoral studies, focusing on pivotal moments in which my method took shape. These moments of self-re-cognition, in which I became increasingly self-conscious of the art of crafting a work of fiction, were crucial in the development of my theoretical framework.

The research began when I was hired as a mathematics teacher in an all-female private school in Toronto, Ontario. I began crafting *speculative* notes about the cultural meaning of specific incidents and particular school practices, inspired by the silences and the unsaid in such moments. I perceived the school as a highly exotic context because of my prior personal experiences. My reflections were an attempt to negotiate some sort of legitimacy in a radically unfamiliar space. My re-visioning of the phenomena was always mediated by my sense that fictionalizing was a means of making the invisible visible. Fluck (2003) argues that fiction has a stake in social justice precisely because it is responsible for carving out a space where other faces can be seen and other voices heard. The writing became an act of defiance and hope.

First Impressions

My first notes were vengeful and visceral. I was the shock-victim immersed in a strange culture, and the writing was highly therapeutic. A familiar anxiety repeatedly gripped my conscience and demanded that I write my way through the confusion. My notes allowed me to structure the surge of emotion and sustain my attention on what I believed to be absurdities specific to my participation in the context. These notes are for the most part polemical and incisive, roaring with the thunder of my anger and surprise. I could not bear the apparent artifice of the institution, the deceptive portrayal of permanence and meaning, the assumption that virtue and truth were captured and known, and ultimately and, perhaps, most profoundly, I was deeply troubled by the implications of my complicity as a participating teacher.

The writing, therefore, despite or perhaps because of its speculative nature, was immediate and highly sensory. The process of inquiry *was* the writing, as though the act of fictionalizing came first, before any notion of re-presentation. I was instantly part of the play, negotiating the meaning of the context. I am not speaking here about my teacher identity per se, although my teaching philosophy is equally disruptive of the status quo. I am speaking as a writer. I perceived the school context as a fluid process of construction and I felt immediately at odds with the perceived, prevailing ideology that seemed intent on pretending it was immoveable. Indulging my outsider privilege, I reconstructed the others, imposed an imagined transparency, and created hidden motives and alternative outcomes. This was my method of reading the context "otherwise". I cannot claim to have witnessed a detached phenomenon nor to have created an objective account. I entered the context with the intention of storying the teaching experience. I was drawn to the private school context because I was able to imagine myself as a writing self mapping out alternative cognitive, affective, and cultural experiences through fictive accounts. By selecting a school that represented, in my own field of experience, oppressive institutional norms and elite class privilege, my writing self envisioned its own doubling as a fictive teacher identity struggling against inequity. I arrived with the assumption that I would pursue artful storying as a form of inquiry into the regulative regimes of truth and tradition. The resulting novel is both my story and a story of others, a story that teases the borders between self and other in its method of construction, its form of address, and its thematic content.

Imagining Otherwise

My first notes were replete with emotion and judgment. Most of these early experiments in thinking were attached to the fictional character Agnes Fu who, like me, was painfully aware of the privilege enjoyed by the school community:

Disrupting Character Development

Agnes Fu contemplates the prefects with fear and trembling. She finds their massive display of exuberance disturbing, their mob-like connections troubling, and their evident self-possession a sign of profound privilege. She wonders how they imagine world poverty. She wonders if their understanding of global hunger involves charming grateful children. (de Freitas, 2003, p. 52)

The anger of these fictional notes was later tamed by further character development, and the emotion was harnessed to a linear narrative. With time I interrupted the desperate and almost tyrannical sense of closure enfolded in these first reflections. These initial notes reveal a reciprocal miss-recognition on behalf of myself and the community. There was a shared failure to identify and warrant distinctive differences, and I fell victim to self-gratifying delusions that the context exhibited a seamless, coherent, and unitary culture. I was the alienated outsider: the sensitive writer, the impoverished teacher, the uninvited inquirer. And they were the privileged community of insiders without rift or contradiction.

Only after a temporal sense of self was established in the community was I able to explore the proliferation of conflicting voices given sound through my own fictive projections. Despite this growing awareness, the struggle to recognize and nurture difference remains within the thesis in both thematic and technical elements. I did not abandon these initial declamatory assessments, although many were redrawn through alternative perspectives that troubled or interrupted the original seamless portrait. In the process of locating these first traces of speculation within an increasingly complex imagined world, I devised strategies for characters to alter their social environment and effect change. This reflexive process of attending to the layers of the imagined other was in itself a profound educative experience. But it was important that this initial voice still be heard and not be completely erased by the sometimes too righteous voice of the reflexive narrator. Retaining the voice of misrecognition was a deliberate attempt to keep the story provocative, to trouble the reader, and disrupt any false intimacy that reflexive writing might evoke.

The Burden of Narrative

After reading the first draft I realized that my character development appeared awkward and unconvincing. I decided to revise the narrative from the end backwards, knowing where I intended the characters to arrive. The retrospective glance forced me to assess the beginning chapters and the characters as they walked onto the scene. Agnes Fu seemed overly naive for where I intended to take her. I had documented her anguish at the outset and intimated how that anguish might fuel her desire for change. But her debilitating self-doubt dominated her scenes and it was hard to imagine her personal growth. I wanted the story to offer more than a tragic end and I wanted Agnes to embrace a form of agency. Depicting the development of agency was perhaps the most difficult challenge in my work.

A work of fiction should cultivate ambiguity; prescription for action and change undermines the power of speculative thinking. Experimental thinking generates potential spaces, as opposed to specific models. The difficulty lies in crafting characters so that their promise for action is plausible. In the case of Agnes, I decided that her journey started from a far more informed space than I had originally imagined. She had reservations about teaching mathematics and returning to high school but she also had an incredibly rich background in the humanities and was an avid reader of philosophy and sociology. I had initially introduced her as the novice math teacher, hoping that her vulnerability would be her defining trait. But I soon realized that vulnerability is debilitating unless it is in relation to a particular past and a potential future, unless it is located within a narrative. There was a life his-

tory to Agnes that needed to be there so as to flesh out her character and give her voice an appropriate strength, even in those first
few encounters. I wrote new chapters in which Agnes spoke with
informed understanding about political motives and change. I
rewrote introductory paragraphs about Agnes so as to open up her
person and potential for the developments later in the novel. In
doing so, I began to wonder how much of our narrative research
misrecognizes beginnings and to what extent are we trapped in
formulaic notions of a life trajectory. The very structure of narrative tension and resolution demands a movement from less to
whole. It is difficult to hold onto the
partial truth that both begins and ends the story. Under further
revisions, I relaxed the parabolic path of enlightenment in the lives
of the characters, by complicating the incidents at the end of the
story and raising the consciousness of the characters at the very
outset.

Contingent Positions

   I invented the character Martha West during a graduate course
which focused on the alternative forms of arts-informed research.
Her name conjured "Martha Quest", the self-scrutinizing character of Doris Lessing's *Children of Violence* series, and underscored
her western perspectives on issues of knowledge and representation
(Lessing, 1997). Martha became a medium for expressing and
questioning my method of experimental thinking. She was the
conflicted voice of traditional inquiry, searching for a new relational encounter between the knower and the unknown. She
entered the story as an educational researcher who had been hired
by the school's board of directors to write a popular history book
celebrating its centennial. Her pursuit of a meaningful form of
authorship at the school evolved through various topologies. Her

desire to write against the grain was compromised by her need to affirm the status quo. Many of her scenes depict the inner turmoil of her ambivalence around research and representation. The following excerpt dwells on her ruminations in the school archives, glancing through black accounting books:

> Martha, alone, her mind free of feelings, knows that numbers cannot lie. They have no intentional propensity. Numbers are the perfect existential being. They bring on nausea, our sickness unto death. Now, thinks Martha, here is a feeling. Nausea is the ultimate visceral feeling. She wishes she could eat the numbers up and swallow them whole and feel that gut-wrenching nausea. She finds the last entry in one of the black books, selects a finely sharpened pencil from the jar, and begins scratching numbers down. She is unaware of how long she stays there, and how many pages of sabotage numbers she enters. (de Freitas, 2003, p. 62)

Conflicted feelings dominated Martha's scenes from the outset. I crafted her character as a place of ongoing and indefinite negotiation. She was strategically positioned to embody ambivalence and lack of closure. Inspired by the critical poststructural theory I was reading at the time, I aimed to problematize her epistemic authority as the researcher and to subjunctify her knowledge claims. I refused to let her idly enact the power of research without also reflecting on the asymmetry of that power. Fiction writing allowed me to explore an imagined world of contingent and partial truths. My hope is that the reader will vacillate with Martha as she indulges in her dubious acts of inquiry. The sustained examination of Martha's motives shifts from one vantage point to another, creating an unstable ground of speculation.

Belonging to Language

As the writing evolved, the story was increasingly dominated by Martha West's interior monologues. It was as though she had wrestled the story away from me. Martha's chapters depicted a sort of self-disturbing form of sustained reflection, a "rigorous disorientation" (St. Pierre, 2002) that interrupted the flow of the narrative. Martha dwells on her ethnographic intentions, naming the constraints that regulate her voice, questioning the process of re-inscription in the school archives, and tracing the path of power relations across the school terrain. She thoroughly subjunctifies all future action, transforming her intentional state into a detached conditional, and dislocating herself from her purpose. Such extreme doubt disrupted the linear flow of narrative and stalled the temporal development of the plot. Her intentions no longer functioned as reasons for action in a diachronically structured story. Martha stopped herself from entering narrative time, locked in a moment of resistance which was not a moment of traditional agency precisely because she refused to author herself into a pre-scribed future. The reader wants to move on, wants to move with her, senses her potential, imagines a future, anticipates action, and expects development. But the reader is made to dwell in the moment of resistance.

John Caputo (2000) suggests that hermeneutic inquiry intersects with deconstruction when the researcher rigorously attends to the situated facticity of her intentions and allows her horizon of meaning to be breached by the irreducible alterity of the research subject. The character of Martha West is inspired by the risk involved in pursuing this form of radical hermeneutics. I wanted to write a research story that depicted the turmoil of a researcher who "pushes facticity to its limits", disrupting the border between in-side and outside, and yet maintaining the "structural non-knowing" of the other, and resisting the desire to resolve the *aporia* and fuse the horizons. The resulting novel became strangely melancholic, as though the character Martha West knew all along that her intentions were always already traces of yet other traces, indeed as though she was aware of this impossible situation even before me.

Caputo's (2000) critical hermeneutics is my character's dilemma. And it is not one she lives easily. Her story is almost a non-story, a rhizomatic writing that works the ruins of post-foundational inquiry. Such writing, as Elizabeth St. Pierre (2002) states, has given up on intentions and cannot see far down the road. "It stalls, gets stuck, thumbs its nose at order, goes someplace the author didn't know existed ahead of time, stumbles over its sense, spins around its middle, forgoing ends, [and] wraps idea around idea" (p. 65).

When I reflected on the narrative as a whole and looked back at the disorientation of my characters, I wondered why I kept them from integrating into the school community. My own life history traces an often self-imposed marginal existence on the edges of communities. But with persistent efforts to introduce explicit moments of belonging in the text, be it between the main characters or otherwise, I began to see how their relation to language was itself the site of their belonging. Each attempt to articulate a research agenda or pedagogy was always (and already) swallowed up by systems of signification in which they dwelled. Each telling of their "interior" motives was torn from them and dispersed through the medium of language. It is language they belong to and language that abandons them. For in performing language they become immediately conscious of their contingent embodied limits and this awareness demands its own deconstruction, and so they wander, disoriented, in search of other limits not yet imagined.

References

Caputo, J. (2000). *More radical Hermeneutics: On not knowing who we are.* Indianapolis, IN: Indiana University Press.

de Freitas, E. (2003). *The wrong shoe and other misfits: Fiction writing as reflexive research.* Unpublished doctoral thesis, University of Toronto, Toronto, ON, Canada.

Ellsworth, E. (2005). *Places of learning: Media, architecture, pedagogy.* New York, NY: Routledge

Fluck, W. (2003). Fiction and justice. *New Literary History 34*, 19-42.

Iser, W. (2000). *The range of interpretation.* New York, NY: Columbia Press.

Lessing, D. (1997). *Martha Quest.* London, UK: Hart-Davis MacGibbon.

St. Pierre, E. (2002). Circling the text: Nomadic writing practices. In N. K. Denzin & Y. S. Lincoln (Eds.) *Qualitative inquiry reader* (pp. 51-69). Thousand Oaks, CA: Sage Publications.

About the Author

ELIZABETH DE FREITAS is Associate Professor at the Faculty of Education, Adelphi University. She is the author of *Keel Kissing Bottom*. She has published arts-informed research articles in the *International Journal of Education and the Arts, Journal of the Canadian Association of Curriculum Studies, Educational Studies in Mathematics,* an l *arts-informed.* As a faculty advisor, she encourages her graduate students to explore alternative forms of research.

The Wrong Shoe and Other Misfits: Fiction as a Reflexive Form of Inquiry, Liz's doctoral thesis, consists of three parts: The first is an introductory chapter which recounts the emergence and rationale of her theoretical framework, the second is a novel consisting of twenty-three short chapters, and the third is a final interpretive chapter reflecting on the impact of using specific literary devices in the structuring of research fictions.

16. Sketchy Lines

by SHARON SBROCCHI

In less than two minutes I draw a memory map. My hand hesitates, momentarily, as I ask myself, "What point in time do I draw?" I quickly resolve to create a map that depicts my childhood home, as it was, when I was between seven and 12 years of age.

Drawing the map helps me focus a broad range of stories, emotions and general information from within. It gives birth to a rapid flow of memory. I translate my knowledge and my way of knowing with a distinct measure of confidence. I finish the task, carefully slip the precious "artifact" into an archival quality plastic sleeve and file it away for safekeeping. Done.

It took less than two minutes to draw the memory map and three more years to complete the thesis — a process that is complete for only a moment.

I enter my thesis inquiry by asking, "What is the significance of a childhood sense of place within an adult's life? How do childhood place-based experiences, in the out-of-doors, influence adult perspectives concerning notions of self and place?" As I toy with the questions I resist admitting they are rooted in *my* life history — albeit a small element of it. My preconceived ideas about doing autobiographical work — such as, concerns that the text will appear self-absorbed and wondering where to find "content" worth writing about within the "context" of my life — slow me down. And, yet, the inquiry texts that inspire me are those firmly rooted in the autobiographical. I need to adjust a few underlying assumptions about what "counts" as research, knowledge development, and how we come to know. I must do this in a personally meaningful way in order to understand the underlying reasons for the decisions I make within the process of inquiry. These decisions not only reflect the position of the researcher *within the text* but the position of the researcher — as *a researcher*.

I sit in a large open lounge space that overlooks the City of Toronto. Sunlight radiates through the cloudy glass and an intense heat beats down on me as I wait for Gary, my thesis supervisor, to arrive. I am nervous. His presence leaves me feeling unsure of myself because I have so much to learn and so far to go. This understanding is entrenched in the notion that obtaining a doctoral degree is rooted in the "quantity" and "expertise" of accumulated knowledge combined with "extraordinary" intelligence. Hmm?

I cannot remember the purpose of our meeting that afternoon but I do remember the focus of our conversation. We discussed the place I call Zorra Street, my childhood home. Then, in mid-conversation, Gary suggests I draw a "sense of place" map. Right now. At this moment! He hands me a sharpened pencil. I look perplexed. "Now?" I ask. I draw it with ease. I know the place. Extraordinary intelligence? Ordinary knowledge. Hmm?

The stories swirling within me, evoked by the image of the map, quickly find their way into my conversations and onto pages of my inquiry. As I literally walk through the place depicted on the map — again and again and again — I flesh out the stories held within the lines on the page. My presence *in place* breathes life into the remembrances I hold within me. I follow the pathways I travelled as a child and gather artifacts. I photograph the significant spots I see, listen to the sound of cherished memories, feel the presence of place beneath my feet, and drink in the changes that envelop me.

I continue the inquiry in the company of childhood friends (Lillian and Amalia) and begin the collective part of the process by asking each of the women to draw a "sense of place map". I am struck by the similarities and the differences between their sketch maps and mine. Each memory map tells a distinct story and places the artist centrally within it as she sketches the lines of her life. I gather the precious "artifacts", carefully slip them in an archival quality plastic sleeve, and file them away for safekeeping.

"Wait a minute! I want to see her map." Lillian chuckles to soften the tone of her request. "Show me Amalia's map." I open the binder to where I have carefully filed documents, photographs, and other accumulated pieces of information. "This is Amalia's map. This map is mine." I offer her the artifacts. "This is unlabelled!" she bursts, "You can't make a map without labeling it or attaching a legend. It has no meaning." Meaning. My sense of place map is a blank white page with sketchy lines traced across it. There are no words on the page but I *know* there is meaning in it.

Throughout the process we gather photographic images of places that evoke memories of our childhood experiences in the out-of-doors. We collect images as we walk and talk about our experiences growing up on Zorra Street, in the south end of the former city of Etobicoke, during the 1960s and 1970s. We photograph remembered places while walking through the current state of deterioration and abandonment of the neighbourhood. The photographic images we collect powerfully juxtapose the childhood stories of our experiences-in-place as we wonder "What happened here?" The past and the present meet in the moment of our shared remembrances as we stand in the exact spot we played when we were children. We stand in the midst of a continually changing urban context and search for traces of our history.

I pull into the parking lot of the city archives. I love it here. The walls of "boxed" treasures intrigue me. "Time in a box." I chuckle to myself as I walk toward the entrance of the building. A melody sneaks up on me and, quite unexpectedly, I softly hum the Jim Croce (1972) tune, "Time in a Bottle." Sentimental fool. I laugh, swing open the large glass door, and check in with security. I sprint up the stairs, place my bag in the locker, and cruise once around the small library before asking for a little help. In a short while, I am searching through computerized records for information connected to our childhood home.

When I find box 80069-5 and box 80069-6, series 3, files 452 and 453 respectively, on the database my heart begins to pound. Maybe this is it. I complete the request for the boxes to be retrieved from the walls of storage and I wait. An archivist arrives carrying a pair of white gloves. "You will need these to handle the photographs," he says, as he offers me a pair of gloves and rolls a cart of boxes up beside the desk where I am seated. I carefully read the numbers on the boxes, checking to make sure they are correct. I open box 80069-5. There are fourteen photographs carefully slipped into protective sleeves taken of The Queensway (the major road located at the "top" of our street) in 1967. I open box 80069-6 and there are twenty more photographs to add to the series. Held there within the photographs, suspended in time, is the landscape of my childhood. Places I have not seen in years because they no longer exist in exactly the same way. I sit poring over the photos, one by one, laughing. As I gaze at the photos a flood of stories fills me.

A few weeks later, I carefully pin copies of the archival images along the wall of my office. I follow the panorama and look for points of intersection. Where can I see my life in these photographs? What purpose can they serve in the text? What form will it take?

I search for different perspectives on the questions we ask within the piles of municipal documents on my desk and rummage through other volumes of work that echo the sentiments and speculations concerning notions of place we touch upon within our conversations. I weave the voices of academics and artists who engage with the question of the relationship between self and place — self and other — within their work, and juxtapose the words with the photographic images of the place we are exploring. The notion of domicide is guided by the work of J. Douglas Porteous and Sandra E. Smith (2001) while the concept of ecological identity and the use of a "sense of place" map is rooted in the work of Mitchell Thomashow (1995). The scholartistry of J. Gary Knowles and Suzanne Thomas (2001), as inspired by Canadian artist Marlene Creates (1990, 1991), awakens me to the significance of developing a structure in the design of the text. I continue to gather multidimensional layers of meaning as I search for a way to pull it altogether. I know each element is intimately connected and, yet, the work feels scattered.

The archival images remain stretched across the wall of my tiny office. An organized mess of strategically arranged municipal documents sits next to a few neatly sectioned binders of transcribed conversations that correspond to a selection of photographic images. Everything is carefully sorted and slipped into *more* plastic sleeves. Tucked away at the back of one of the binders are the memory maps.

One afternoon I carefully remove our penciled maps from the back of the binder and lay them out on the kitchen table. I step back from the work and put the kettle on the stove to make a cup of tea. As I turn around and look at the maps I see the sketchy lines of continuity drawn across the crisp white pages as if I were seeing them for the first time. Amazing! It comes to me quickly. I look at my unlabelled map and see the stories in context. We labelled our maps. We fleshed out the meaning and gave them significance. The decision to label my map to create the visual representation of where we grew up and chart the pathways we followed through the process of inquiry locates the position of the researcher centrally within the text — this is my life history. But my voice is not alone, it is part of a collective story, one of many collective stories. I dash to my tiny office across the hall from the kitchen and take a few archival photographs off the wall. I lay them on the kitchen table beside the collection of memory maps. The photographs add a layer of depth to the work and provide a way for the reader to visually engage with our memories, while telling a story about our city. The photographs are special to each of us in different ways. However, they share a common element. They depict a part of our lives that is gone.

The stories we gathered are not just part of an abstract theory — they are rooted in lived experiences and drawn together in this place. Our intimate place-based experiences are located visually on the map as collective remembrances evoked by the power of place itself. We express our relationship to the place we call home and our relationship to one another as we wander through the unfolding memory map that depicts our experience of Zorra Street. Our conversations chronicle the sharing of collective memories: their stories, my stories, and our stories-in-place. The voices of the women who shared these childhood place-based experiences with me are explicitly honoured in the form of a written dialogue within the text. The shared remembrances of childhood experiences are the result of focused remembrances returned to again and again within our conversations. The physical locations are returned to repeatedly because they are significant *places* in our lives. We belong to these places; these places belong to us. Each story told in the text is a fusion of perspectives and an honouring of the uniqueness of each woman's life.

To be able to listen for the story the other person is telling I need to know my own story. I need to see where the line of my story takes a pause, intersects, and deviates from their stories. I need to be able to see the sketched lines of their lives in this place.

The strength of the reflexive process is depicted in the fusion of collective remembrances and, although, the sketchy lines that become the central organizing construct are the lines of my life, the representation of the interconnection of our shared experiences is crucial to the rigorous quality of the work. To be able to know another one must know one's self. We must learn to see the lines of another story in creative ways.

As it turned out the memory map structures the text of the thesis. It draws lines of continuity through the process and is the element that provides visual and logical coherence in the form of the representation. It answers the question, "How will the inquiry look?" as it traces a path through the process and exemplifies the conceptual significance of a focused repetition as a central construct in place theory. We share moments of re-enactment of intense sensory-based experiences of our childhood landscapes (Stilgoe, 1995) in the stories we tell one another and along the literal and metaphoric pathways we travel. We return to these moments, these focused repetitions located along the lines of our memory maps as a source of strength and creativity while we begin to explore the significance of these place-based experiences in our lives. We flesh out the sketchy lines drawn across the crisp white page....

At its conception — but without knowing the power of its

simplicity at the time — my memory map became a metaphor for the processes of inquiry I was to find in my work. It also inhabited my work as a key structural element of the manuscript, one that tied together the weavings of lives lived as children and as adult reflections upon them. Inspiration came from an unanticipated source — at the hand of a sharpened pencil and a crisp white sheet of paper in a room with a view and an insistent mentor.

References

Creates, M. (1990). *The distance between two points is measured in memories, Labrador 1988.* North Vancouver, BC: Presentation House Gallery.

Creates, M. (1991). *Places of presence: Newfoundland kin and ancestral land, Newfoundland 1989-1991.* St. John's, NL: Killick Press.

Croce, J. (1972). Time in a bottle. On *You don't mess around with Jim.* [Album, 1972]. ABC (Dunhill).

Knowles, J. G., & Thomas, S. (2001). Insights and inspiration from an artist's work, envisioning and portraying lives in context. In Cole, A. L. & J. G. Knowles, Lives in context: *The art of life history research* (pp. 208-214). Walnut Creek, CA: AltaMira Press.

Porteous, J. D., & Smith, S. E. (2001). *Domicide: The global destruction of home.* Montreal, QC & Kingston, ON: McGill-Queens's University Press.

Sbrocchi, S. (2005). *Remembering place: Domicide and a childhood home.* Unpublished doctoral thesis, University of Toronto, Toronto, ON, Canada.

Sbrocchi, S. (2007). *Remembering place: Domicide and a childhood home.* Halifax, NS & Toronto, ON: Backalong Books and Centre for Arts-Informed Research.

Stilgoe, J. R. (1995). Boyhood landscape and repetition. In G. F. Thompson (Ed.), *Landscape in America* (pp. 183-202). Austin,

TX: University of Texas Press.

Thomashow, M. (1995). *Ecological identity: Becoming a reflective environmentalist*. Cambridge, MA: MIT Press.

About the Author

SHARON SBROCCHI is a PhD graduate from the Ontario Institute for the Studies in Education, University of Toronto. Her research interests include the use of arts-informed processes to articulate a sense of place in community contexts. Sharon explores life histories of people and places whose stories are embedded in the phenomenon of domicide. She is currently working on a community sense-of-place project that fuses the notions of artist as researcher and researcher as activist.

Sharon's thesis is entitled, *Remembering Place: Domicide and a Childhood Home*. Her work focuses on the relationship between self and place in a rapidly urbanizing world wherein she maps a process of learning that embraces the transformational potential held within an arts-informed approach to inquiry to inspire reconnection to the communities where people live and reclaim the art of dwelling in place. Sharon's thesis is published by Backalong Books and the Centre for Arts-Informed Research.

Finding and Working with Form

17. Riding the Waves, Reading the Sea

by S<small>UZANNE</small> T<small>HOMAS</small>

This text is a representation of elements and processes associated with the development of my thesis, *of earth and flesh and bones and breath: Landscapes of Embodiment and Moments of Re-enactment* (Thomas, 2003, 2004), in which I organically created form in a movement from whole to parts and parts to whole rather than in a linear, sequential process. I began with the bare bones of a skeletal structure layering the flesh and substance of my phenomenological encounters in the natural world. Through the design of my scholartistry method, voice and form became inextricably intertwined and connected.

209

Finding and Working with Form

In the following poetic text I reveal the complexities associated with envisioning, imagining, creating and trans/forming form. Inspired by Robert Bringhurst's, *Ursa Major: A Polyphonic Masque for Speakers and Dancers* (2003), I play with the notion of polyphony, intertwining voices of scholar and poet, scholartist, and sea traveller. As in Bringhurst's text, voices are interwoven with one another — their crossing is as continuous as the restless, unrelenting waves of the sea.

In search of navigational guides
  feeling vibrations shudder through hull
  as seas breathe and roll
  sensing beyond compass points, markers
  maps, scales, charts

exploring form, genre, medium
  choosing a route,
  finding a course, direction of nautical flow
  seaworthiness of vessel

metaphorical structure
  sleek body,
  sharp prow slice waters,
  carving smoothly, while tapered stern
  resists yawing
  in alternating thrust of stroke

aesthetic elements
  cords fastened between gunwale and keel
  sea faring travel
  securing rudder, skeg, rescue lines, hatches

refining skills, methods, perspectives
  swift, narrow, balanced, buoyant,
  moving in a dance of body rotation

arms, thrust of legs,
feet anchoring
roots of ontology, epistemology, methodology

underpinnings
undercurrents,
rearing, erupting, tensions of push / pull motion
manoeuvring

an episteme,
riding the waters,
thrust in a myriad of shapes and forms, surfaces
riding the waters,
rolling in swells, heaving, propelling positionings

an embodied, transitional nature of being
riding the waters
above blurring, fitful, swaying depths

Seeking clarity of vision
mists lifting and unveiling
channels, beacons, buoys, safe harbours,
shoals and reefs

messengers of seas, a symphony of sounds
leaning into the winds
leaning into the world
in expectation, hope, vision.

Encountering obstacles, altering forms
swirling colours, reflections of light — drama
foreshadows, wave shadows,
gathering gales, unfathomable storms, pacing

facing complexities, obscurity, ambiguity
reading the seas

riding the dark side of the crest,
shifts in wind patterns, wave patterns
reading the seas
peaks, complex pulses,
surge of energy
lost — in dissipation

anticipation
reading the seas
moving relentlessly, discerning
origins of deep musculature
force of crossings, fetch of winds
rip tides, chops, currents

chaos
combs break, crests topple, tumble
waters bend towards shore in lines of spilling, plunging
breakers

Finding integrity, coherence, cohesion
in undulating, varying speeds,
waves complement one another, cancel each other
into a synchrony of movement
equilibrium, balance

in mindfulness, reflection
paddles stilled
gesturing contemplation
as surf spray flattens into a calmness, sereneness

deepening
steepening
in the power of art
lost in the illumination
of shimmering surfaces, shallows of land
the spirit of movement

spirit of passion
*a stroking flame
solo search,
in grasp of that pure,
elusive moment
when kayaker and sea are one.*

References

Bringhurst, R. (2003). *Ursa Major: A polyphonic masque for speakers and dancers.* Kentville, NS: Gaspereau Press.

Dowd, J. (1997). *Sea kayaking: A manual for long-distance touring.* Vancouver, BC & Toronto, ON: Greystone Books.

Thomas, S. (2003). *Of earth and flesh and bones and breath: Landscapes of Embodiment and Moments of Re-enactment.* Unpublished doctoral thesis, University of Toronto, Toronto, ON, Canada.

Thomas, S. (2004). *Of earth and flesh and bones and breath: Landscapes of embodiment and moments of re-enactment.* Halifax, NS & Toronto, ON: Backalong Books & Centre for Arts-informed Research.

About the Author

SUZANNE THOMAS is an Assistant Professor at the University of Prince Edward Island. She teaches courses in arts-informed research, qualitative research methods, place-based community arts, and Island Studies. Suzanne's book *Of earth and flesh and bones and breath: Landscapes of embodiment and moments of re-enactment* is published by Backalong Books and the Centre for Arts-informed Research. Her scholartistry is inspired by kayaking journeys along the Eastern shores of Mahone Bay, Nova Scotia, where she revels in the mystery of sea encounters.

Of earth and flesh and bones and breath: Landscapes of embodiment and moments of re-enactment, Suzanne's doctoral thesis, represents an eco-phenomenological inquiry focusing on issues of place and placelessness, embodied knowing, and transformational qualities of an aesthetic understanding. Experiences in the natural world are rendered in moments of dwelling poetically and attending photographically to engender an ecological consciousness. The reader is invited to enter into phenomenological encounters that reveal worlds of imagination and experience.

18. from the corner of my eye

by NANCY VIVA DAVIS HALIFAX

Figure 1. Nancy Viva Davis Halifax, 2001. *this red interior (c)*. Digital photograph. 11.65. cm x 10.41 cm.

Finding and Working with Form

We do not have to establish the primary principle: that the thought of the heart is the thought of images, that the heart is the seat of imagination, the imagination is the authentic voice of the heart so that if we speak from the heart we must speak imaginatively. (Hillman, 1992, p. 4)

This chapter is a rereading of one of my notebooks in which writings and drawings of my thesis, *Of rose petals and sutures, marks on a woman's body: an aesthetic and oblique inquiry into dysbody, solace, and vulnerability* (Davis Halifax, 2002) are found. A careful reading of my notebook allows me to consider and articulate some of their influence on the final thesis.

I wrote on a daily basis, always moving closer toward my subjects. I wrote on sidewalks, in grocery stores, while doing dishes. I wanted to be able to re-present my experience of the world not so that when writing "there is nothing left of the sea but a word without water" (Cixous & Jenson, 1991, p. 65). I wanted the sea to persist with its salt water and tides, and the earth to remain filled with worms.

•

I pick a notebook at random from my bookshelf. It's the fourth one; it commences June 21, 2001 and ends October 17, 2001. In between its black covers are 200 pages of notes, thoughts about what I'd been reading, small drawings, fragments of poems. This particular journal covers a portion of the period of time I was readying my final draft. I commenced it in Toronto, Ontario and remember finishing it at Artspace on Big Tancook Island, Nova Scotia. A quick review tells me the pages are well marked. On some pages a struggle seems clear as I tried to make a decision or clarify a thought. I wrote over some words, placed stars near others, pasted in a note or drawing.

I experience a sense of pressure, of "wanting to be done", when I am nearing completion of a notebook. I write more. But the last page is difficult to fill. This one is half filled with phone numbers, Email addresses. The name of a CD that one of my daughters liked. Flight numbers. Lists of words to follow etymologically: *solace, shovel, solve.* The first pages usually have observations from the previous notebook, things I do not want to let go of. There are red notes penned about hermeneutics. This first page is composed of the colours red, blue, black, the marks in pencil are beginning to fade.

•

I need to remember I am here to dream
Rough rocks, bleached bones
And I stare into the mirror trying to find a reflection of what I want
to write
On the frame of this face.

No matter. This room. Maybe this room is where she took you
Like a child takes a cookie, hungrily,
And this is where she planted the seeds
That grew into you on a dark violet night.

My room has no window. I couldn't
See the blur of a pigeon caught by a stone
Falling.
She'll be here soon. She'll take her payment.

From the corner of my eye
She gallops toward me with her
Delicious grin and the colours of the waves crashing
On the shore are silence.

•

Not a focus on meaning but on experience. I wanted, still want, my writing to focus on the expressive elements of form, image, word. My writing does not hold as its goal an ability to

217

argue or persuade. The paradigm that dominates institutions still relies on knowing about the world from a distance that privileges the rational. I want to write a text that wholly supports an emergent manner of encountering the world from within it. Not a work of linear perspective but a work of imagination and multiple perspectives.

•

How do we start writing?

I became passionate about worms. Everywhere I went there were small soft bodies, dead, and dying. These bodies became a language that would allow what was unnamed to emerge. *Their bodies, sighs upon the earth that I cannot find letters for.*

In my body the worm performed her grave presence. She was not in the category of a group or thing. I wrote that the worm had become more than herself. She bore an enormous burden. She was now a body through which I began contemplating the wounds and wounding of bodies. She made me look at knowledge from a different point of view; she made me look at the ground upon which we stand as artists and scholars and researchers (Davis Halifax, 2001). On certain days I felt substantial discomfort in my non-canonical reading of this embodied text until I read Charles Darwin (1972) whose example made me delight in this passion:

> Worms do not possess any sense of hearing. They took not the least notice of the shrill notes from a metal whistle, which was repeatedly sounded near them; nor did they of the deepest and loudest tones of a bassoon. They were indifferent to shouts, if care was taken that the breath did not strike them. when placed on a table close to the keys of a piano, which was played as loudly as possible, they remained perfectly quiet. (p. 29)

This was an inquiry full of rich description and imagination. I sensed that Darwin, dare I say, loved these worms. He proposed that worms did, indeed, have a mind of some kind, arguing that because they displayed excitation in response to the presence of different foods and attended in a differential manner to things around them, not all of their behaviour could be explained on an instinctual level. *Imagine playing the violin to the ever-present white mouse, the handmaid to science, reading Rilke to her. Carefully noting her responses to each phrase so we could better understand her intelligence.*

•

How do we start writing, representing? How do we trust that the words we use will move, delight others? How do I trust the forms that arise from a body that has been schooled to listen to the voices of authority? I learn that these questions do not matter, at least at first. At first I must just write. I re-educate myself to attend closely to the world and to write it over and over again. It is like drawing. Thinking about writing as drawing is one of the only ways that I keep my discipline. I know that as a drawer I have to keep going, keep making mistakes, wrong lines. I bring this learning to my writing. I learned to trust imagination, worms, passion, errors.

I become a close reader, looking into the cracks inside walks, under leaves, touching, and being touched by whatever I am attending to. My struggles to make decisions or clarify thoughts are clear in the markings on each page. Some pages contain annotations with dates scribbled beside them; sticky notes refer the reader back and forth through the series of journals. This worn cover is decorated with the hearts of a worm, anatomically correct, shown in a dissection, stickers of the body that a friend brought back from Japan; a price tag from a set of six needle files, and, in the lower right on the back cover, the ground of a moon is pictured against sparkly paper. What travelled from this notebook cover to the thesis itself was the image of the hearts of a worm (Figure 1). The other adornments rest on the cover as private imaginings.

•

At one point I had to understand more of the being of the worm. I wanted to draw worms. But I soon knew that was not enough. There was something fundamentally missing between the image that I held within and the worms as they existed on the page; there was no weight in my hand. The worms had a mass and my hands would feel overfull of their bodies.

I began to search for a medium that would convey this new knowledge. Clay, plaster, bronze, wax, silver. I began with a brown wax that jewellers use and which is soft enough to be molded by body heat. For hours I rolled the tiny coils that would be the segments, knowing each worm has over one hundred. I made a central coil for the body and turned her over and over to receive her muscles. I made dozens of these bodies as I strived to find a technique. While doing this I thought again about the material for casting. I decided to have them cast in pewter, a relatively soft metal with the right weight for my hand to be convinced. Inside the notebook there are scribbles leading me to the past. These notebooks contain more than my thesis. The notebooks are my encyclopedias, my reference texts. The entire shelf of a bookcase behind me is lined with them.

•

Some days I curl up in my rocking chair. Waiting. Eyes closed. I have just read a scribbled quote from Cixous and I am thinking about it. "We have forgotten that the world is there prior to us" (Cixous & Jenson, 1991, p. 65). The worm existed before my walking past it. The worm is what I tried to write with earth and water and death.

My thesis is long past and I continue to try to write and think with whatever materials come to hand. Notebooks persist in their assembly on the shelf behind me. My education continues as I explore new ways of teaching and learning and imagining. I still make sense of the world through the reversible touch of flesh to

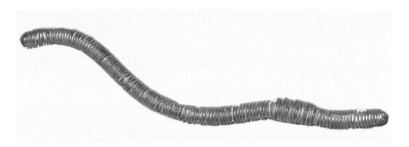

Figure 2. Nancy Viva Davis Halifax, 2002-ongoing. *underground.* Cast pewter. 110 cm x 5 cm.

flesh; knowing this touch carries a dense materiality through which an ethics of call and response is being articulated.

References

Cixous, H., & Jenson, D. (1991). *"Coming to writing" and other essays.* Cambridge, MA: Harvard University Press.

Darwin, C. (1972). *The formation of vegetable mould, through the action of worms, with observations on their habits.* New York, NY: D. Appleton. Original work published in 1896.

Davis Halifax, N. V. (2001). *journal number four.* Unpublished manuscript.

Davis Halifax, N. V. (2002). *Of rose petals and sutures, marks on a woman's body: anaesthetic and oblique inquiry into dys-body, solace and vulnerability.* Unpublished doctoral thesis, University of Toronto, Toronto. ON, Canada.

Hillman, J. (1992). *The thought of the heart; and, the soul of the world.* Dallas, TX: Spring Publications.

About the Author

NANCY VIVA DAVIS HALIFAX is an Assistant Professor, Critical Disability Studies, York University. She received her PhD from the Ontario Institute for Studies in Education, University of Toronto.

Her research interests include: the experienced body, gender, health, and ability as they are represented aesthetically. She recently held a Post-doctoral Fellowship at the University of Toronto where she focused on knowledge translation. At the time of writing Nancy worked as a consultant in knowledge media design and translation.

In Nancy's doctoral thesis, *Of rose petals and sutures, marks on a woman's body: anaesthetic and oblique inquiry into dys-body, solace and vulnerability,* disability and illness are represented as experiences that collectively enrich and challenge our understanding of embodiment, narrative, social structures, identity and politics — what it means to be human. The thesis text, congruent with life, is discontinuous, fragmented. The inclusion of photographs of illness and disability mark this work as an artful text.

19. *Currere* and Cloud-sculpting

by WARREN SELLERS and NOEL GOUGH

Noel (November 2004)

My engagement with arts-informed inquiry draws, for the most part, on narrative and poststructuralist theorizing which I perform through narrative experiments that follow (more-or-less) a process that I summarize elsewhere as, "read intertextually, write an essay, make a rhizome" (Gough, 2004a, p. 209). The "materials" from which I produce my narrative experiments include genres of literary fiction and popular media, including crime fiction (e.g., Gough, 2002), science fiction (e.g., Gough, 2004b), and particular fictional works (e.g., Gough, 1996).

Pictures rather than words are Warren's first language (e.g., Sellers, 2003). Although our respective preferences for representing and performing curriculum inquiry in prose (Noel) and pictures (Warren) have never produced anything resembling a language barrier, our different dispositions nevertheless produced occasional problems of translation. Warren lives near Wellington, New Zealand, and undertook his doctoral degree in Education at Deakin University (Melbourne, Australia) as an off-campus student under my supervision. We mostly communicate by Email.

We focus here on what the editors of this volume might call an "epiphany of process". Early in Warren's doctoral degree candidacy he produced a variety of poetic musings on, and picturings of, the objects of his inquiry: *currere*, generativity, learning, complexity, and so on (see Figure 1).

I did not always understand Warren's musings and picturings (I would have had a hard time telling someone else what *he* meant in *my* words) but I found them pleasingly puzzling. To support and

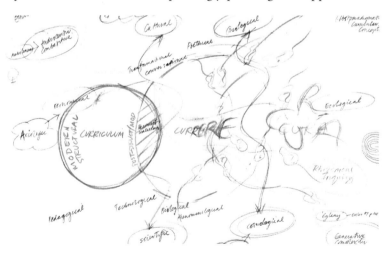

Figure 1. Warren Sellers, 2003. *Musing and Picturing*. Colour pencil on paper. 42 cm x 59 cm.

guide Warren's creativity I did not try to persuade him to *represent* his conceptual refinements and inventions in academic prose but encouraged him to perform them in ways that made their effects and consequences accessible to his audience(s).

We elaborate on an episode that illustrates how our respective modes of scholartistry meshed in generative ways. It began with an Email in which I responded to one of Warren's draft chapters — and which also demonstrates my disposition to read academic texts for their intertextual relations with many (any) other texts: "Some of what you wrote reminded me of J. G. Ballard's (1973) surreal short stories from collections such as *Vermilion Sands*, e.g., The *cloud-sculptors of Coral D*. Maybe I see you doing some cloud-sculpting...."

Warren (March 2003)

The story (Ballard, 1973) concerns a pilot (grounded by injury) who has retired to a surrealistically dangerous desert resort. The pilot adjusts to this environment by engaging with flying craft — kites, then gliders — tethered by cables from the ground. Others join the pilot to launch an enterprise which evolves from the remark of one which "contained a complete understanding of my motives. He pointed to the coral towers rising above us into the evening sky. 'With silver iodide we could carve the clouds'" (p. 12). Practically, this involves spraying iodide crystals at the clouds carving away "the flock-like tissue", and forming it into "drops of condensing spray" (p. 14). Drama emerges through the narcissistic desires of a *femme fatale* who challenges the sculptors to render her from the "storm-nimbus" that swirled over their heads. "For clouds like these I need a Michelangelo of the sky.... What about Nolan? Is he too frightened as well?" (p. 26). The challenge is accepted: One sculptor is devoured and destroyed but Nolan, the pilot, rides the whirlwind with fatal consequences for the *femme*.

My reading of Ballard's story recognizes the intertwining of his skeptical commentary on *man*ipulating illusory reality with his visionary allegories for emergent creative potential. The pilot represents the disrupting reality of the emasculate modern world: Conventional consciousness, damaged and shoved aside by more ambitious worlds of ideological reality. Nevertheless, awareness of potentials beyond the rose-tinted virtual horizons sustains challenges. Flying remains a very male domain and, perhaps, it signifies the quintessential challenge towards reconceptualizing control as other than the egoistic pursuit of omnipotence. That is, to recognize "control" *with* the world not *of* it, in the sense that William Doll (2002) writes of it as "within, not lying outside or imposed on, situations, as arising naturally and complexly from rather simple interactions" (p. 54).

My interpretation of Gough's musing on "doing some cloud-sculpting" interacts with this reconception of control through our interactions with each other and the idea and this writing, and so on…. I will explain this by using Ballard's story: I am the pilot with a past in a technical medium. I have retired from the modernistic controls of the commercial world to the vermilion sands of the academy. Within academe I have been able to review how "Many paths of change are potentially possible, and which one is selected is an expression of the particular kind of structural coherence the unit has, in a continuous tinkering" (Varela, 1987, p. 61). This notion of tinkering and its coherence is, I believe, reflected in the metaphor of cloud-sculpting. However, like the pilot, I am nervously cautious about cutting loose the tethers and flying free to re-vision and sculpt the clouds. I therefore cast Gough in the *femme fatale* role — to challenge me to the call for a "Michelangelo of the sky" and to remind me of the intrinsic difficulties involved in responding. Gough's (and Doll, 2002) curriculum visions pertain to the realm of clouds — they have presently used the metaphor of Ghosts — but both are conceptually nebulous. Thus a significant challenge for emerging curricularists is

226

generating conceptual forms within nebulous nuances, such as reconceptualising "control". Cloud-sculpting is a useful and pertinent analogy for a prospective approach to this control imaginary because it elaborates the complexity embodied in conceiving "controlling" — not as a force but as spirit in the vivifying sense. Clouds are analogous with spirit in this sense too, by representing energies not otherwise recognizable. In short, "doing some cloud-sculpting" is a way (among many) for continually expressing reconceptualizing control or, as Doll (2002) suggests, "another, new, livelier spirit of control" (p. 28).

Noel and Warren (November 2004)

This episode seems to be rich in possibilities for understanding some of the ways in which scholartists can be supported in what are still somewhat risky endeavours. Borrowing from Joni Mitchell, "We've looked at cloud-sculpting from both sides now" and see that Warren could have chosen much less demanding paths to explore and more obvious and explicit questions to investigate (and we suspect that some supervisors might have encouraged him to take such lines of less resistance). We conclude with Warren's more recent musings on cloud-sculpting as an invitation to interpretive, recursive, and enactive processing of embodied curriculum inquiry.

Warren (November 2004)
Cloud-sculpting…*Currere*

When reading I often think visually; it is like having a picture dictionary / thesaurus always running in my mind. I contextualize a word or words in a pictorial phrase that exemplifies the meanings I make through thinking. I read / see these pictures not as static literal objects but, dynamically, in an almost dreamlike way that opens to complex generativity. Consider this brief passage by Jacques Daignault (1992):

The history of arts and the history of sciences are a struggle against prejudices and clichés of an age, while it seems the history of education is an irreducible struggle to find the best prejudices and clichés…. Curriculum, I believe, is the excluded middle in the debates between art and science. (p. 209)

As I read Daignault's words — *arts, sciences, struggle, prejudices, clichés* — concepts associated with chaos and complexity come to mind and begin to generate a picture, in this instance Maurits Escher's (1950) *Order and Chaos*. In *re-collecting* this picture (Figure 2), the words resonate with a complex concept of curriculum or, rather, its reconceptualising which William Pinar (1994) called the "method of *currere*". I sense Escher's image as a trope for curriculum / *currere*, although I am not able to recall why until I revisit the picture with its paradoxical central element pointing to the fragility and reflecting the intangibility of objects

Figure 2. Warren Sellers, 2004. *Re-collecting* Order and Chaos *(after Escher)*. Pencil on paper. 10.5 cm x 14.8 cm.

surrounding the infinity of complexity.

This picture is not a composition of objects from which I make a literal meaning. Instead, I experience it as a complex space opening to meaningful generativity. I do not search for meaning in the symbols but allow the complexity of the imagery to shift my thinking beyond what I think I know. My thinking and reading is not methodically determining the making of meaning, rather, it is methodologically (thinking-reading-thinking) exploring meaning-making.

Writing about doctoral research as writing, Alison Lee (1998) calls for "a way of theorizing the research / writing nexus that destabilizes the naturalized distinction between the two terms and allows for a more dynamic and iterative relationship between them" (p. 125). Lee cites David Murray's (1980) writing process model, which delineates relationships between information / text, and writing / reading and collecting / connecting (Figure 3).

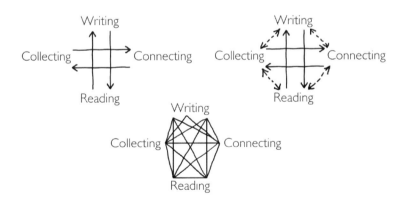

Figure 3. Warren Sellers, 2005. *A Representation of Writing Process Model,* adapted from Murray, 1980, pp. 8-11.

Figure 4. Warren Sellers, 2005. *Writing-process as Clouds*. Digital illustration. 12.7 cm x 8.3 cm.

Reading Murray's model impels me to deconstruct its linear geometry. The Euclidean geometric structures suggest a crystalline formation that is anathema to my reading-thinking about a text that writes of "the bringing together of text and information, or animating information into text". Where Murray saw a crystal, I see clouds... (Figure 4).

My collecting-reading, thinking, connecting-writing envisions a state in which, like Escher's picture, constructs different complex spaces, interacting notions, and other dimensions for research-writing generativity — and in turn inspires this painting (Figure 5). Here I draw on meteorology to turn the literal relations of sun, earth, heat, moisture, condensation towards the dynamic complexity of what is happening. Rather than trying to make things make sense I am sensing what is happening by playing with (performing) reconceptualizing. This is something that many visual artists do so I do not claim a unique grand theory. But, through performing this visualizing-contextualizing-thinking-synthesizing

Figure 5. Warren Sellers, 2005. *Researching-writing...Cloud-sculpting.*
Digital illustration. 12.7 cm x 8.8 cm.

process, I am adopting a poststructuralist approach towards challenging what Lee (1998) termed the "naturalized distinction" that
inheres in writing and reading as separate skilled constructs for
making and communicating meaning. Furthermore, I consider
this approach to be not only effective for cognition but also for
learning because both processes are complexly co-implicated in
each other's generativity.

References
Ballard, J. G. (1973). *Vermillion sands.* London, UK: Jonathan
    Cape.
Daignault, J. (1992). Traces at work from different places. In W. F.
    Pinar & W. M. Reynolds (Eds.), *Understanding curriculum as
    phenomenological and deconstructed text* (pp. 195-215). New
    York, NY & London, UK: Teachers College Press.

Doll, W. E. (2002). Ghosts and the curriculum. In W. E. Doll & N. Gough (Eds.), *Curriculum visions* (pp. 23-70). New York, NY: Peter Lang.

Gough, N. (1996). Textual authority in Bram Stoker's Dracula; or, what's really at stake in action research? *Educational Action Research, 4*(2), 257-265.

Gough, N. (2002). Fictions for representing and generating semiotic consciousness: The crime story and educational inquiry. *International Journal of Applied Semiotics, 3*(2), 59-76.

Gough, N. (2004a). Read intertextually, write an essay, make a rhizome: performing narrative experiments in educational inquiry. In H. Piper & I. Stronach (Eds.), *Educational research: Difference and diversity* (pp. 155-176). Aldershot, UK: Ashgate.

Gough, N. (2004b). RhizomANTically becoming-cyborg: Performing posthuman pedagogies. *Educational Philosophy and Theory, 36*(3), 253-265.

Lee, A. (1998). Doctoral research as writing. In J. Higgs (Ed.), *Writing qualitative research* (pp. 121-133). Sydney, NSW: Hampden Press.

Murray, D. M. (1980). Writing as a process: How writing finds its own meaning. In T. R. Donovan & B. W. McClelland (Eds.), *Eight approaches to teaching composition* (pp. 3-20). Urbana, IL: National Council of Teachers of English.

Pinar, W. F. (1994). The method of *currere*. In *Autobiography, politics and sexuality: Essays in curriculum theory 1972-1992* (pp. 19-28). New York, NY: Peter Lang.

Sellers, W. (2003). Review of curriculum visions. I*nternational Journal of Education & the Arts 4* (review 1). Available at: http://ijea.asu.edu/v4r1/

Sellers, W. (2008). *Picturing currere towards c u r a: Rhizo-imaginary for curriculum.* Unpublished doctoral thesis, Deakin University, Melbourne, Australia.

Varela, F. (1987). Laying down a path in walking. In W. I.
Thompson (Ed.), *Gaia a way of knowing: Political implications
of the new biology* (pp. 48-64). Great Barrington, MA:
Lindisfarne Press.

About the Authors
WARREN SELLERS has worked as a designer, director, and producer
in visual media. His later involvement in professional development
training and tertiary education motivated his move to researching
alternative conceptions for curriculum. He has continued his "lifelong learning" by gaining an MEd and by researching and performing a PhD dissertation at Deakin University, Australia.
Warren lives in New Zealand and continues to perform research-
writing with pictures concerning changing conceptions for curriculum.

  Picturing currere towards c u r a: Rhizo-imaginary for curriculum,
Warren's doctoral thesis, is a critical inquiry in curriculum studies.
The thesis uses poststructuralist and Deleuzian rhizomatic
approaches alongside an original "picturing" methodology. Warren
genealogically maps historical and contemporary curriculum theorising to deconstruct curriculum development and foreground
currere (curriculum reconceptualising). In performing Deleuzian
philosophy, his proposed c u r a reimagines curriculum via currere
to envision generativity living-learning.

NOEL GOUGH is a Professor of Education at the School of
Education and Community Studies, University of Canberra,
Australia. His teaching and research interests include curriculum
inquiry (with particular reference to the implications of globaliza-
tion and multiculturalism for curriculum work), research methodologies in education, cultural studies of science, and environmental education. He is co-editor (with William Doll) of *Curriculum
Visions* and founding editor of *Transnational Curriculum Inquiry*.

20. Listening for the Heart of the Story

by LOIS KUNKEL

Once upon a time...time, as Spider Ananse would tell it, seven-year-old Lois moved with her family to Liberia, West Africa. There, at a birthday party, as she was putting a taste of cake into her mouth, a spider dropped down on a dragline right into the cake. Since she was a good girl, Lois made no sound and caused no upset. She swallowed that spider and felt it wriggle down her throat with a lump of moist cake. Along with her sisters she was sent away from her parents to live at a missionary-run boarding school. Lois and her sisters were lonely sometimes but they did their schoolwork and played and grew. Even though Lois and some friends were sexually abused at this school, they did not talk, and they did not tell. The children did not want to disturb their parents who were there to help the Liberian people learn about God. And, then, one day, life in Africa was over.

Once upon a time…time, I was forty and haunted by memories of the loneliness and abuse in that boarding school. I had been grappling with my doctoral thesis topic and having a terrible time writing a proposal. I wondered how the missionary children I had known in the boarding school were doing. Were they struggling to understand God too?

Now I knew that I wanted to honour, to give form to missionary children's recollections and reflections at midlife. I sensed that the spider and the silent suffering were important.

I poured out my dilemma to my colleague and friend Agnes. With Agnes, a former schoolteacher who now works as an Expressive Arts Therapist, I discovered my ways of knowing and learned to value my learning style. When I initially had no words to express my ideas she asked me to make art and let the art help me. I drew a picture of a web with a spider dropping down on his dragline onto my cake and into my first weeks as a missionary child. I drew a picture of the spider ensnaring and entangling my family in the web of the missionary world. I wondered about how I might be a spider, ensnaring the stories of my research participants, and I created another web drawing to represent that.

These drawings became my working notes, hanging on the wall in my writing space and were included in the methodology section of the completed thesis. Through the art I could visualize my thesis questions and imagine my inquiry. I learned that I needed to make time to nest with my ideas, gaze inward to find the words to articulate that which stirred inside. I needed to talk with someone. I needed to use that person as a sounding board so that I could hear myself say what I knew and have it reflected to me. I needed to use myself congruently — body, mind, and spirit — in order to create. So together, we talked, and I made art and wrote and we danced the ideas awake.

I sat down at my computer and felt like the secretary to my thoughts. My fingers flew over the keys and my thesis proposal was created and accepted. I contacted my research participants and listened to their stories of being missionary children raised in church-run boarding schools and how that legacy lingered in their lives now. Their suffering touched and ignited my own grief. I had to retreat, to care for my own childhood's suffering. Galvanized by our stories I decided to spit out the spider that had silenced me. I talked with my family and, with their support, I pursued a case with the church we had gone to Africa for. I sought and received financial compensation for the pain of the sexual abuse I had suffered as a child in their boarding school.

I paused in my thesis journey to have a baby. Midwives assisted me with pregnancy and birth. Each one offered a distinctive gift. I learned to listen to the growing of my baby and to feel the contours of my baby's shape. The home birth did not go as planned. The midwives wisely took me to the hospital. Solace: The doctor was from West Africa. Kindly, the doctor told me that the baby would have to be delivered by Caesarean section — and so he was. My gorgeous son, Matthew, arrived with a lusty cry! Like the thesis, my son was born in a different way than I had planned. Like the thesis, he came in his own way and in his own time. Over the following weeks the midwives were there, helping.

Once upon a time…time, the birth of my son resolved something wounded inside me and returned my creativity to myself. As with him, I saw that I needed midwives to listen to, attend to the growing of my thesis and its birth.

I found them. There were the research participants, of course.

And the spider of my swallowing spun a new dragline and dropped down beside me. It wanted to be part of the telling. In fact, it wanted to be the metaphor for the telling and so the Ananse spider story from West Africa, the *anansesem*, became the hermeneutical framework of the inquiry. I spun the design of my telling with Ananse's orb web.

I already had Agnes assisting me with the gestation of my thesis inquiry.

I found a new thesis supervisor who encouraged me to use the artifacts of my story in my thesis inquiry. He invited me to use a midwives' Doppler to listen for the heartbeat in the story, and thus listen for what the stories wanted. Old photographs, child-hood letters, and diaries became a medium through which the story came alive. Many of them found their way into the complet-ed thesis text allowing the reader to resonate with the story through the script or the photo of a child.

I looked across my side fence and found Barbara, who listened and offered to read and edit what I wrote. Writing pieces went back and forth over the fence, like the shuttle of a weaver's loom. Over coffee the stories lived between us. Barbara, an English teacher and minister's daughter, knew a similar childhood to me and my research participants. With Barbara, I learned to recognize and palpate the silky thesis threads in my belly.

There were, too, my university classmates. Some of us formed a thesis group and over time, we created the trust to listen to each other's work with care and critique. In regular meetings, we faith-fully helped each other develop our ideas and, sometimes, even find the right words.

I completed my doctoral work and, with my supervisor at hand, I brought forward a healthy, scholarly, and creative thesis. My mentors and professors judged it worthy and awarded me a degree. Ananse was pleased with the silk of my spinning and the web of my weaving. All the midwives danced with joy.

Once upon a time...time, I turned 47 and looked back with an eagle's eye. I ponder the conception and pregnancy of my thesis process. I witness the ongoing influence of my scholartistry in the lives of my research participants and the ripples it has made to other doctoral students and former missionary kids and even my midwives. I see how my thesis inquiry represents my *anansesem,* or spider story, a spider process of spinning, weaving, moulting, eating the silk of old webs, and weaving anew.

Bibliography
Belenky, M. F., Clinchy, B. M., Goldberger, N. R., & Tarule, J. M. (1986). *Women's ways of knowing: The development of self, voice, and mind.* New York, NY: Basic Books.
Cole, A. L., & Knowles, J. G. (2000). *Researching teaching: Exploring teacher development through reflexive inquiry.* Boston, MA: Allyn & Bacon.
DeSalvo, L. (1999). *Writing as a way of healing: How telling our stories transforms our lives.* Boston, MA: Beacon Press.
Hollis, J. (1993). *The middle passage: From misery to meaning in midlife.* Toronto, ON: Inner City Books.
Kolb, D. A. (1984). *Experiential learning.* Englewood Cliffs, NJ: Prentice Hall.
Kunkel, L. (2000). *Spiders spin silk: Reflections of missionary kids at midlife.* Unpublished doctoral thesis, University of Toronto, Toronto, ON, Canada.
McCarthy, B., & Leflar, S. (1983). *4-Mat.* Obrook, IL: Excel.
Pelton, R. D. (1980). *The trickster in West Africa: A study of mythic irony and sacred delight.* Berkeley, CA: University of California Press.

About the Author
LOIS KUNKEL completed her Doctor of Education at the Ontario Institute for Studies in Education, University of Toronto, delighting in her arts-informed, reflexive inquiry. Lois is a psychotherapist in private practise in Toronto, Ontario. She brings her artful

inquiry into her psychotherapy work. When Lois was seven, she swallowed a spider and it changed her life forever.

Spiders Spin Silk: Reflections of Missionary Kids at Midlife, is the title of Lois's doctoral thesis. Mid-life offers an opportunity for those raised as missionary children to come to terms with their unique childhood experience. Using reflexive and arts-informed inquiry processes, Lois was one of the participants of her investigation. Artifacts are used to enhance a connection with this life experience. The West African trickster spider, Ananse, provides the hermeneutic framework and metaphor.

21. Finding Form and Inspiration

by KAREN SCHALLER

Whenever I am asked how I chose my thesis form (Schaller, 2002) I reply that I did not find form, form found me. In fact, at times, it seems I had very little to do with it — it came to me in a moment of uncertainty and fear, after a year of work, as an inspiration.

I spent January to June doing "pure" research. Reading, taking notes in well-organized binders with numbered lines and quotations, references to the gurus of writing and emotion. Books spread out on the tables in the research rooms of the library, laptop diligently packed and unpacked every day as I built an outline, a vague skeleton of the body my thesis would become.

From July to August my work went outside, to the beach, the park, lying on the grassy greens in front of the library and administration buildings. The careful notes turned to sticky notes stuck on the margins of articles, underlines, and the occasional pithy quotation written on scraps to be tucked inside a battered notebook. The sea crashed around me and I played in the ocean and sand and remembered how it feels for the water to rush around my feet, pulling strange particles of rock and glass with it, taking balance out from under me. In these months my hand would shake, dash with impulse across the page, and I would find myself writing words that made no citable sense but seemed to me to be the clearest articulation of everything I knew about my thesis subject. I left August and entered September with the accumulated notes and outlines of those cold months juxtaposed against a messy collection of poetry, insouciant comments about theories and their makers, and the residue of salt on my skin, all gathered in the sun.

In the strange heat of September I sat down to write. But every day found me empty, unable to conjure the heavy metaphors I felt, unable to commit to the page. The days of September slipped away and I sat less often at my desk. Laundry took over the great piles of notes, books, and articles on my desk and by the end of October I had not written anything. Then, in that first week of November, I began to read again. Theories settled against one another, forming strange bodies of thought, layered into and against one another, dense packages of history and humanity, with small gaps where the strata lifted and heaved.

In December I began walking. Every morning I woke at six and walked for an hour, breathing deep the chilling air. Authors argued in my head, as I traced my route, and I found myself racing home the last few steps to write the emerging connections and patterns.

At home each day I would write till late into the dark then run again, this time revisiting every word I had written, revising in my head and allowing my own argument to propel me. I would translate my revisions upon returning then close my lights and eyes when there were no more left to do.

In January I finished. When I returned to my thesis the next day for proofreading, however, fear struck. What I found was not what I thought I had left. Rather than an articulate, careful, and mindful reading of my subject I was struck by the stiffness, the formality, the authority of this work and, worst of all, the disjointed fragments that, rather than walk gracefully in body, instead struck out at odd angles and lurched with a lumbering gait. This was not the thesis I meant to write. This was a thesis that did everything I did not want it to do — it backed me into corners, it declared without exploring, and it spoke from a voice outside myself, the one I critiqued. This thesis stood on the page as if it was written standing alone, of itself, connected to no one and no time. This thesis worried me. I had managed to defeat myself and was left here, in the middle of January, with the sudden knowledge that I did not know how to write my argument in a form that would tell it in flesh.

I began to panic and knew I needed to leave my desk, get away from my computer, and get out of my apartment. I took myself, naturally, to the campus bar and sat down with a beer to contemplate what I was going to do. Through the first drink I considered quitting. People dropped out of graduate school, I reasoned. It happens all the time. Through the second, I panicked. There was no way I could drop out and, yet, I knew I could not possibly turn this thesis into work I could submit for defence. It was simply not defendable. My heart beat wickedly. Through the third beer, I sat and stared out the window, taking in the snowy patio and awnings. My heart slowed, heavy in my chest, and I slept with my eyes open. In this waking dream I saw myself sitting there

242

gazing then the image turned to the scenes of my research — the library, the beach, my bedroom, the café, the mental no man's land that staged my arguments while walking, and finally, I returned to the bar scene: Me, sitting at a table with only a notebook, drinking at two in the afternoon. I uncapped my pen and opened the notebook to a new page. I wrote without seeing, my eyes still in that vision: "Karen, a Master's degree student, is trying to write." Finally, I had that heady moment when time stops and words, once reluctant and shy, come strong and certain. I wrote as if dictated to. My fingers could hardly keep time and, four hours later, I had Act One of my thetic play. My eyes refocused, the words were gone, my fingers tired, and I read what I had written. I felt a strange certainty that this was what I had been meant to write. Four weeks later I typed "End of Play".

Three years have passed and I still know that no other form could have expressed what I knew and had to tell. And I am humbled by the knowledge that the stepping of this work from authoritative composition to artful inquiry relied upon the intervention of inspiration. I have always believed in inspiration but find it troubling too, now, as I find myself writing doctoral proposals and discussing my thesis. Three thoughts strike me. I find myself calling into question the reliability of inspiration, integral though it is to my inquiry. It is a difficult position for a graduate student to propose research that must, at some point, despite the careful notes and outlines, await the "moment, a pulsation of the artery" (Blake, 1920) in which inspiration comes. As scholartists, we find ourselves at odd angles to those students who can predict their methodology with the sureness of their traditions. At the same time, inspiration presents a difficult notion for research in that it involves "some invisible influence, like an inconstant wind," which awakens the mind "to transitory brightness" (Shelly in Press, 1955, p. 25). If I accept this sense of an "other" that writes my research, am I shirking my accountability for what I write? Am I re-enacting dis-embodiment just as my inquiry purports embodied knowing? Finally, if I accept that inspiration, rather than intentionality, will bring voice to my inquiry, then do I risk denying the mindfulness that guides scholartistry?

References

Blake, W. (1920). Time. In Yeats, W. B. (Ed.). *Poems of William Blake*. New York, NY: Boni & Liveright.

Press, J. (1955). *The fire and the fountain: An essay on poetry*. London, UK: Oxford University Press.

Schaller, K. (2002). *A writing story, on being written: A thetic play on words*. Unpublished Master's thesis, Mount Saint Vincent University, Halifax, NS, Canada.

About the Author
KAREN SCHALLER graduated from Mount Saint Vincent University, Nova Scotia with an MEd in 2002. Karen is now a doctoral candidate at the University of Sussex, UK. Her doctoral research draws together interests in emotion theory and post-structuralism through a close engagement with the short fiction of Elizabeth Bowen.

A Writing Story, on Being Written: A Thetic Play on Words, Karen's Master's degree thesis, positions academic writing as a cultural text, open to discourse analysis. Deconstructing emotion from an historical and inter-disciplinary perspective, this work draws on post-structuralism to posit emotion as cultural and inseparable from writing. From this position this thesis argues for arts-informed representations of research, demonstrating this through a "thetic" play: a combination of scholarly writing, play writing (including soundtrack), and poetry.

22. A Grim Fairy Tale:
Taboo, Mythopoetics, and Truth-telling

by KEVIN KIRKLAND AND CARL LEGGO

i believe writing we value is writing which springs from necessity. the necessity to speak the unspoken, the taboo of our lives. if we do not, we BETRAY: trans-, over + dare, to give ourselves over, turn ourselves in, become agents of our own absence. (Warland, 1990, p. 60)

Writing is ⸱ ⸱ay…to open up the word and the world, and our lives within that ⸱ ⸱orld for attention, discussion, understanding, re-imagining and re-⸱ ⸱ting. (Chambers, 1998, p. 26)

Finding and Working with Form

We have to begin not only by lying less but by telling the truth more.
(Rule, 1986, p. 92)

In sharing these dark shards, I hope to encourage
others to bite open the bullet of pretense in which we
live. Telling the truth is powerful medicine. It is a fire
that lights the way for others. (Chrystos, 1995, p. 130)

On March 2, 2004, Kevin Kirkland successfully defended his doctoral thesis, entitled *A Grim Fairy Tale*, in the Faculty of Education at the University of British Columbia (UBC). Carl Leggo was the supervisor. Kevin uses arts-based research methodologies, including mythopoetics and narrative inquiry, to address issues of taboo, truth, identity, and pedagogy. His research opens up much needed conversations about experiences and emotions that have been mostly rendered silent and prohibited; his research promotes ways of living with a commitment to seeking wellness in the world. Among the questions that Kevin's thesis addresses are: How do we write from the position of I in the academy? How do we write about life stories that are uncomfortable, even *dangerous*, especially, when they are no longer approached from the perspective of the Other? What stories are privileged while others are silenced? When does the scandalous constitute research? What are the ethics of writing about taboo subjects? What narratives are (not) told, written, and lived in the academy?

Through our interaction in the embodied and complex roles of doctoral candidate and doctoral supervisor we struggled to find our way amidst the tensions and possibilities of researching taboo topics. In this chapter we examine not only the tensions that erupt and emerge around researching and writing about taboo subjects in the academy but, also, how arts-informed theorizing and practices can facilitate a scholarly engagement with all experiences, including complicated personal experiences that are frequently

246

silenced. In writing about experiences we write our lives and living in the social, cultural, political, and ideological contexts that shape and inform our worlds, and we learn to read our lives and living in creative and critical ways that open up possibilities for living well. This chapter focuses on a gay student's thesis research that seeks performatively to re-work and rewrite, even right, a history of mother-son incest. Informed by Miller's (1993) contention that writing is an indispensable precondition for healing, we examine the benefits and challenges of engaging with dangerous discourses in the academy and how exploring personal writing and reflexivity through a literary genre enables progress, activism, and inclusion. There are many challenges, especially in educational contexts, connected to opening up silenced topics that include both homosexuality and sexual abuse. Drawing on sources about mythopoetics, arts-based research, performative inquiry, and anti-oppressive pedagogy, we demonstrate how people can reclaim their voices through narrative approaches, focusing on the fairy tale but, also, touching on poetry, music, sketches, photographs, and autoethnographic fiction or, as Kuhn (2000) might call it, revisionist autobiography.

Individually and collectively educators must determine what constitutes legitimate knowledge for curricular and pedagogical purposes. Despite increased attention to cultural pluralism and diversity, experience teaches us that some subjects are regarded as more marginal than others and hence more subject to silence and rejection. We believe that this is particularly true of the topics of incest and sexual orientation. Their silencing reflects individual and cultural forms of classroom knowledge "brokering". This brokering in turn reflects "in"clusive and "ex"clusive pedagogies. Decisions to honour or reject social taboos in the classroom serve to validate or invalidate different forms of educational participation. Transformative learning, by contrast, demands creative forms of participation and a willingness to transgress traditional

247

boundaries of theory and practice (hooks, 1994). Engaging taboos on these terms may identify teachers and students as "academic outlaws" (Tierney, 1997). Breaking codes of silence for us speaks to our roles as educators in the "practice of freedom" (hooks, 1994) and social responsibility. As relational constructs, taboos help to shape, define, and mediate personal and collective knowledge systems. Making sense of these systems is crucial for understanding the broader roles that identify us as teachers, learners, and social science researchers.

Our collaborative research journey was often challenging with many twists and turns that had to be navigated creatively in the process. Nevertheless, ultimately the journey was full of affirmation and hope because we were successful in pursuing the research that we felt called, even compelled, to pursue. In the following section we weave Kevin's words (regular font) and Carl's words (*italics font*) in a double-voiced text that highlights some of the key moments of the thesis journey that we lived together.

•

Kevin decided that he wanted to change his thesis focus after he confronted the terrible truth that when he was a child he was sexually abused by his mother. He now wanted to research auto-ethnographically the experience of mother-son incest. I cannot imagine a more difficult experience to write about but I was also convinced that Kevin felt compelled to write about this experience and, therefore, I was eager to support him.

Memory was cast into language when I revealed to a psychologist that my mother had sexually abused me throughout childhood. The taboo of mother-child incest is so great that I was 37 before confronting the realities of my childhood. I was not alone in my experience: Two other siblings, a brother, 49, and a sister, 62, had endured the same experience. Schools did not teach about sexual abuse when I was a child. I was all too familiar with a pedagogy of silence, having grown up gay in a predominantly Catholic, small town in Northern Alberta. But now here I was, pursuing a doctoral degree with a supervisory committee willingly engaging with the [socially constructed] ultimate taboo. I was ready to write a thesis about it and let the text flow — but there would be a boulder in the stream.

The chair of UBC's Behavioural Research Ethics Board (BREB) responded to Kevin's application for ethics approval to write autoethnographically about his experience of mother-son incest with a letter that highlighted several grave concerns. The board was concerned about issues of libel. Also, the board was concerned for Kevin's well-being. Will this kind of research and writing harm Kevin? Does he have the kind of psychological support needed to address such a difficult topic? The board expressed concern that the supervisory committee would not be able to sustain a sufficiently rigorous approach toward Kevin's research in order to evaluate it appropriately for its academic merit. Above all, the board was very concerned with the question: Is this research?

The *I* of the storm. BREB said *No* for many reasons, too complex to expound upon at length here. The concerns warranted a six-page reply to re(ad)dress their concerns. Ultimately, an uncategorical *No* indicated BREB would not sanction my application. It was suggested I change topics. My goal of demonstrating that "personal memory is always connected to social narrative as is social memory to the personal" (Antze & Lambek, 1996, p. xx) was dashed on the rocks.

I spoke to the chair of BREB, as well as the lawyer for UBC, and Kevin addressed the concerns in an eloquent and thoughtful letter of response. But it eventually became clear to Kevin and me that we would never get ethics approval for an autobiographical or autoethnographic research project about mother-son incest. I struggled with this difficult impasse. I was always eager to support Kevin in the research that he most wanted to pursue. I had complete confidence in him to handle the challenges of his proposed research. Above all, I was concerned about the ethics involved in prohibiting and silencing research about taboo topics. I feared that the university was seeking to render Kevin's experience unspeakable, insisting that it be buried once again, as it had been for decades.

This could be viewed as retraumatizing: keep the silence. Authority says "hushhhh". When a student writes from the position of *I* in the academy, another taboo is encountered: first person narratives. Can we allow people to write from the position of *I*, even when the writing might include uncensored claims about others? Is the real problem the nasty content? Does academic writing favour distanced, impartial, polite (re)presentations of others? What constitutes truth? Is there veracity to my research if I cite my brother instead of published authors? Can my memories constitute a methodology (Radstone, 2000)? BREB does not know me. They won't dialogue with me: it's technically Carl's research. Where am I in the research? I debated taking up the cause and fighting the decision tooth and nail. I learned from Carl, with spiritual warriorship, how to circumnavigate the boulder in the stream.

I have abiding respect for the members of BREB. I know several of them as inspiring colleagues and I fully support the careful and conscientious and considerate work of the board. I have no wish to offend or undermine the necessary and crucial service of the board. Of course I am committed, like all researchers, to ethical conduct in research. Therefore, Kevin and I decided to navigate our way down the river by flowing around the boulder that seemed to block our way. Instead of trying to scale the boulder or dash ourselves against it, we turned and flowed past it. Kevin decided to write a fictionalized drama with a fairy tale as a part of the drama. He chose to write a fiction within a fiction, even a fictionalized appearance on the Larry King Show. *He would write about mother-son incest from the "objective" and (less) objectionable distance of a story that is made up, a story where truth is convoked and evoked and provoked as only the creative arts can.*

Kumashiro (1999) believes that anti-oppressive pedagogy calls us to performatively rework oppression and to shift inaction to action. Such writing is bound to be seen as contentious and disruptive, even inappropriate. It challenges our resistance to envisioning education as a place for speaking and teaching about difficult subjects, social change, and emotionally charged topics.

All my writing, including my autobiographical, narrative, and poetic writing, is part of a lifelong, intense, pedagogic practice and process of exploring, learning, and transforming. I am heartened by Gass' (1983) perspective that "one's complete sentences are attempts, as often as not, to complete an incomplete self with words" (p. 175). We are all in process, none of us is complete and, therefore, we all need to write, and we need to write with courage and boldness and imagination in the pursuit of truth.

I came home stressed out from the committee meeting and complained to my partner Brent that my writing was stale. "Carl suggested I begin with a character mulling over the central issues." Brent was quick to respond, "You should be happy. You love creativity." He was right. I do. I needed permission to engage with it. To run with it. *Currere.* To tell my story. *Narrare.* I would have to start my thesis again from page one. I began with an old curmudgeon who is a librarian and, after a page of self-talk and reflection, I was stuck. It was not working. He needed dialogue. Discourse. Counter-narratives. Difficulty. Process work. But dialogue meant

it would have to be a play. *I'm not a playwright!* What about the
fairy tale? Drawing on the fairy tale genre's tradition as a vehicle
for imparting moral and ethical messages, the encompassing play
creates a forum for dialogue and disruption of its content. Fairy
tales usually have pictures. *I'm not an illustrator. I can't draw!* But
creativity demands a foray into undiscovered country. Wouldn't I
betray myself and others by abandoning autoethnography and
truth-telling, and resorting to fiction? *No! I'd use the very devices
that had traditionally oppressed and silenced me and turn them on
their ears!* I would write music, songs, use old photographs. I
would draw, I would sing! Breaking the silences demands telling,
demands discourse. What began with one character mulling over a
tenet soon emerged into dialogue, debate, and deconstruction.

*Out of this conviction about human learning and becoming, I
turn to Vanier (1998), the philosopher, educator, and spiritual leader.
Vanier asks:*

*Is this not the life undertaking of us all...to become human?
It can be a long and sometimes painful process. It involves a
growth to freedom, an opening up of our hearts to others, no
longer hiding behind masks or behind the walls of fear and
prejudice. It means discovering our common humanity. (p. 1)*

*I think that Vanier's perspective on human becoming is an apt
description of the process and aims of pedagogy: "To be human is to
create sufficient order so that we can move on into insecurity and
seeming disorder. In this way, we discover the new" (p. 13).*

Bliss (in Perrin, 2000) describes mythopoetics as "the creation
of new myths in our own lives" (p. 60). Plot is *mythos, poesis*
means *"making"*, thus a plot for making meaning in one's life.
Bliss argues that a person can embrace a more positive, hopeful,

and inspirited life by intentionally letting go of destructive attitudes, practices, and values through the mythopoetic interpretation of texts. As a methodology it can be a means of reinventing social traditions and beliefs. Hillman (1983) claims that the act of meaning-making is done by way of the imagination cast into language, or the art of speaking and hearing, writing and reading. My research called for a mythopoetic text that challenges the foundations of ways of knowing and being or as Doll (2000) writes, the "constructed fictions of tradition" (p. 10). Trauma necessitates a critical and creative reconsideration of social science research as a site of narrative inquiry and healing.

I often write about family, always seeking to know who I am, to gain a clear sense of identity and positionality in the midst of memory, desire, heart, and imagination, especially in relation to others. One of the ongoing challenges I face in my writing is trying to sort out what is true and what is not. This is, of course, the central question of epistemology and certainly a question that all of us ask all the time. As I write about family and personal experiences, I realize that I am always keeping so much secret. For every experience and emotion and event that I write about, I also hold back so much more, as if I am not yet ready to share most secrets. I hold firmly to a conviction that writing truthfully is integral to good health, and that writing truthfully invites productive communication among people, and that writing truthfully opens up possibilities for creative living. But, at the same time, I also know that I hold so much back. There is a careful winnowing of the stories I am willing to tell. And, then, even with the stories I am willing to tell, there is a great deal of selection, fabrication, manufacture, and interpretation. I know that I am never really telling the whole truth.

Through mythopoetics I can understand my incest experience on a global scale, on the archetypal level. It is an avenue to restor(e)y myself. I was working on the fairy tale and it suddenly took on a stronger and deeper meaning. I struggled to find words that were impactful enough to carry the meaning. How do I write about something I have never had language for? It is a strange, liminal space. It suddenly moved forward into a poem about the wound. This was a poem I began several weeks earlier and I occasionally came back to painstakingly edit. This time I was in a full frame of mind to write it, possessed by memory and a stream of unconsciousness. The words poured out and the embodied feelings bound up with the pent-up energy of the text brought me crashing down into an abyss. I left the computer, and curled up on the floor, all too familiar with this state of being. I wanted to cry but could not. I printed the poem and read it again. I was back in this place of despair that literally forced me yet again to the floor in a stupor. It was a mood that lasted several days until it finally burst when I accessed the emotions and wept uncontrollably to the point of rushing to the toilet to purge once again. All through the terrible feelings of those few days I knew I had to carry on. This time I knew what was going on right from the moment I completed the poem. I knew the best thing for me would be to keep writing, to work through it. To exercise my body so as not to hold everything in. To bask in autumn light. I began to understand, I think, for the first time, how transformative writing can be. For if it elicited such a strong response in me in writing metaphoric passages, I knew that if I could stay with the tale, it would unfold as majestically as I needed it to, and, in some ways, as powerfully as it wanted me to. As Feldman (2003) explains, "in self-study we delve into our existential ways of being in the world, which may best be made public through artistic representations of research" (p. 26).

As a teacher and poet, I am committed to supporting others so they can develop as writers, in both their desire for writing as well as their confidence in writing. I invite my students to write creatively, inter-rogatively, and expressively. I encourage them to take risks, to experi-ment with diverse discourses, to challenge conventions, and to seek truth but, in spite of my enthusiasm for writing that is personally rele-vant, even transformative, I continue to be fearful, too. I am always concerned about inviting people to walk in the tangled places of their hearts and memories and experiences, fearful that they might be lost, fearful that they might not be strong enough to make the journey.

•

In this collaborative research journey we asked (and continue to ask) many questions: What are the conventions and expectations that govern the stories that are told and written in classrooms? In what ways are students encouraged and constrained in writing the stories of their lives? Why is it valuable for students and teachers to write their stories? We are always engaged in a meaning-making process of becoming human. We write and tell stories as part of a hermeneutic process of truth-seeking. Hutchinson (1999) spells out a comprehensive and compelling case for the importance of students' personal writing:

> Two things schooling can do are, first, to reflect the narrative nature of the self as it develops and, second, to provide a place for students to come to know many different stories as well as articulate their own stories. Both endeavours sustain dignity and hence, the creation of lives. (p. 72)

When we write our stories — autobiographically, ethnographically, mythopoetically, fictionally — we seek to understand our lived experiences and we seek to understand our connections in the world, connections to others and to the earth and even the uni-verse.

As creative scholars, Kevin and I seek to nurture vibrant research relationships where differences of opinions, beliefs, experiences, and personalities can be celebrated. We write and share our writing with one another. We tell stories of our lives, and we reveal ourselves in intimate ways, and we grow more confident in our conviction about the power of words for writing our lived stories, and transforming our living stories, and creating possibilities for more life-enhancing stories. Our hope is that our words will invite others to enter into dialogical relationships of word-making founded on risk-taking, trust, truth-seeking, courage, encouragement, nurture, desire, and unwavering commitment to the power of words for singing our worlds into creation.

In this commitment, we especially appreciate Winterson's (1995) advice:

> The question put to the writer "How much of this is based on your own experience?" is meaningless. All or nothing may be the answer. The fiction, the poem, is not a version of the facts, it is an entirely different way of seeing. (p. 28)

If we do not learn to write truthfully about human experiences, both joyful and terrible, in classrooms, where will we ever learn to write in ways that foster the heart of education as questioning, researching, learning, and transforming? Writing truthfully is a practice. We learn to write truthfully or we learn silence.

References

Antze, P., & Lambek, M. (Eds.). (1996). *Tense past: Cultural essays in trauma and memory.* New York, NY: Routledge.

Chambers, C. (1998). Composition and composure. Alberta English, 36(2), 21-27.

Chrystos (1995). *Fire power.* Vancouver, BC: Press Gang Publishers.

Doll, M. A. (2000). *Like letters in running water: A mythopoetics of curriculum.* Mahwah, NJ: Lawrence Erlbaum Associates.

Feldman, A. (2003). Validity and quality in self-study. *Educational Research, 32*(3), 26-28.

Gass, W. (1983). Interview. In T. LeClair & L. McCaffery (Eds.), *Anything can happen: Interviews with contemporary American novelists* (pp. 152-175). Urbana, IL: University of Illinois Press.

Hillman, J. (1983). *Healing fiction.* Woodstock, CT: Spring Publications.

hooks, b. (1994). *Teaching to transgress: Education as the practice of freedom.* New York, NY: Routledge.

Hutchinson, J. N. (1999). *Students on the margins: Education, stories, dignity.* Albany, NY: State University of New York Press.

Kirkland, K. (2004). *A Grim Fairy Tale.* Unpublished doctoral thesis, University of British Columbia, Vancouver, BC, Canada.

Kuhn, A. (2000). A journey through memory. In S. Radstone (Ed.), *Memory and methodology* (pp. 179-196). Oxford, UK: Berg.

Kumashiro, K. (1999). "Barbie," "Big Dicks," and "Faggots": Paradox, performativity, and anti-oppressive pedagogy. *Journal of Curriculum Theorizing, Spring,* 27-42.

Miller, A. (1993). *Breaking down the wall of silence: The liberating experience of facing painful truth.* New York, NY: Penguin Books.

Perrin, D. B. (2000). The mythopoetic interpretation of texts: Hermeneutical considerations. In E. R. Barton (Ed.), *Mythopoetic perspectives of men's healing work: An anthology for therapists and others* (pp. 59-74). Westport, CT: Bergin & Garvey.

Radstone, S. (Ed.). (2000). *Memory and methodology.* Oxford, UK: Berg.

Rule, J. (1986). *A hot-eyed moderate.* Toronto, ON: Lester & Orpen Dennys.

Tierney, W. G. (1997). *Academic outlaws: Queer theory and cultural studies in the academy.* Thousand Oaks, CA: Sage Publications.

Vanier, J. (1998). *Becoming human.* Toronto, ON: House of
Anansi Press.

Warland, B. (1990). *Proper deafinitions: Collected theorograms.*
Vancouver, BC: Press Gang.

Winterson, J. (1995). *Art objects: Essays on ecstasy and effrontery.*
Toronto, ON: Alfred A. Knopf Canada.

About the Authors

KEVIN KIRKLAND graduated with a PhD from the Centre for
Cross-Faculty Inquiry, University of British Columbia, in 2004.
He works as a music therapist with the elderly and writes articles
on the silences and stigma around sexual abuse. He is also writing
a lyrical memoir on childhood mother-son incest called
Motherf*cker and is intrigued by the interactions of memory, trau-
ma, narrative, myth, and historical (un)consciousness. He lives in
Vancouver with his life partner and cat.

Kevin's doctoral thesis is entitled *A Grim Fairy Tale.* "Fairy tales
can come true, it can happen to you...." His mother taught Kevin
everything he knows about incest. The rest he learned when writing his thesis. Broken silences, homosexuality, taboo, trauma, and
transformation come together in the land of mythopoetics and
narratives that (en)counter *inbedded* oppression in the cultural curriculum. In the land of *make believe* readers awaken to discourse,
drama, and disruption.

CARL LEGGO is a poet and professor, Department of Language and
Literacy Education, University of British Columbia, where he
teaches courses in writing and narrative research. His poetry, fic-
tion and scholarly essays have been published in many journals.
He is the author of three books: *Growing Up Perpendicular on the
Side of a Hill, View from My Mother's House, Come by Chance,* and
*Teaching to Wonder: Responding to Poetry in the Secondary
Classroom.*

Scholartistry in Relation

23. Re-becoming a Supervisor: Extending Possibilities

by ALMA FLEET

Having been given an opportunity to indulge myself by becoming immersed in a pile of theses shaped by arts-informed inquiry, I wondered about the possibilities of encouraging graduate students to pursue the tantalizing possibilities that this form of inquiry offered. Fortuitously, I was invited to crystallize my ramblings in a form that might be useful for others entering the forum of supervision of postgraduate arts-informed inquiry.

Scholartistry in Relation

In an Office

"How many words?" was my unexpected response. Standing there, being still and no doubt looking rather blank, I responded as other students do, using a place-holder to imply the unformed blur that came to mind when the task was proposed. As shorthand for, "Probably yes, but I'm not sure what is expected here; what sits around it? Who is the audience? What offerings might I make that could be a useful contribution?" The only question that hung in the air was, "How many words?" I must remind myself to be more sympathetic the next time (regularly and predictably) a student asks the same thing. Remember to look behind the question. Implications might range from anxiety about the minimum acceptable size of the project, to enthusiasm for the topic being constrained by space available or, in toddler style, "Whaszat?" standing in for "Explain more please." Three words acting as an unformed invitation for clarification.

The Springboard

My own experience of being supervised was a puzzle to me, one where the supervisor's intentions mismatched the actuality I experienced. I had chosen him on the recommendation of a respected colleague, without fully understanding the process or the importance of that decision. The resulting journey was disastrous. From this distance it is unfathomable how a decade could have passed without one of us seeking a change of supervisor. Perhaps it had to do with the notion of disparate identities as explained by Grant (1999). The grayness of the time is summarized elsewhere (Fleet, Holland, Leigh, & Patterson, 2001) but the legacy is my commitment to finding ways of supervising that are responsive, flexible, and empowering; offering input, editing, and advice as the situation unfolds. Mutuality is essential.

Beginning

The journey towards becoming a helpful, challenging, and creative supervisor of arts-informed inquiry seems to me to contain two elements. Firstly, there is the essence of being an empowering, nurturant, informed supervisor and, secondly, there is the extension of that role into a way of being in relationship to a graduate student interested in alternative representation.

David Smith (2001) has written about how his experience of being supervised helped shape his personal goals as a supervisor, goals related to gaining trust and respect, with communication founded on a "successful relationship" (p. 132). These elements certainly seem to be key and resonate with the literature I read as a beginning supervisor. For example, in her reflections on being a supervisor, Phillida Salmon (1992) spoke of lessons learned from her own experience:

> The importance of trusting in one's own struggle for meaning, the courage to live with uncertainty and to resist quick and facile answers…. Only where there is a mutual respect, a sense of reciprocal resonance with the other person's way of seeing things, can these kinds of messages be conveyed. With students whose seriousness I can feel, whose projects clearly carry personal depth and urgency, I feel confident in undertaking supervision…. I have learned to my cost that it is fatal to disregard, on either side, these personal feelings. (p. 114)

To assist in my musings about those elements in my experience that supported me on this new journey, I sought out the minutes made in 1992 / 1993 with a co-supervisor (Catherine Patterson) of meetings held with our first research postgraduate student. We were working with a Master's degree candidate who found academic work a challenge but who was exploring an area of interest to each of us. She was working as a full time classroom teacher and wanted to investigate her practice. In March, the notes recorded that,

> Sharon [pseudonym] is still at an early exploratory stage, not yet being clear about the nature of the problem which she wishes to investigate or confident about initiating directions for the research…. She wants to study problem-solving behaviours in formal academic classrooms as opposed to classrooms which are more developmentally appropriate, because she believes that such behaviours will be fostered more in the latter settings….

As time went on the focus shifted to action research within her own classroom. Sharon tabled summaries of her current thinking or examples of observations and children's work from her classroom. As supervisors, we encouraged ways of "managing data" (e.g., an annotated photograph register and regular summaries of events) and suggested readings. There were clarification about differing interpretations of key concepts and variations in perspective about the roles of teachers as well as the importance of language use with words like "play", "games", and "activities" for children. Catherine and I continued to struggle with ways to supervise in useful and effective ways just as Sharon continued to struggle to get her head around the complexities of the study and to fit her research into her busy life. In August we

> asked if Sharon would be interested in having us write on her work as a form of interactive response. She was pleased with the suggestion as she is seeking feedback on whether she is noticing and recording "the right" or useful things. We expressed doubts about the notion of "rightness" but will respond to and post back her report in a week.

As an action research project, the work unfolded with excerpts of classroom practice and the teacher's journal as well as photographs as data. We encouraged Sharon to write up her work as "story", in the sense used by Jean Clandinin (Clandinin & Connelly, 1994). Supervisory sessions were punctuated with Catherine's "I wonder if…" as a lead in to challenging thinking. The project laboured on for several years, eventually reaching a successful conclusion. It would have been interesting to have tried to extend the experiential perspective into an arts-informed project but Sharon did not seek interpretive approaches to representation and I was not yet familiar with work such as that by Lorri Neilsen (2001) and Suzanne Thomas (2001).

Time continues to meld the years together. My work has slid from action research to practitioner inquiry, honouring silenced voices in a world of multiple realities (Fleet, Scrimshaw, & Winkler, 2004; Fleet & Winters, 2004). I am also informed by third space conceptualisations (Soja, 1996), avoiding the dualities of modernist interpretations and seeking simultaneous engagement of potentially conflicting constructs through both / and interpretations (Dahlberg & Moss, 2005; Dahlberg, Moss, & Pence, 1999).

There is undoubtably a combination of predisposition and learner respect for elements of the arts which combine to provide a basis for an arts-informed inquiry. Thinking about these components leads to another phase in my redevelopment as a supervisor.

Conversing with Texts

Perhaps, I thought, it was time to step back from what I knew of myself as a supervisor and look more closely at the supervisors I found in my reading. Thinking tangentially, I looked at Robert Coles' (1989) memories of his supervisors when he was a student psychiatrist, remembering Dr. Binger (the "brilliant theorist") as offering authority, explanations, and exhortations, while the hard of hearing Dr. Ludwig sent him on the path of clearer listening, the seeking of stories as a way into the things that mattered. Coles remembered himself as he presented to these highly regarded supervisors, torn between saying very little "lest I reveal my stupidity, my inadequacy", and "talking at a brisk pace, lest awkward silences develop, a clue no doubt to — well, my stupidity, my inadequacy" (p. 3). In thinking about how new students might be presenting themselves to me I thought about Robert Coles' expectation of interaction with supervisors:

> My own phobias had always urged upon me a policy of with drawal, escape, silence, or at best, brief and softly spoken com ment. That was the way I handled professors whose promi nence and outspokenness intimidated me, made me feel in fact, speechless: no words of mine could have any value to people who had used words as they did, thereby becoming the impor tant people they were. (1989, p. 4)

This sobering reminder of the power differentials inherent in the context I now inhabit, reminded me again of how inadequate I felt each time I presented myself at my supervisor's door, a threatening and depressing experience, not one to be passing on to the next person who arrives at my office. Somewhere in the proposed scenario must be an empowering human relationship underpinning the dance between the roles of mentor, instructor, editor and colleague.

> I would notice over the months that his more trenchant and, for me, lasting comments often came just as we were ending our time together, almost as if he wanted me to think about something in my own good time, and maybe wanted to remind himself of what he, too, might occasionally forget. "Supervision" is after all a meeting of two persons, a shared possibility for each of them. (Coles, 1989, p. 9)

This reminder sent me off to another source, a conversation reported in the context of educational supervision as a site for mentoring within friendship. This discussion between Janis Jipson and Petra Munro (1997) was reported as part of a contribution to a piece in *Daredevil Research* (Jipson & Paley, 1997).

Petra: I mean when I switched advisors and decided to work with you that was very difficult…. I knew intuitively that it was the right thing…. I think the thing I got the most out of it was this sort of unbridled path that you seem to facilitate. You know, there were no boundaries, no bars, I guess with other faculty, as I think about it now, there was this set intellectual path that you were supposed to follow…. I don't think my interest to work with you was solely your interest in feminist theory or curriculum…. It was that there were no constraints on my explorations — no matter how fragmented or how disorganized I was….

Jan: But you see, first you have the right to do that and secondly, that's what I do too. I love the excitement of being able to just charge into these things…. I criticize myself for reading all over the place….

Petra: Again, we write well together because we know each other so well and therefore can be critical of each other's work and, because of the trust inherent in the relationship, we can also be critical in a positive sense….

Jan: What I see is a facilitator role where I can respond to individual needs and provide a safe environment to explore questions, focus on issues, all outside of the traditional academic environment…. The whole idea is that if knowledge is socially constructed it doesn't have to occur with someone who has more knowledge, it has to be with someone who has as much commitment to the process. (pp. 204-208)

Theses Speak

So, given the multiple possibilities of creating one-self as a supervisor, how does one enter the world of alternative presentations? While a belief in the potential of the process is fundamental, it helps to have a range of possibilities to consider. (Again I can hear myself exhorting students to imagine what might be possible, with little to guide them, while being frustrated by those who want concrete examples. How similar we are as learners!)

An opportunity to study at the Centre for Arts-Informed Research, at the Ontario Institute of Studies in Education (OISE) of the University of Toronto, enabled me to consider examples of this work. Reflecting through a pile of theses, mundane things surfaced in the midst of intense personal revelation and photographic reflection. What options had people found in the forms and representations that they chose to give voice to in their explorations? Each included some form of analytic frame as well as a study presented in multiple languages (in the sense used by the educators and philosophers in Reggio Emilia; see, Edwards, Gandini, & Forman, 1998). The collection of work included: a play involving five men (shaped by interviews with 11) considering their working lives and shifts from that space (Miller, 2001); a piece of readers' theatre enabling the voices of seven women, in jail in Ecuador for drug trafficking, to be heard (Bastidas, 2001); personal art expressions of wounded pasts (brown, 2000), and an exploration of Hungarian heritage through digitally interpreted artifacts (Cutcher, 2004). The topics all had extraordinary emotional power related to matters of importance to each author, often in the context of life history work.

Each of these theses was considered to have constructed a meaningful piece from varying components, exploring an area with integrity and reference to related thinkers and creators. Accessibility was contested. Certainly each succeeded within its own frame but each was dependent on audience intention and experience for transparency. Nevertheless, the academy was satisfied.

While presentation might seem a lesser concern than content, in this case, presentation often (but not always) represented content. Physical format varied from the traditional (hard bound in strong red, navy blue, or apple green with single coloured lettering) presenting a solid academic front, to those with small metaphoric individual messages on the cover or frontispiece, to those with fully illustrated covers creating an invitation to the reader to become involved in the text (a painting of the café where the reported conversations transpired [Miller, 2001]or the skeletal frames that led to reflections on landscapes [Thomas, 2004]). Opening pages led to a discovery of individuality in the Tables of Contents. For example, each piece included an analytic frame for an artistic piece, either independently or integrated in the body of the work, depending on the forms being used for representation. Page layouts moved from the straightforward to the poetic, with page placements and white space carrying particular messages, including the use of different fonts and iconic features to guide or challenge the reader. Metaphors were used often as glue to hold together an investigation. In Kunkel's (2000) work, a striking grey binding included a dangling silver spider, signifying her use of the tale of Ananse the spider as the metaphor for spinning the story. As she was raised in West African missionary schools this approach was salient and grounded her investigation in a culturally relevant context.

I wandered through the multi-coloured pile, immersing myself in wonder. The focus of each inquiry grew from very individual contexts, often engaging with topics causing personal hurt or concern, but all seeking engagement through multi-layered investigations and representations. Many of the pieces were a delight to hold, with interesting paper to caress, and often a lyric presentation to enjoy. Angela Rotundo (2001) explored her pathway as a teacher through a dance with Dante's *Divine Comedy*. Liz de Freitas (2003) used "writing and performative language" to "mediate the construction of community and the experience of alienation within the school context" (p. iii). brenda brown (2000) and

Nancy Davis Halifax (2002) confronted topics personal and silenced in ways that invite a reader to partake in the sharing of a circle of wounded souls who have moved through grief and confusion to find expression and light. brenda writes of "pulling together fragments of words and images to find ways to express the forbidden and disowned" (p. 14). She offers pictures of installations and re-creations of melded stories. Nancy's black end pages and translucent photographs warn the reader that a melee of dark and light await within the constructed text. She claims her work as

> poetic, fictional, aesthetic. This is an arts-informed inquiry where words and images participate with imagination to exhibit an embodied narrative of disability.... This is a work of ficto-phenomenology, a work of the embodied literary and aesthetic imagination. (Davis Halifax, 2002, p. iv)

Varied fonts and condensed quotations in margins, the process becomes part of the content. Lyric reflections confront stark realities, introspection framed in intellectual inquiry.

In her work on the Raging Grannies, Carole Roy (2003) used an oversized horizontal framework to enable four column presentation on a two paged frame. Her work includes historic photographs and texts of activist songs, as part of a tale of humour and strategy employed by diverse older women in pursuit of important causes. "This is an attempt to preserve the recent heritage of this group" (p. 1). As with other theses developed in these ways her work was published subsequently as a book in its own right (Roy, 2004).

Suzanne Thomas (2003; published version, 2004) also began with black, followed quickly by a sandy page, that transposed into the opening title page photograph, reconstructed sections of a skeletal cream fish, swimming past us on a background of black, framed in white — stark, unexpected, but inviting consideration.

Turning the page, the same image and title, re-presented, essence of fleshless fish remaining but transported into a gleaming whiteness with silver words, alerting the reader to the unexpected, highlighting the aesthetic. The "Tissue of Text" announces itself in poetic form as "a tale of placelessness and a longing search for place…a series of fragments

> threaded together
> with invisible seams, wisps of thought,
> re-enacted moments
> of earth and flesh and bones and breath —
> fleeting traces of blood memory.
> (Thomas, 2003, p. ii)

These pieces resonate; they are extraordinary. But would they be recognized elsewhere as doctoral theses? Might they be dismissed as something less than they are? The context is all. If there are supervisors to support, students to inquire, and examiners to accept, the process must be considered legitimate within the academy and nurtured in the context of a supportive learning community.

How to Provoke These Possibilities?

The first challenge for someone wishing to support arts-informed inquiry may be the attitude of the host university. Much will depend on how much autonomy is available at department or faculty level and how flexible the postgraduate committees (or equivalent) might be. Presumably the argument, from those inexperienced with these forms of inquiry, will rest on a definition of "knowledge" since the task of the doctoral student can be defined as making a contribution to the knowledge base. Perhaps the implication of that expectation is that information will be generated that can contribute to an understanding of the area in question or be useful for policy-making. If, by extension, the task is defined as expanding the field of investigation, then arts-informed inquiry "simply" becomes another tool, not a source of concern in terms of legitimacy. What if, however, the topic being investigated is, loosely speaking, one's self? Does this not become an exercise in self-indulgence rather than scholarly investigation? (I can hear my supervisor scathingly dismissing a piece of work that was "based on an N of 1!") At this point, a consideration of the convergence of case study and life history methodologies can rescue the debate. These approaches are recognized as offering insights into the social context, indeed the construction of the human condition, and are, therefore, by definition, legitimate under the academic umbrella although, of course, some individuals may not be sympathetic to the full range of investigative and representational possibilities. Given that the degree granting institution (or some influential members within it) can accept these arguments, the stage is set for promoting (and supervising) arts-informed inquiry.

What invitations does a supervisor offer if the local context is not currently provoking students to consider alternative approaches to the construction of a thesis? Perhaps the offering of opportunity through example and guided reading will be enough to excite those with a predisposition to this kind of representation and theorizing. In the absence of courses of study about possibilities inherent in these approaches, extended discussions with sympathetic colleagues and reference to illuminative literature will help. In this case, a useful place to start is in the work contained in *Provoked by Art: Theorising Arts-Informed Research* (Cole, Neilsen, Knowles, & Luciani, 2004).

Consideration of intersections also informs these musings. A grey autumn morning dog walk in the park with Ardra Cole helped consolidate some of the elements to be considered here. In entering the realm of supervision in this arena, there is the interplay of the opportunities of arts-informed inquiry, the positioning in time and space of the graduate student, and the nature of the content to be investigated. There are myriads of ways in which these elements might interact and might engage with the orientation, expertise, and personality of a supervisor. The content, for example, might seem to slide towards the personal, whereas the academy might presume that there is some expectation that the personal inform the general that there will be resonance for a reader, and implications for increased understanding. There may be a subtle difference between a self-indulgent personal reflection (which may be useful for the individual and part of a family's history) and the investigation of the personal in ways that include multiple paths and interpretations or resonance in larger contexts (that may contribute to the knowledge base of the community). Intellectual links with literature that can be consulted by others is a critical component.

Clothed in the shapes of traditional academe, my movement towards arts-informed inquiry felt like a struggle through the firm ground of early spring, wriggling out of constraints to emerge in the light. I had been richly fertilized with a home that valued music and literature, moving through the spaces of macramé knots, guitar playing and photography, accompanied by journals bursting with observation, reflection, and poetry; I was ripe to grow in this inviting environment.

Dark 4 AM Self-doubt

Suppose I make myself available to support arts-informed inquiry? What if I find I am offering students something that I can't deliver? Upon reflection, I suspect that two people who have "quit" / decided not to proceed with postgraduate research, might have been more safely engaged in an arts-informed inquiry, rather than finding that the requirements of their employment overwhelmed their study and made the academic path too troubled. Both were working with children in early childhood services and had serious time constraints. For both students (and with two different co-supervisors), we explored interviews, video, and dialogues. Perhaps we needed to stretch the boundaries, explore different readings and move into other representations of voice. One was anxious not to "pollute her nest" and over-rely on her workplace as a research site, so situating the work more heavily there (to reduce the space between work and study reflections) was not an option. Nevertheless, her passion about the area of investigation leaves room for re-entering the dialogue in the future. The other student who is caught currently in a sense of the impossible, may yet be re-enticed through an invitation to alternate forms of representation; the fact that her co-supervisor is a visual artist energizes me to reframe our discussions.

Light Mid-day Optimism

So let's assume this is both a possible and a desirous thing, encouraging and supporting students who are so inclined to enter the world of arts-informed inquiry. This belief takes me back to my reading of 1992:

> In supervising someone engaged in their own line of work, I am free to speak from my own real experience, to offer what I can in support of a project in which I believe. I have intimate and privileged access to a unique intellectual journey, to the excitement and the challenge of personally creative thinking.... (Salmon, 1992, p. 120)

In addition to personal belief in the possible, there is the appropriate expanding literature to be considered, the similarly minded colleague to engage in the creation of inspirational contexts, and the offering of supportive conversational challenges. I am already a photographer and need to learn more; I am already a writer and can explore more forms; I have already explored non-traditional formats for presentation and can expand my repertoire. I am an enquiring learner. I think, perhaps, I am in a position to begin.

References

Bastidas, H. J. (2001). *Listen to the (In)mate: A life history, readers' theatre (re) presentation of women in Ecuador jails accused of drug trafficking.* Unpublished Master's thesis, University of Toronto, Toronto, ON, Canada.

brown, b. (2000). *Lost bodies and wild imaginations: Expressing the forbidden tales of childhood sexual abuse through artful inquiry.* Unpublished doctoral thesis, University of Toronto, Toronto, ON, Canada.

Clandinin, J., & Connelly, S. M. (1994). Personal experience methods. In N. K. Denzin, & Y. S. Lincoln (Eds.). *Handbook of qualitative research* (pp. 413-427). Thousand Oaks: Sage Publications.

Cole, A. L, Neilsen, L., Knowles, J. G., & Luciani, T. C. (Eds.). (2004). *Provoked by art: Theorising arts-informed research.* Halifax, NS & Toronto, ON: Backalong Books & Centre for Arts-informed Research.

Coles, R. (1989). *The call of stories: Teaching and the moral imagination.* Boston, MA: Houghton Mifflin.

Cutcher, A. J. (2004). *The Hungarian in Australia: A portfolio of belongings.* Unpublished doctoral thesis, University of Sydney, Sydney, NSW, Australia.

Dahlberg, G., & Moss, P. (2005). *Ethics and politics in early child hood education.* London, UK: RoutledgeFalmer.

Dahlberg, G., Moss, P., & Pence, A. (1999). *Beyond quality in early childhood education and care: Postmodern perspectives.* London, UK: Falmer Press.

Davis Halifax, N. V. (2002). *Of rose petals and sutures, marks on a woman's body: An aesthetic and oblique inquiry into dys-body, solace and vulnerability.* Unpublished doctoral thesis, University of Toronto, Toronto, ON, Canada.

de Freitas, E. (2003). *The wrong shoe and other misfits: Fiction writing as reflexive enquiry within a private girls school.* Unpublished doctoral thesis, University of Toronto, Toronto, ON, Canada.

Edwards, C., Gandini, L., & Forman, G. (1998). *The hundred languages of children: The Reggio Emilia approach advanced reflections.* Greenwich, CT: Ablex Publishing Corporation.

Fleet, A., & Winters, P. (2004, September). *The impact of practitioner research on curriculum quality in the early years.* Paper presented at the European Early Childhood Education Research Association Conference. Malta.

Fleet, A., Scrimshaw, K., & Winkler, T. (2004, November). *Seeking the unexpected: Staff collaborative inquiry.* Paper presented at the Centre for Equity and Innovation in Early Childhood Conference, Melbourne, Australia.

Fleet, A., Holland, S., Leigh, B., & Patterson, C. (2001). Fragile relationships. In H. Byrne-Armstrong, J. Higgs & D. Horsfall (Eds), *Critical moments in qualitative research* (pp. 92-105). Sydney, NSW: Butterworth Heinemann.

Grant, B. (1999). *Walking on a rackety bridge: Mapping supervision.* Paper presented at the HERDSA annual international conference. Melbourne, Australia.

Jipson, J., & Munro, P. (1997). Deconstructing wo / mentoring: Diving into the abyss. In J. Jipson & N. Paley (Eds.), *Daredevil research: Re-creating analytic practice* (pp. 201-217). New York, NY: Peter Lang.

Jipson, J., & Paley, N. (Eds.) (1997). *Daredevil research: Re-creating analytic practice.* New York, NY: Peter Lang.

Kunkel, L. I. (2000). *Spiders spin silk: Reflections of missionary kids at midlife.* Unpublished doctoral thesis, University of Toronto, Toronto, ON, Canada.

Miller, E. (2001). *Closing time: Men, identity, vocation and the end of work: A stage play as a representation of lives.* Unpublished doctoral thesis, University of Toronto, Toronto, ON, Canada.

Neilsen, L. (2001). Scribbler: Notes of writing and learning inquiry. In L. Neilsen, A. L. Cole, & J. G. Knowles (Eds.), *The art of writing inquiry* (pp. 253-272). Halifax, NS & Toronto, ON: Backalong Books & Centre for Arts-informed Research.

Rotundo, A. (2001). *A teacher's soulful inquiry: Exploring professional development using "The Divine Comedy as a guide".* Unpublished doctoral thesis, University of Toronto, Toronto, ON, Canada.

Roy, C. (2003). *The Raging Grannies: Meddlesome crones, humour, daring, and education.* Unpublished doctoral thesis, University of Toronto, Toronto, ON, Canada.

Salmon, P. (1992). *Achieving a PhD: Ten students' experiences.* Stoke-on-Trent, UK: Trentham Books.

Smith, D. (2001) Learning through supervising. In H. Byrne-Armstrong, J. Higgs, & D. Horsfall (Eds), *Critical moments in qualitative research* (pp. 128-135). Sydney, NSW: Butterworth Heinemann.

Soja, E. W. (1996). *Thirdspace: Journeys to Los Angeles and other real-and-imagined places.* Boston, MA: Blackwell Publishers.

Thomas, S. (2001). Reimagining inquiry, Envisioning form. In L. Neilsen, A. L. Cole, & J. G. Knowles (Eds.), *The art of writing inquiry* (pp. 273-282). Halifax, NS & Toronto, ON: Backalong Books & Centre for Arts-informed Research.

Thomas, S. (2003). *earth and flesh and bones and breath: Landscapes of Embodiment and Moments of Re-enactment.* Unpublished doctoral thesis, University of Toronto, Toronto, ON, Canada.

Thomas, S. (2004). *Of earth and flesh and bones and breath: Landscapes of embodiment and moments of re-enactment.* Halifax, NS & Toronto, ON: Backalong Books & Centre for Arts-informed Research.

About the Author

ALMA FLEET is Coordinator of Teaching and Learning, Institute of Early Childhood, Macquarie University, Sydney. She is interested in educational change and working with preservice and inservice teachers to stretch the boundaries of traditional practice. She draws on the philosophies and work of the educators in Reggio Emilia, Italy to confront mundane approaches to work with young children. Her most recent publication is an edited book considering the intersections between pedagogical documentation and social justice.

24. Creating Spaces for Artful Ways

by Lynn Butler-Kisber, Christina Rudd, and Mary Stewart

In this chapter we briefly examine the context of a qualitative research course and document, with the help of three student stories, how this space ignited their interest in arts-informed inquiry and how they subsequently developed it in their thesis journeys. We suggest some of the implications that three different approaches — collage, concept mapping, and photographs — have for research and to try to tease out some important elements for advancing arts-informed research.

In 1999 Lynn proposed and began teaching an advanced

qualitative methodology course ("Interpretive Inquiry") for graduate students who were working with their data and were familiar
with the basics of qualitative research. The course is predicated on
the notions that form influences knowledge and mediates understandings in interesting and different ways (Eisner, 1991;
Richardson, 1995), and artful approaches provide compelling
avenues for expression (Butler-Kisber, 1997; Gardner, 1983,
1999). These approaches not only push the boundaries of understanding and communication but also provide powerful ways to
interrogate our traditions and practices (Butler-Kisber, 2007).

The "Interpretive Inquiry" Context
The "Interpretive Inquiry" course actively engages students in a
range of inquiry approaches that can be used in different ways to
help students make their processes transparent, and to expose
them to the possibilities that exist in arts-informed qualitative
research. It is a three credit, pass / fail course that takes place over
one semester. The pace of the course is fast, and the work is
demanding, but the pass / fail grading encourages risk-taking —
and the student-oriented classes build trust and a sense of community in what we are calling "artful collaboration" (Butler-Kisber,
2002). Each week students are required to read theoretical pieces
and practical examples of research that include narrative, collage,
found poetry, work with photographs, and drama. They come to
class prepared to discuss the theoretical pieces and with an analytic
exercise they have applied to their data. Students respond to the
readings in class and share, in pairs or small groups, the work they
have done. At the end of a class the exercises are submitted for further feedback and each student writes a reflective memo about
"where they are" in their thinking and doing. Direct instruction is
guided by needs as they arise, often signaled in the memos, and
frequently graduate students who are further along in the process
come to present. The course culminates in an exhibition of visual

products or performances, accompanied by short, oral presentations where the students synthesize the connections they have made during the course.

Student Journeys

Three former students who have taken the course and who have used different artful approaches in their thesis work, agreed to share their stories. We are grateful to Pamela, who uses collage, Tiiu, who uses visual mapping, and Teri, who uses photographs. We engaged in an iterative process of talking and writing to respond to their stories and to tease out the elements that are conducive to creating a space for artful inquiry. We have done this by revisiting our respective experiences in the course and those of the students who contributed to this chapter through audio-taped conversations and Email exchanges.

Finding the Words by Pamela Markus
(Pamela, on completing the first full draft of her doctoral thesis.)

In the spring of 2001 I was introduced to artful methods in research in the Interpretive Inquiry course. To say that I was resistant to these alternative methods would be a vast understatement! This original doubt, however, grew into gradual acceptance and, eventually, into great enthusiasm that has convinced me to use artful methods in my doctoral research (Butler-Kisber, et al., 2002-2003).

One of the exercises in this course was to use collage as a way of contextualizing our data. Donna Davis, a collage artist and former student, led the class. Before we engaged in the process Donna informed us that collage allows for multiple ways of looking at phenomena (Davis & Butler-Kisber, 1999). As a student with a fine arts background, and many years of studio experience, I was skeptical. Donna outlined directions for constructing the collage, suggesting that we look for images that did not necessarily represent our data.

As I began choosing images from magazines, I found that I was unable to find the exact "picture", in the photographic sense, to represent my work. Instead, I intuitively chose images that "felt" like what I was investigating in my research at the time. In my own artwork spontaneity rarely came into play and, here, spontaneity was the key. Hesitant and highly reluctant, however, I did complete one collage. In response to the finished work fellow students wrote comments on small pieces of paper next to the collage. Their reactions offered alternate ways of looking at the phenomena, views that I had not imagined before. The open-ended space created by the images allowed for multiple views to exist. Thomas Brockelman (2001) explains that collage retains a sense of ambiguity, where "each element exists in two 'worlds' (the one from which it was drawn and the one into which it is pasted), that it must speak with two voices" (p. 31).

Several months later while I was working on my thesis, an autobiographical study entitled "Drawing on Experience", I tried to put into words the context of where I teach art, that of summer camp. Camp is so familiar to me that I find it almost impossible to describe. It is like being farsighted; you cannot read anything clearly because it is too close. I needed to find the words to present a vivid picture of this place, particularly because my research focuses on how place influences how I "see". I thought that collage might help. When I think of camp, I think of being in the woods, immersed in nature. The green surroundings feed me, comfort me, and energize me. We spend nights lying out on the docks, below the immense open sky, searching for shooting stars and sharing conversation. We walk down the road to the bridge, talking, picking flowers and wild strawberries. I walk down the road when I am in need of solitude.

The first image that resonated with me was of many hands

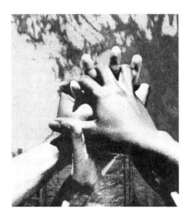

Figure 1. Pamela Markus, 2002. *Memories of Summer Camp*. Found magazine photographs and glue on cardstock, 21 x 15 cm. (Used with permission.)

grasped together. Camp is about working together, collaborating, and reaching up. It is a celebration of that collaboration. Clearly we could not do it on our own. We need people to help. I need to work with others. At home we are isolated but there collaboration is everything. The words started to flow; collage provided a way to find the words.

Besides the satisfaction that I get from bringing the visual into my work, literally "playing" with images, I learn from these images. With support from the members of my thesis committee, all of whom are interested in arts-informed work, I continue to construct collages based on phenomena in my research that will be part of my thesis. Through this I develop a more methodical, step-by-step approach to "finding the words" (Markus, 2005). Collage invites multiple interpretations which not only contribute to its relevance in research but also within contemporary culture.

Reflections

Collage, in this case the process of pasting found images from magazines to cardstock, has attracted interest in qualitative work because it allows the researcher to work in a non-linear and intuitive way by arranging image fragments that reveal unconscious connections and new understandings. It is the reduction of conscious control over what is being presented that contributes to greater levels of expression and, therefore, greater areas for expression and interpretation (Williams, 2000). In fact, "collage reflects the very way we experience the world with objects given meaning not from something within themselves, but rather through the way we perceive they stand in relationship to one another" (Robertson, 2002, p. 2).

For the novice, collage can be a non-threatening medium because it does not require sophisticated artistic skills to produce interesting forms of expression (Butler-Kisber, 2007). For Pamela, however, her fine arts background and experience with collage initially made her resistant to working intuitively from feelings to ideas. We suggest that artists, who become researchers rather than the reverse, have often kept their art worlds quite separate from their research and may find crossing these boundaries unsettling initially. During one of our Email exchanges, Christina corroborated this when she wrote:

> My biggest struggle was with the idea of bringing art into the academy…. My feeling was, if you want to be an artist, get into your studio and shut up. You want to write a novel? Great. Find a publisher and good luck but don't call it a doctoral degree. The idea that art in any form, from any perspective, could be married with whatever it is we call traditional acad eme made me extremely nervous. I worried that "art"…would be used the way a bad cook uses someone else's great recipes. However, I was being way too literal. When I let go of words and created a response within a collage activity I began to re-frame my expectations and trust what might happen. I needed

to experience an artful way of making connections that I knew could not have been made in any other way.
(October 24, 2004)

Pamela's approach of using collage as a form of elicitation for writing autobiographically is indeed interesting and, we hypothesize, a quite novel approach. We eagerly look forward to the imminent completion of her thesis.

Mapping My World by Tiiu Poldma
(Tiiu, on completing her doctoral degree in 2003.)

As an interior design teacher and professional I approach both my work and teaching using visual methods, such as drawing and visual mapping, and integrate them with narrative. In the spring of 2000 I was in the initial stage of data collection for my doctoral thesis. I was investigating how students learn design processes and what teachers do to guide them. I realized that I needed some analytic tools, so I enrolled in the Interpretive Inquiry course. I had no idea how profoundly arts-informed work would influence the development of my thesis.

I found it exciting when I tried out an approach and felt the intuitive aspects of my own designer side resonate with the inquiry techniques. During one of the class exercises I discovered how my conceptual sketching had evolved from the ways that I had drawn in childhood. I was stunned! I came to realize that my tendency to express my ideas visually had worth and could be a valuable part of my research.

About nine months later I analyzed my work using various artful approaches. I coded the research data to cull emerging themes and, then, as issues were uncovered I used analytic memos, narrative, poetic re-transcription, concept maps, and diagrams to grasp the emerging phenomena. Concept maps, juxtaposed with narrative, helped me to visualize the phemomena and make interesting connections. For example, through the concept map below I was able to realize the value of juxtaposing earlier with later data and envision the research process I would follow (Vaikla-Poldma, 2003).

I had positive reactions from my doctoral thesis committee to the use of artful forms during the exploration and analysis phases of my work. In the end, however, there was some opposition about including the visuals in the thesis. I resisted, and with the support of my supervisor, created more "geometric" rather than free-hand maps to include in the thesis itself and retained some of the "original maps" in the appendices. In the end this helped make my methodology transparent and retained the context of my work.

Reflections

Concept maps permit the viewer to understand complex phenomena at a glance in order to make new connections, build new knowledge, and / or analyze difficult topics (Blantchet-Cohen, Ragan, & Amsden, 2003). In fact, Sobel (1997, n.p.) suggests that, "mapmaking in the broad sense…is as important to making us human as language, music, art, and mathematics." Yet, in spite of this and the knowledge that concept mapping is particularly suitable for qualitative work because it retains context, supports qualitative underpinnings, helps reduce data, and has an excellent revisiting capacity, it has received little attention (Daley, 2004). What is particularly noteworthy about Tiiu's journey, is that she used concept mapping with interesting results for many of these reasons, as well as the natural talent she has that she previously kept very separate from her research.

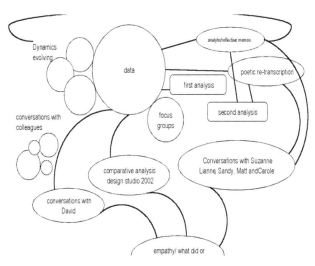

Figure 2. Tiiu Vaikla-Poldma, 2003. *Evolving research process*. Black ink sketch on white paper, 12 x 12 cm. Used with permission.

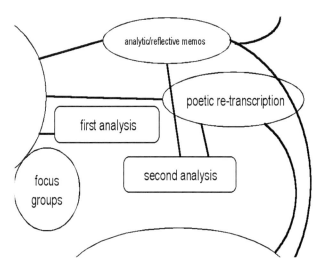

Figure 2. Tiiu Vaikla-Poldma, 2003. *Evolving research process*. Black ink sketch on white paper, 12 x 12 cm. Detail. Used with permission.

Voice for the Voiceless by Teri Todd
(Teri, on completing two out of three of her final "thesis papers".)

As part of my doctoral program I enrolled in the Interpretive Inquiry course in 2002. Though I had engaged in some prior research it was always of a quantitative nature and, while I was curious about qualitative approaches, I wondered if I would find qualitative inquiry scientific enough to meet the rigours of "good science".

At the same time I was at a crossroads in my own research. My area of work is instructional strategies that promote sustained engagement in physical activities and encourage self-determined behaviors for individuals with severe developmental disabilities. It is also an area in which I am personally involved because my son has a severe developmental disability. I wondered whether I could be objective while being emotionally involved. I did not expect this question to be answered in class but it was. I came to understand that all researchers are biased in some way and that, by attending to reflexivity and voice, bias can become transparent and useful. Reflexivity helps to make biases transparent and give voice to participants to ensure their stories and interpretations are told.

The question of voice intrigued me because my participants do not speak, read or write, and have few signs and a limited use of pictures. Yet, we need their "voices" to help guide us in developing good schools and effective programs for them. As the course progressed participant voice became a central theme for me and I pondered how I could access the voices of the participants in my research.

We had worked with words, poems, and collage and were moving into using photographs. I used an adaptation of Lykes' approach (2001). She used photographs taken by research participants to tease out interpretive themes. I decided to take pictures during an exercise session with my participants. I then had my colleagues in class organize the photographs in chronological order

288

and interpret what happened at different times. The outcome was quite amazing. They saw much more than I had anticipated. I began to see the possibility of using photographs with my participants as a way of "giving voice" to them.

Following the course I wrestled with how to find a creative way to get responses to pictures from participants who were non-verbal. Ultimately, I decided to conduct a pilot study and take pictures of my participants at the beginning, middle, and end of exercise sessions during a five month program. I then presented the pictures to the participants and asked them to respond to them as "anxious", "neutral", or "happy" using pictograms of the three emotions. I was careful to exclude pictures that might be seen as compromising to a participant. I was excited when I found participants were able to tell me, in a fairly concrete manner, how they felt during each session. Over time I discovered changes in their engagement that were corroborated by their responses. I might have missed these changes had I not been systematically looking (literally) at what was happening and attending to what they "said".

This discovery led me to design a qualitative part to my study that became a section of my doctoral thesis and built on the pilot work. When I presented this idea to my advisor, a quantitative researcher, he was skeptical at first but was convinced and enthusiastic when he saw my results. Since then we have added an arts-informed qualitative researcher to my committee. Later, I presented some of my qualitative findings at a conference for the North American Federation of Adapted Physical Activity (Todd & Reid, 2004) and it was extremely well received by others in the field. This was both encouraging and legitimizing. I believe that in the adapted physical activity area, mixed methodologies — quantitative to measure physical activity, fitness, for example, and qualitative to understand peoples' reactions, emotions, and well-being — complement each other very well, and hold much promise for the voiceless with whom I live and work.

Reflections

Photo-interviewing has been used to elicit information from participants, particularly by anthropologists, from as far back as the time of Franz Boas' work in the Trobriand Islands (Hurworth, 2003). Its value lies in the fact that it can provide nuances, trigger memories, lead to new perspectives and explanations, and help the researcher avoid misinterpretations (Harper, 1984). Teri's use of photograph elicitation is unique in that it mediates communication in non-verbal participants and gets at social and emotional understandings that otherwise could not be documented. It pushes the notion of what constitutes voice in qualitative work, and opens the doorway to many exciting possibilities.

Salient Features for Encouraging Arts-informed Inquiry

In summary, our work suggests there are many possibilities for opening spaces that encourage arts-informed research in the thesis process. A course is just one means of doing this. The advantages of such a course are that it exposes students with diverse research perspectives and disciplines, to the potential and range of arts-informed work, and to each other. At times, the work legitimizes existing talent that has been kept very separate from research as witnessed in Pamela and Tiiu's stories. In other instances it provides a catalyst for "non artists" to explore new avenues with innovative results, as in the case of Teri. A distinct disadvantage is that students, who become excited about the prospects of pursuing an arts-informed dissertation, can find themselves with insufficient support to carry out and / or get recognition for the work.

We suggest that spaces to help researchers imagine arts-informed theses should:

- provide a collaborative environment that attracts a range of researchers from different disciplines, where an "artful tone" elicits risk-taking, empathy, and playfulness;

- create opportunities where participants can explore their data using a range of clearly articulated arts-informed approaches that are supported by theoretical readings, discussions, and reflection;
- be an environment that encourages sharing "works-in-progress" rather than final products in order to decrease pressure and self-consciousness, and
- use peer mentoring / presenting to scaffold the work.

Furthermore, we believe that more inter-institutional exchanges are needed to help create spaces for this kind of research. Some of these do occur at conferences, through existing electronic communications, and in journals. More mechanisms need to be established to ensure this kind of research will continue to flourish and grow.

References

Blantchet-Cohen, N., Ragan, D., & Amsden, J. (2003). Children becoming social actors: Using visual maps to understand children's views of environmental change. *Children, Youth, and Environments, 13*(2). Retrieved February, 11, 2005 from http://www. colorado.educ.journals/cye/13-2/Fieldreports/ Mapping/Mapping.htm

Brockelman, T. P. (2001). *The frame and the mirror: On collage and the postmodern.* Evanston, IL: Northwestern University Press.

Butler-Kisber, L. (1997). The practical: Classroom literacy through stories, questions and action. In V. Froese (Ed.), *Language across the curriculum* (pp. 183-213). Toronto, ON: Harcourt Brace.

Butler-Kisber, L. (2002). Artful portrayals in qualitative inquiry: The road to found poetry and beyond. *The Alberta Journal of Educational Research, XLVII*(3), 229-239.

Butler-Kisber, L. (2007). Collage as analysis and respresentation in qualitative inquiry. In J. G. Knowles, T. C. Luciani, A. L. Cole, & L. Neilsen (Eds.), *The art of visual inquiry* (pp. 265-280).

Halifax, NS & Toronto, ON: Backalong Books & Centre for Arts-informed Research.

Butler-Kisber, L., Allnutt, S., Furlini, L., Kronish, N., Markus, P., Poldma, T., & Stewart, M. (2002-2003). Insight and voice in artful analysis: A co-operative inquiry. *Arts and Learning Research Journal, 19*(1), 127-165.

Daley, B. J. (2004). Using concept maps in qualitative research. In A. J. Cañas, J. D. Novak, & F. M. Gonzales (Eds.), Concept maps: Theory, methodology and technology. Proceedings of the *First National Conference on Concept Mapping*. Retrieved February 12, 2005 from http://cmc.ihmc.us/papers/cmc2004-060.pdf.

Davis, D., & Butler-Kisber, L. (1999). Arts-based representation in qualitative research: Collage as a contextualizing analytic strategy. Paper presented at the American Educational Research Association Annual Meeting, Montreal, QC. *Resources in Education, 34*(11), 135.

Eisner, E. (1991). *The enlightened eye*. New York, NY: Macmillan.

Gardner, H. (1983). *Frames of mind: The theory of multiple intelligences*. New York, NY: Basics Books.

Gardner, H. (1999). *Intelligence reframed: Multiple intelligences for the 21st century*. New York, NY: Basic Books.

Harper, D. (1984). Meaning and work: A study in photo elicitation. *International Journal of Visual Sociology 2*(1), 20-43.

Hurworth, R. (2003). Photo-interviewing for research. *Social Research Update, 40*. Retrieved January 14, 2004 from http://www.soc.surrey.ac.uk/sru/SRU40.pdf.

Lykes, M. (2001). Creative arts and photography in participatory action research in Guatemala. In P. Reason & H. Bradbury (Eds.), *Handbook of action research: Participative inquiry and practice* (pp. 363-371). Thousand Oaks, CA: Sage Publications.

Markus, P. (2005, March). *"Seeing" place*. Paper presented at the National Art Education Association Conference, Boston, MA.

Richardson, L. (1995). Narrative and sociology. In J. van Maanen (Ed.), *Representation in ethnography* (pp. 198-221). Thousand Oaks, CA: Sage Publications.

Robertson, B. (2002). *Why collage?* Retrieved April 5, 2004 from www.collagetown.com.

Sobel, D. (1997). *Mapmaking from the inside out: The cartography of childhood.* Retrieved January 25, 2005 from http://www.haveo.net.deep/council/sobel.htm.

Stewart, M. (2003). *Literacy instruction in a cycle one classroom: A qualitative study.* Unpublished doctoral thesis, McGill University, Montreal, QC, Canada.

Todd, T., & Reid, G. (2004, October). *Understanding enjoyment and engagement in physical activity for adolescents with ASD.* Paper presented at the Bi-annual Conference of the North American Federation of Adapted Physical Activity, Thunder Bay, ON.

Vaikla-Poldma, T. (2003). *An investigation of learning and teaching practices in an interior design class: An interpretive and contextual inquiry.* Unpublished doctoral thesis, McGill University, Montreal, QC, Canada

Williams, B. (2000). Collage as a medium for guided reflection in the clinical supervision relationship. *Nurse Education Today, 20,* 273-278.

About the Authors
LYNN BUTLER-KISBER is an Associate Professor in the Department of Integrated Studies in Education, McGill University, Montreal. She is Director of the Centre for Educational Leadership and the Graduate Certificate Programs in Educational Leadership. Lynn is the Editor of the new journal LEARNing Landscapes. Her research and development activities focus on classroom processes, literacy learning, student engagement, educational leadership, professional development, and qualitative methodologies. She is

particularly interested in the role of arts-based analysis and representation in qualitative research.

CHRISTINA RUDD taught in Montreal elementary and secondary public schools for many years and at the time of writing was a PhD student and lecturer in the Faculty of Education at McGill University. She also teaches at the National Circus School. Her research interests are teacher education, teacher identity and community-based literacy and art projects. She was twice awarded the "Teacher Appreciation Award" by graduating classes.

MARY STEWART graduated with a PhD in Integrated Studies in Education from McGill University. She Managing Editor of the new Journal LEARNing Landscapes and is Quality Control Manager for the Leading English Education and Resource Network (LEARN) of Quebec, Canada. Her research interests include literacy, professional development, adoption and research methodology. She is one of the founding members of the Artful Analysis and Representation in Research Collective (AARRC).

Mary's doctoral thesis, *Literacy Instruction in a Cycle One Classroom: A Qualitative Study*, explores literacy instruction in a grade one classroom. She discovered that exemplary instruction was characterized by three dimensions: fine-tuned precision, student choice and variety. Found poetry was particularly useful in her research because it enabled her to incorporate contradictions she encountered in interviews with parents. Mary believes this led to more nuanced, sensitive, and honest work than she might have done otherwise.

25. Light Out of Darkness: (Re-)staging a Collaborative Inquiry

by CHRISTINE VAN HALEN-FARBER AND C. T. PATRICK DIAMOND

Prelude: A Program Note to Our Audience

Our chapter finds its beginnings in one of our collaborative arts-based inquiries; in this instance, that of Christine's doctoral thesis as supervised or co-imagined by Patrick. Midway through the first year of *Seeing Through Apples: An Arts-based Exploration into the Ethics and Aesthetics of a Teacher-educator-researcher's Arts-based Beginnings* (van Halen-Faber, 2004), Christine intuitively turned to the ancient Indonesian art form of *batik*.[1] This technique became central to her methodology and formed a key representational strategy in the inquiry. Drawing upon an array of different fabrics, dyes, and wax she co-created six fragmented apple images to mediate her exploration of her own beginnings as an arts-based inquirer who was working in the presence of six other collaborators who were themselves student-teachers / beginning teachers. As a result of her ongoing self-reflection and exchanges with her co-inquirers and Patrick, Christine came to re-present the six individual batik apple images as characters in a shadow play in which she took the role of a beginning or apprentice *dalang* — shadow master[2] who eventually graduated to become a shadow master herself. By learning to "hang fire," or watch and wait and to remain open to a series of arts-informed intimations she gradually came to realize the significance of her family's emigration from the Netherlands to Canada. This in turn resurfaced Dutch (former colonial) connections with Indonesia, its art forms, and experience of liberation. These culture-straddling threads were strengthened further by revisiting Clifford Geertz's (1960) pioneering symbolic auto-ethnographic inquiries in Indonesia, forming a spreading web of ghostly imaginings that foreshadowed things to come.

We two have come to understand that we are seeking to examine not just a culture (that of doing an artful thesis) but experience itself — in ways similar to reading or interpreting a text. Our goal is not to perpetuate a specific form of arts-based methodology but, rather, to set an inquiry tone or mood that others can react toward or against. Seeing the interplay of light and shadow for themselves.

In this chapter we extend this shadow play image as a metaphor for tracing the contours of a collaborative development between a thesis candidate and her supervisor. We now re-present Christine's arts-based inquiry experience by placing it in a re-focused light and accept that in the presence of light there is always a shadow. The shadow side was revealed as an integral part of us as inquirers, symbolizing our individual and joint presence, and providing the backdrop to our emerging text. Our experience confirms that the first wavering steps of the inquiry warranted being followed.

Setting the Scene

Our chapter consists of a collaborative self-study of how we conducted our inquiry by choosing to follow an evolving arts-based form and by constantly re-imagining its possibilities. Our informing theme is that such an inquiry needs to be non-linear and to honour the central place both of "imaginative rationality" (Lakoff & Johnson, 1980) and the play of intuition. We also consider the complexities that are entailed when reflexivity, subjectivity, and presence are invited into the research process. When the need for supportive relationships with the other thesis committee members and the external examiner is acknowledged.

For our centrally informing analogical form and structure here we take that of the Indonesian *wayang purwa*[3] or shadow play. We extend the implications of this form to illustrate the collaborative inter-play between a master-puppet-master (Patrick, supervisor) and an apprentice-puppet-master (Christine, thesis writer) and their journeying toward ever more artful imaginings.

The intermingled moves or tone are thus intro- and retrospective: Introspective as we follow both Christine's use of the shadow play as a form to introduce and showcase her six research participants and Patrick's "in-the-shadows" or behind the scenes role as her thesis supervisor. Retrospective as we re-trace his development and role as an arts-based thesis supervisor (and beginning novelist), and Christine's own "in-the-shadows" role as a beginning arts-based inquirer and writer herself.

The *wayang purwa* plays are epic, all-night performances in which the shadows cast by puppets are considered to mediate between the visible world and the unseen realm of the spirits. So too our re-inscribed arts-based thesis play, within the confines of academe, follows pre-scribed performance practice. The members of the audience (that is, the thesis committee, external examiner, university-appointed examination chair, and present readers) are actively engaged as they sit and watch on either side of the screen. They can somewhat anticipate the overall story line and its musical accompaniment but need to remain open to the (apprentice) puppet master's (or thesis candidate's) improvisations and re-voicings of inquiry. Ready for the unexpected. The audience members closely follow the sequence of the play's ritualistic patterns believing that those who have gone before (as cited from the literature) might be "brought to life as shadows" (Geertz, 1960, p. 268) to give advice and guidance in the ways of the super-natural: That of "sur-real" arts-based inquiry.

In the *wayang purwa*, the flickering of a coconut oil flame (or that of the arts-based inquirer's intuition and imagination) behind the screen adds mystery and excitement, lending an unearthly and compelling beauty to the lacy shadow figures of the puppets (or the co-participants in the study). An interplay of informing light and concealing shadow. Well-known, time-honoured stories allow the members of the audience to see themselves and others in or through the mirror of collective history and to re-view current situations through more expansive perspectives.

Like the shifting scenes of a shadow play our chapter text is divided into sequences. Each of these re-captures some of the inquiry dilemmas or sensory memories that turned out to be crucially important to reconstructing our personal history of shadow-mastery and of becoming collaborative arts-based educational researchers. The sequencing of the scenes follows the chronology of the "apprentice's" (Christine's) arts-based experiences and is inter-voiced with the "master's" (Patrick's) recollections of and references to other supervisory experiences. The text draws on fragments from thesis journals, conversations, co-written texts, and our extensive Email correspondence. As our working-together develops, thoughts, words, and lines of text run into each other naturally like the wax and dye upon the fabric apple images. Roles shift and change. And then recur. The apprentice becomes her own mistress and the master the apprentice.

Light out of darkness. We turn to Christine's oral defence to show how "cultural [and academic] forms can be treated as texts, as imaginative works built out of social [and academic] materials" (Geertz, 1973, p. 449). It then follows a sequence of inciting moments or scenes (as in a shadow play) that represent the trajectory of our work alone-together. Showing how a collaborative arts-based thesis can be staged. A dramatizing of the inquiry sequence from sharing doctoral level arts-based courses to conducting and then writing up and defending the whole thesis process. Simplifying while honouring the complexity. The text is shaped to reflect the interplay between con-text and contents: We use separate and overlapping voices as columns to in/trans-form our script. Light and shade, movement and stasis.

Scene One: The Oral Exam

November 20, 2003.

Christine

The scene is set. The theater a square, nondescript room. Institutional and un-adorned beige walls. No windows. Two doors to be closed. I re-arrange the furniture, placing the chairs equidistant around the rectangular conference table.

In anticipation of today's per-

Patrick

Shortly before 2:00 PM and the defence. I have just returned to my office on the 10th floor of my academic tower. I stand at the window and gaze over the cityscape toward the lake with its pale horizons. The route Christine would have followed earlier.

Like Henry James's (1881 / 1995) window vantage point

formance, I set out my props on smaller tables lining the walls:

Six batik panels featuring distinct apple fragments.

Silent participants.

These are the six characters in my thesis play, waiting to be re-animated yet once again. As *wayang* (shadow play) puppets are displayed in the soft juicy flesh of a banana tree, so my six characters are sorted and placed in order of appearance but on hard wood veneer.

At rest for now.

Quietly waiting until I, their *dalang* (or shadow master), decide their time has come. November 20, 2003. The day of my defence. My timing. My husband had patiently awaited my timing. As had Patrick.

on Venice, mine has offered me a breathing space during the past years. Lunch was pleasant: Served in the hospitable ambiance of a bustling bistro, framed in collegial exchanges. I learned about dry foam for cappuccino.

I had lunched with Christine's external examiner, a very distinguished scholar, for the first time in person. He had flown in the night before and assured me that his stay in the hotel next to my tower was comfortable. He had already visited an art gallery and reminisced about the time he too worked in "our" tower. I felt I knew him through his writing and our Email exchanges but now, as we spoke, we shared other connections: Favourite authors and other Australian specialties (must remember to present him with the Penfold Thomas Hyland shiraz).

Time to knot an unaccustomed tie. One last check in the mirror.

Time to put in my appearance.
Not just another defence.

Today is a golden apple day for me: One that marks my entrance into the academy. The day that signals my appearance as a shadow master in my own right.
Initiation day.
Patrick, my master-shadow-master and mentor, has assured me that I am ready. The final draft of my shadow text is finished. During the past week I have performed versions of my shadow play at several dress rehearsals. And it passed the scrutiny of others. I now feel that I am ready. Let the audience come. Let the shadow play begin.

On my way down in the elevator, I let my thoughts drift back to the class when I first met Christine. January 6, 1999. The Feast Day of the Epiphany. By way of introduction I had shared a diamond-shaped name-poem, a "self-narrative or signature piece…[as a] geometric miming and aesthetic expression of self" (Diamond & Mullen, 1999, p. 440). In a response to the course readings and the poem, Christine shared how, for her, the last two letters of my name and poem took on a very different meaning: *nd* became a *new day*. She then invited the class and me into a relational setting based on the fragments of our life histories we had chosen to share. Later when she asked if I would consider becoming her "supervisor," I did not hesitate: She genuinely seemed to be "a student whose research interests matched mine" (Diamond,

It is almost 2:00 PM
The members of the audience

301

enter the room one at a time.

Patrick is first to arrive. A
quick hug and a kind glance. I
am ready.

The external examiner enters
next. An imposing, almost
magisterial, presence in dark
suit and white shirt. Patrick
offers introductions and,
before long, we two speak
with each other in Dutch, our
mother-tongue.
The others follow. More introductions and small talk: three
committee members and lastly
the university-appointed chairperson.

Members of the audience, yet
all are master-shadow-masters
in their own right.

I am asked to leave the room.
Time to gather my thoughts.
Some deep-breathing.

The door opens.

The final call.

1994, p. 59).

I enter the now quiet examination room and quickly check
the staging: Apple portraits
against the wall. Yes, Christine
is ready. The audience is arriv-
ing. I smile at the examiner.

The chairperson sees that the
paper work is completed and
the order of appearances is
determined.

I invite Christine back in. Let
the play begin.

And I am on stage.
In the spotlight.

Quietly I begin.
"As the author of [my] own
personal story, [I] select what
belongs to the story and what
lies outside" (Diamond, 1991,
p. 91).

For the next two hours, this
enclosed room will become a
light-filled "box in the theater
of the world"
(Benjamin, 1999, p. 6).

I improvise.
I weave my shadow text into
the text prepared by the
external examiner.
I speak of darkness and light.
I speak for my co-inquirers.
I re-animate them one more
time.
I let their shadows dance.

A dancing exchange between
Christine and her audience.
Play and ritual.

Interlude One

In the light and shadow world of a *wayang purwa*, the *dalang* is
the puppeteer, the so-called mastermind, or shadow-master behind
the scenes. Often there is a strong familial connection, a clear lineage, and an important oral tradition that supports the *dalang*. His
training usually begins spontaneously at a very young age, growing
up in the profession: While a father performs, the young child is
encouraged to keep busy (and out of trouble) by imitating the
shadow-master using small cardboard puppets on the non-shadow
side of the screen (Herbert, 2002; Ulbricht, 1970; van
Groenendael, 1985; van Ness & Prawirohardjo, 1980). There is
also the more formal training offered at institutions for the

performing arts where the apprentice shadow-master "acquires 'experience' primarily from two sources — reading and performance...and [must demonstrate he is] inquisitive by nature" (Mrazek, 2002, p. 119).

Scene Two: Past in the Present

Christine

I let my shadows dance by going back to my beginnings as an (arts-based) inquirer. "For me to return to my distant childhood is a necessary act of curiosity" (Freire, 1996, p. 13).

My "*dalang* training" took place in a safe place: Behind the screen of my father's study, surrounded by the many books in his theological library, I learned to "read and underline" (van Halen-Faber, 2004). Sacred moves.

For many years I resisted walking in my father's doctoral footsteps. Even when two of my younger siblings chose to follow that path.

Patrick

Every defence stirs memories of my own academic beginnings. My own play set within an Australian context: "The three page abstract, like the thesis, was written in the third person, in the past tense, and mainly in the passive voice. It now reminds me of a campus novel with a cast of shadowy players." (Diamond, 1994, p. 54)

Tensions between committee members. But not with my external examiners.

I, too, remember the play of shadow and light when I moved in my doctoral inquiry from words to numbers to words.

Light out of Darkness

My epiphany occurred in the light of arts-based narrative inquiry:
When I (re)cast traditional research into arts-based and experimental text.
When I (re)placed the neutrality of cognitive knowledge with intensely personal and autobiographical knowing.

And now years later to arts-based writing.
Seriously.
I read. I write.
I re-read. I re-write.

I now re-trace my present shadows in the light of my past, re-membering that also in my (con-)text, "memory is not an instrument for exploring the past but its theater. It is the medium of past experience." (Benjamin, 1978, p. 26)

Once again I experience how "writing about a topic presupposes previous and parallel readings, as well as the reading of one's own writing. And none of that can be done without effort, dedication, and responsibility." (Freire, 1996, p. 172)

Light out of darkness.

Serious engagement as exemplified by Christine.

Interlude Two
From then to now to then.
Before and after November 20, 2004, in our work together as supervisee and supervisor, we each and together move forward on our life-and-work course. We continue to live our personal experience of inquiry as currere (Pinar & Grumet, 1976). "The play thus is not a static object but an active process constantly mediating [the dalangs'] personal experience" (Mrazek, 2002, p. 119).

305

Also our own.
Together we celebrate the different

ways in which the arts, in particular, can release imagination to open new perspectives, to identify alternatives. The vistas that might open, the connections that might be made, are experiential phenomena; our encounters with the world become newly informed. When they do, they offer new lenses through which to look out at and interpret the educative acts that keep human beings and their cultures alive. (Greene, 1995, p. 18)

Scene Three: Present into Future

Christine	*Patrick*
And so here we are.	This is an award-winning thesis in the making.
Two arts-based *dalang* masters at different ends of the academic career continuum: Beginning and ending.	
As I begin my academic writing career, Patrick moves towards writing fiction. From what he has shared with me he shows that "an author's curiosity, risk-taking, and adventurous spirit may be of more value than a well-behaved one that reveals fear. It is not possible to create	Through our arts-based inquiries, while "on our way to a new consciousness," Christine and I (along with many others) have discovered that we "can't hold concepts or ideas in rigid boundaries.... Because the future depends on the breaking down of paradigms, it depends on the

without serious intellectual discipline; likewise it is not possible to create within a system of fixed, rigid, or imposed rules." (Freire, 1996, p. 169)

We read each other's (and others') texts.
Alone-together.
We make connections.
We remark on our epiphanic moments of synchronicity.
We co-script our moves.
We spin our gossamer cyber-web.
We track our ways with words carefully,
knowing that we can co-construct new meaning "if we keep notes and hindsight accounts of the connectedness of things that seem to have happened: pieced-together patternings." (Geertz, 1995, p. 2)

straddling of two or more cultures." (Anzaldúa, 1987, pp. 78-79)

I know that inquiry cultures continue to collide as unlikely worlds and inconsistent frames of reference clash.
But I also know that "life is a constant search that cannot, even when writing [or supervising] theses and dissertations, be immobilized."
(Freire, 1996, p. 167)
And so I move on.
As I respond to the insistent pull of heart-strings, I prepare to return to my native home, Australia.
Some day.
My own play of light and shadows.

Opening up other ways.

Postlude

Now that we have shared some of our experiences of becoming arts-based educational co-researchers we invite you, our readers, to view our shadow play in the light of your own shadow-text. Perhaps like us you may choose to ask yourself, "What is [my] substance, whereof [I am] made / That millions of strange shadows on [me] tend?" (Shakespeare, *Sonnet 53*). Your "strange shadows", when you trace them back to external and internal sources such as academic norms, non-arts-informed thesis formats, top-down forms of supervision, memories, and self-doubts, may provide intimations of future inquiries. As our own collaboration deepens we know that, while a thesis text has "substance" like a novel, it also needs its shadows. Throughout a text there must be tensions at play between light and dark, between imagination and rationality. A play of contrasts. As we have shown above, "this shadow [play] is a *bit* of ideology, a *bit* of representation, a *bit* of subject: ghosts, pockets, traces, necessary clouds: subversion must produce its own chiaroscuro"[4] (Barthes, 1975, p. 32). When imagining and completing an arts-based thesis, opportunity for such multidimensional play to enter in can be provided by allowing intuitive knowing to declare itself through the use of artful forms. Even the most unlikely experience, as of a thesis-defence, filtered through the screen of an arts-based sensibility, can be dislodged from its usual context and assigned a new and more enlightening role.

As in a shadow play art speaks to art.

End Notes

1. *Batik* is the process by which a design is produced on fabric through the use of a dye-resist. According to Indonesian tradition, batik was considered to be a way to develop spiritual discipline: Each time the batik artisan executes a particular intricate pattern the design is not only fixed to the cloth but the meaning of the design is engraved ever more deeply in the soul of the artisan.

2. A *dalang* is a puppeteer or shadow master who single-handedly stage-manages, directs, and conducts the gamelan percussion

orchestra, while giving voice and movement to all the puppet-actors in a *wayang* performance. The *dalang* is said to be able to communicate between the spiritual and physical worlds.

3. *Wayang* [shadow] *purwa* [ancient] is a traditional form of Indonesian theatre in which shadows created by flat cut-outs of leather puppets are used to convey sacred stories of cosmic events and divine will. *Wayang purwa* plays provide moral and social instruction along with entertainment and the audience is said to be protected from evil while a play lasts.

4. *Chiaroscuro* is an art term that describes the bold contrast between light and dark. The use of highlights and shadow to suggest the illusion of depth on a two-dimensional surface was first developed in 15th century painting in Italy and Flanders.

References

Anzaldúa, G. (1987). Borderlands / La frontera. *The new mestiza.* San Francisco, CA: Spinsters / Aunt Lute.

Barthes, R. (1975). *The pleasure of the text* (R. Miller, Trans.). New York, NY: Hill & Wang.

Benjamin, W. (1978). *Reflections. Walter Benjamin — Essays, aphorisms, autobiographical writings* (P. Demetz, Ed., & E. Jephcott, Trans.). New York, NY: Schocken Books.

Benjamin, W. (1999). *The arcades project* (H. Eiland & K. McLaughlin, Trans.). Cambridge, MA: Harvard University Press.

Diamond, C. T. P. (1991). *Teacher education as transformation: A psychological perspective.* Milton Keynes, UK: Open University Press.

Diamond, C. T. P. (1994). From numbers to words. In A. L. Cole & D. Hunt (Eds.), *The doctoral thesis journey. Reflections from travelers and guides* (pp. 53-60). Toronto, ON: Ontario Institute for Studies in Education Press.

Diamond, C. T. P., & Mullen, C. A. (Eds.). (1999). *The post* modern educator: Arts-based inquiries and teacher development. New York, NY: Peter Lang.

Freire, P. (1996). *Letters to Cristina. Reflections on my life and work.* New York, NY: Routledge.

Geertz, C. (1960). *The religion of Java.* London, UK: Collier-MacMillan.

Geertz, C. (1973). *The interpretation of cultures. Selected essays by Clifford Geertz.* New York, NY: Basic Books.

Geertz, C. (1995). *After the fact. Two countries, four decades, one anthropologist.* Cambridge, MA: Harvard University Press.

Greene, M. (1995). *Releasing the imagination. Essays on education, the arts, and social change.* San Francisco, CA: Jossey Bass.

Herbert, M. (2002). *Voices of the puppet masters. The wayang golek theater of Indonesia.* Jakarta, Indonesia: The Lontar Foundation.

James, H. (1881 / 1995). *The portrait of a lady.* Oxford, UK: Oxford University Press.

Lakoff, G., & Johnson, M. (1980). *Metaphors we live by.* Chicago, IL: University of Chicago Press.

Mrazek, J. (2002). *Puppet theater in contemporary Indonesia. New approaches to performance events.* Ann Arbor, MA: University of Michigan Centers for South & Southeast Asian Studies.

Pinar, W., & Grumet, M. R. (1976). *Toward a poor curriculum.* Dubuque, IA: Kendall / Hunt.

Shakespeare, W. (n.d. / 1962). Sonnet 53, In *The complete works of William Shakespeare* (p. 1078). London, UK: Abbey Library.

van Groenendael, V. M. C. (1985). *The dalang behind the wayang.* Dordrecht, Germany: Foris Publications.

van Halen-Faber, C. (2004). *Seeing through apples: An arts-based exploration into the ethics and aesthetics of a teacher-educator-researcher's arts-based beginnings.* Unpublished doctoral thesis, University of Toronto, Toronto, ON, Canada.

van Ness, E. C., & Prawirohardjo, S. (1980). *Javanese wayang kulit. An introduction.* Oxford, UK: Oxford University Press.

Ulbricht, H. (1970). *Wayang purwa: Shadows of the past*. Kuala Lumpur, Malaysia: Oxford University Press.

About the Authors

CHRISTINE VAN HALEN-FABER is Principal and lecturer at Covenant Canadian Reformed Teachers College, Hamilton, Ontario. Her research interests include visual and literary forms of arts-based narrative inquiry into self / other as artful pathways leading towards pre-service and in-service teacher-educator-researcher development. Her doctoral thesis was given the Canadian Association for Teacher Education 2004 Dissertation Award. She is a founding co-editor (with Patrick Diamond) of the Special Series on Arts-Based Educational Research in *Curriculum Inquiry*.

In *Seeing Through Apples: An Exploration with the Ethics and Aesthetics of a Teacher-educator and Researcher's Arts-based Beginnings*, Christine's doctoral thesis, she explores the ethics and aesthetics of her arts-based beginnings in the presence of others. She uses apple batik panels to re-present her six co-participants who are then re-animated in a shadow play. As a teacher-educator-researcher drawn to artful forms of development, Christine experiences her self-inquiry in non-linear and layered ways.

C. T. PATRICK DIAMOND is Professor Emeritus, the Center for Teacher Development, the Ontario Institute for Studies in Education, University of Toronto. He specializes in literary forms of arts-based narrative inquiry, mentorship, and teacher-educator-researcher development. Pat has published many works and has co-edited special arts-based issues of the *Journal of Curriculum Theorizing* and *Curriculum Inquiry*. He is author of *Teacher Education as Transformation*, and co-author of *The Postmodern Educator: Arts-Based Inquiries and Teacher Development*.

26. Hanging On and Flying

by Bronwyn Davies and Susanne Gannon

This chapter is written, first, from the point of view and in the voice of the doctoral candidate, Susanne and, second, from the point of view and in the voice of the supervisor, Bronwyn. We each discuss the genesis and production of Susanne's arts-informed thesis and we analyze the nature of our pedagogical relationship, which developed in the process of working together.

Susanne's Story
Flying, when I'm working well and the words flow out like a

*thread that I'm just hanging on to and following. I'm high in my
tree-house and looking at blue butterflies, bougainvillea, and birds.
I don't know where I'm going, where these words are taking me
but I know I'd rather be here, hanging on and flying, than any
where else.*

Hanging On and Writing

My doctoral thesis began with an interest in writing and
became an exploration of what poststructural theory makes possible in writing and research. Rather than looking solely at other
writers and what their theoretical orientation made possible in
their writing, my own textual performances, and my own processes of writing became my points of departure. Writing itself was the
red thread that I followed into the doctorate from my Master's
degree research (Gannon, 1999) in which I explored the ways
thinking shifted with different modes of writing. I wrote *Hanging
On and Flying* during my doctoral candidacy and it captures the
pleasures and surprise of the writing experience where writing
itself becomes a way of coming to know differently (Richardson,
1997; Richardson & St. Pierre, 2005). It also evokes the isolation
in which I wrote the final drafts of the thesis, looking out through
the upstairs window of an old house, my tropical "treehouse",
looking out at butterflies and brilliant bougainvillea and birds.

Though I worked in isolation, hundreds of miles away,
Bronwyn and her other students were very much present in my
writing and in my thinking. Bronwyn visited me, when she could,
in Cairns, Queensland, and I visited her in Townsville when I
needed to talk face-to-face. And twice a year, we met on Magnetic
Island, off the coast of Queensland, Australia for a week-long collective biography workshop with other students and with visiting
scholars.

In those workshops we gathered together from all corners of
Australia and Papua New Guinea and Europe. We told and wrote

memory stories that arose from and informed the topic we had collectively chosen for study. The practice of writing and of story-telling is central to the collective biography method (Davies & Gannon, 2005, 2006). Collective biography is a feminist research method we have developed from the work of German sociologist Frigga Haug (Haug, et al., 1987). In collective biography a group of researchers works together on an agreed topic of interest drawing on their own memories relevant to that topic. Through the shared work of telling and listening and writing they move beyond clichés and explanations to the point where written memories come as close as they can make them to an embodied sense of the past. These memories become data that are collectively subjected to fine-grained discursive analysis.

The fragment that begins this chapter emerged during a collective biography workshop on the theme of "embodiment at work" (Davies, Browne, Gannon, Honan, & Somerville, 2005). During the workshop the hanging on and flying metaphor extended into a description of the doctoral candidate as a woman on a flying carpet ride, still hanging on and flying but not alone on her journey nor contained in her own backyard. The story emerged from an exercise in which we each chose an image that best reflected our ideal of academic work. I described my chosen image — two figures on a flying carpet — thus:

She is exhilarated, holding on to her hat, her mouth wide open with joy and surprise. She doesn't know where the ride is taking her but she trusts it will be fantastic and the feeling will stay with her. She's not alone on her flight. She's experiencing all this with someone else who's with her, who trusts her and who she can trust and who also trusts the benevolence of the journey, and there may be more of them all on their own fantastic adventure but together at the same time. She's flying over the mundane landscape that she knows well and that was her life and when she lands, even if it's in the same place, it will be transformed for her because she is. She's open to everything and though perhaps she should be scared she's not. She's clever and she's lucky.

Coming Along for the Ride

Bronwyn accompanied me on that journey and, at different times, provoked, inspired, cajoled, and challenged me. Most of all, she trusted me. Sometimes she frustrated me. Sometimes I wanted simple answers, shortcuts, or linear thinking. She answered my questions clearly and promptly but always refused binaries and clichés and familiar discourses. Initially I despaired of my ability to comprehend the ideas and language of slippery poststructural theorists but Bronwyn assured me that, if I just kept reading and writing, I would get used to the language. As well, the collective biography workshops, each with a poststructuralist focus and a collaboratively written academic paper as the outcome, served as an apprenticeship in academic discourse and poststructuralist discourse in particular. The workshops were a vehicle for establishing a supportive collegial network with shared ideas and projects (Davies, Dormer, et al., 2001; Davies, Flemmen, Gannon, Laws & Watson, 2002; Davies, Browne, et al., 2004; Davies, Brwone, Gannon, Honan, & Somerville, 2005). Thus I became part of a scholarly community of women working collaboratively with Bronwyn and writing and experimenting with feminist poststructuralist theory. The discussions amongst us took place not only at the workshops but on an Email listserve where we talked almost daily about our struggles with writing — and with life.

The thesis was thus a busy and collective enterprise and it reached beyond my university, supervisory, and collegial relationships. It began with my participation — with over nine hundred other women from around the world — in the International Women's University summer school in Hanover, Germany in 2000. That was where I began collecting data in a series of collective biography workshops I co-convened on the theme of "breasts" (Gannon & Müller-Rockstroh, 2004a, 2004b, 2005). The data consisted of a collection of short memories written by different women and generated after extensive discussion and analysis of the themes "getting breasts", "dangerous breasts", and "losing breasts".

I used these texts as the starting point and inspiration for a play that I wrote in a community playwriting program, working with dramaturges, actors, and other playwrights over several years. Each draft shifted further away from raw research data towards a script with complex characters, storylines, and themes that would work theatrically and would also materialize the philosophical and sociological analyses in my work. The data with which I began the script merged and disappeared as my script became more and more fictionalized, more and more a work of "art", where aesthetic and affective dimensions became as important to me as the rational dimensions of the text.

Finally the script of the play became one of the eleven chapters of my thesis. It also became a two act play and a night out in the theatre for many people. When it came to life on the stage I wanted it to touch an audience that was not of the academy — many of whom would be unlikely to read my academic writing. I wanted it to touch them in their bodies and their hearts as well as their heads. Bronwyn did not see the play performed and she was not present at most of the events which led to it. She did not meet, or need to meet, the people with whom I worked in these other arenas. Our supervisory relationship required, in part, recognition that the boundaries of candidacy could not be contained neatly in space or time.

Though the route was unpredictable and the journey "fantastic", Bronwyn's supervision provided clear guidance. She responded rapidly to my questions; she took the lead role in drafting our collaborative papers; she recommended readings; she negotiated timelines for multiple drafts of chapters and papers, and she facilitated presentations of work in progress. These all enabled timely and successful completion of the thesis. At the same time, within this safe and orderly frame, I accepted her imperative that I must "write beautifully".

Advice to Intending Scholars...

So.... How might my story be instructive to others who seek to write the an arts-informed thesis? Where to begin? How to proceed? Look at your life, I might say. What possibilities arise from the context that you inhabit, that inhabits (or inhibits) you? What is it that you are passionate about? What question is large enough for you to love for years? For me it was women's lived embodied experience and how writing might make sense of it. How might you make use of all the resources that we have for building knowledge — the rational, the emotional, the aesthetic? What is your medium? What more do you need to learn about poetry, or visual arts, or film, or drama if you want to use these as your entry or exit point, if you want to make work that will stand on its own in the world outside the tower? What do you need to know of theory? How will you find the theorists who set you on fire? I found people like Barthes, Cixous, Derrida, and Richardson but my gurus will most likely not be yours. If you are lucky you will you find the supervisor who suits you, leads you, trusts you, and travels with you.

Bronwyn's Story
Letting Go

Susanne's thesis deconstructs writing itself. It is a radical and dramatic work engaging the reader both emotionally and intellectually. She does far more than simply reverse the binary that has privileged rational, analytic writing over creative writing. She brings them together in such a way that her writing is always both

analytic and creative. She had been teaching, attending creative
writing workshops, and experimenting with writing long before
she began her Master's thesis with me. She came to the work as a
practiced writer. As her supervisor, my contribution, at first
glance, seems small. You could say it was I who held onto my hat
and went for the ride, simply enjoying the interaction with
Susanne's dynamic creative energies. I saw my task as lending
active support for her initiatives, as giving strong encouragement
for thinking outside the usual bounds of what a "thesis" might be,
as giving encouragement and support in writing for publication in
order to get feedback from international journals on the thinking
that was unfolding in her work, and in giving close, prompt, and
detailed feedback on her experiments with different kinds of writing. In addition, my task became one of helping her to decompose
(Barthes, 1977) her surprising and habituated self-doubt and,
closely related to this doubt, to *decompose* the belief that there is a
thesis genre that pre-determines what a thesis will look like. All of
my supervisory activities were supportive of her initiatives rather
than generative of them. No doubt it took the dynamic interaction between the two of us, along with my leadership of the group
of students and scholars in workshops and on Email, to make the
work possible but it was never my idea that lay at the end of the
thread she was following. It was unequivocally hers.

The twice-yearly collective biography workshops were an
important part of my supervisory role. These were not mandatory
and not part of the usual practice of other supervisors. The idea
of them emerged over many years of supervision, inspired both by
a workshop run by Lorri Neilsen (1998) and Sharn Rocco, and
also by the proximity of Magnetic Island, where we could hire a
house and live for a week enjoying each other's company and the
simultaneous immersion in such a tropical landscape. The workshops provided not just a collegial network for students working
in isolation but an apprenticeship in writing — first in learning to

318

write richly embodied memory stories, and second in learning a range of writing skills through the collaborative projects. Arts-informed practices, such as voice work, assemblage, and visual arts practice became part of our way of working together.

Supervision

Good supervision, as I understand it, gives permission to students to push the boundaries of knowledge and of research practice beyond what they imagine is possible. A lot of my work with students involves giving them enough confidence in their capacity to write and think differently — and confidence in my capacity to judge just how much they can get away with in running against traditional patterns and expectations. For this reason it is very important to build a community of students and ex-students who are challenging and who have successfully challenged traditional forms of thesis writing. Such a group can inspire and reassure each of its members along the way.

In the beginning with Susanne, I worked in an open-ended way to help her find an answerable question. Asking a good question is usually harder than students at first imagine. "I don't know what I want to know," Susanne would agonize. The task was to bring together the wellspring of her creative power, the power of theory, and to develop the power of her academic writing, each in relation to the emerging question that eventually became something she passionately wanted to explore.

From beginning to end of each thesis I supervise I insist on, for myself and for my students, a disciplined open-mindedness. As the work unfolds any aspect can change, including the question, the methodology, the theoretical focus, the tone, and the shape of the thesis. Such open-mindedness is absolutely necessary for the arts-based thesis to emerge as a possibility, and then as a reality. The willingness to go with the not-yet-known is crucial.

Letting go of repeated recipes and familiar genres requires a facility with writing. At the beginning of any thesis I focus on what it is the student is struggling to say, the big idea — I ask what is the story here? What is the conceptual work that she is trying to do? What might be getting in the way of the possibility that is emergent here? What might she need by way of thought or form that will enable the idea to come to its full fruition? In Susanne's case, this kind of questioning happened not only in my own responses to draft papers and chapters and plays and poems but, also, collaboratively at the collective biography workshops.

Susanne writes about writing as blissful, as euphoric, as just '"hanging on and flying". I have been asked whether, as supervisor, I share that bliss and if that is why I enjoy supervision. Certainly I take pleasure in being there to help generate those moments. Sometimes I experience moments of intense pleasure in reading a student's work when it leads me to see something I had not seen before. I also take great deal of pleasure in the moment when the student comes to see something new. With the paper I invited Susanne to write for *Qualitative Studies in Education* journal, theorizing the process of writing her play, we worked through many drafts before she had that moment of bliss. When finally she sent me the beautiful piece of writing that became her paper (Gannon, 2004) I was ecstatic. It was a memorable moment for us both.

Barthes (1986) describes the moment of bliss where the pleasurable repetition of that which is already known is punctured with another way of knowing, where the writer is:

> born at the same time as his [sic] text; he is not furnished with a being which precedes or exceeds his writing, he is not the subject of which his book would be the predicate; there is no time other than that of the speech-act, and every text is written eternally here and now. (p. 52)

Embodied moments of bliss, such as those described in the first half of this chapter, punctuate the sometimes painful process, the hard work, of writing a thesis and the papers and other creative productions that come out of it. Part of my work as Susanne's supervisor was to reassure her that the moments of bliss would come and to trust that she had the capacity to make them happen. The trick was not to settle for anything less.

Bronwyn and Susanne

We return in our conclusion to Susanne's image of flying and of the thread that she hung on to and followed. Like Ariadne, the thread cannot be relinquished as it will take her to what she desires. Like Arachne she spins the thread as she goes. The desire for the thesis that is also a work of art is a transgressive desire that breaks up the linearity and predictability of more usual and predictable writing (Davies, 2006). We worked together as student and supervisor and as members of a collegial and collaborative network of writers to make the thesis imagine-able and possible. As well, Susanne set out on her own sub-plots, her own trajectories, her own lines of flight, and she spun a thread of writing inspired by the possibilities poststructuralist theory opened up for her.

References

Barthes, R. (1977). *Roland Barthes by Roland Barthes*. Berkeley, CA: University of California Press.

Barthes, R. (1986). *The rustle of language* (R. Howard, Trans.). Oxford, UK: Blackwell.

Body Project (Ed.). (2004). *CorpoRealities: Interventions in an omnipresent subject*. Berlin, Germany: Ulrike Helmer Verlag.

Davies, B. (2006). Women and transgression in the halls of academe. *Studies in Higher Education, 31*(4), 497-509.

Davies, B., Browne, J., Gannon, S., Honan, E., Laws, C., Mueller-Rockstroh, B., & Bendix Petersen, E. (2004). The ambivalent practices of reflexivity. *Qualitative Inquiry, 10*(2), 360-390.

Davies, B., Browne, J., Gannon, S., Honan, E., & Somerville, M. (2005). Embodied women at work in neoliberal times and places. Gender, *Work and Organization, 12*(4), 343-362.

Davies, B., Dormer, S., Gannon, S., Lenz Taguchi, H., McCann, H., & Rocco, S. (2001). Becoming schoolgirls: The ambivalent project of subjectification. *Gender and Education, 13*(2), 167-182.

Davies, B., Flemmen, A. B., Gannon, S., Laws, C., & Watson, B. (2002). Working on the ground. A collective biography of feminine subjectivities. Mapping the traces of power and knowledge, *Social Semiotics, 12*(3), 291-313.

Davies, B., & Gannon, S. (2005). Feminism / Poststructuralism. In C. Lewin & B. Somekh (Eds.), *Research methods in the social sciences* (pp. 318-325). London, UK: Sage Publications.

Davies, B., & Gannon, S. (2006). *Doing collective biography.* London, UK: McGraw Hill / Open University Press.

Gannon, S. (1999). *Writing as a woman: Collective / autobiographical and transgressive texts of the self.* Unpublished Master's thesis, James Cook University, Townsville, QLD, Australia.

Gannon, S. (2003). *Flesh and the text: Poststructuralist theory and writing research.* Unpublished doctoral thesis, James Cook University, Townsville, QLD, Australia.

Gannon, S. (2004). Out / performing in the academy: writing "The Breast Project". *Qualitative Studies in Education, 17*(1), 65-81.

Gannon, S., & Müller-Rockstroh, B. (2004a). In memory: women's experiences of (adolescent) breasts. In Body Project (Ed.), *CorpoRealities: Interventions in an omnipresent theme* (pp. 195-214). Berlin, Germany: Ulrike Helmer Verlag.

Gannon, S., & Müller-Rockstroh, B. (2004b). In memory: Women's experiences of (dangerous) breasts. *Philosophy in the Contemporary World, 10*(1), 55-66.

Gannon, S., & Müller-Rockstroh, B. (2005). Nurturing breasts: Constructions of contemporary motherhood in women's breastfeeding stories. In M. Porter, P. Short & A. O'Reilly (Eds), *Motherhood: Power and oppression* (pp. 41-56). Toronto, ON: Women's Press.

Haug, F., Andersen, S., Bünz-Elfferding, A., Hauser, K., Lang, U., Laudan, M., Lüdemann, M., Meir, U., Nemitz, B., Niehoff, E., Prinz, R., Rathzel, N. Scheu, M., & Thomas, C. (1987). *Female sexualization: A collective work of memory.* London, UK: Verso Press.

Neilsen, L. (1998). *Knowing her place. Research literacies and feminist occasions.* San Francisco, CA & Big Tancook Island, NS: Caddo Press & Backalong Books.

Richardson, L. (1997). *Fields of play.* New Brunswick, RI: Rutgers University Press.

Richardson, L., & St Pierre, E. (2005) Writing: A method of inquiry. In N. K. Denzin & Y. S. Lincoln (Eds.), *Handbook of qualitative research* (3rd edition, pp. 959-978). Thousand Oaks, CA: Sage Publications.

About the Authors

BRONWYN DAVIES is Professor of Education and Chair of the Narrative Discourse and Pedagogy Research Group at the University of Western Sydney. Her publications include *Gender in Japanese Preschools: Frogs and Snails and Feminist Tales in Japan* (2004), a second edition of *Frogs and Snails and Feminist Tales* (2003) and of *Shards of Glass* (2003). She is co-editor, with Susanne Gannon, of *Doing Collective Biography* (2006).

SUSANNE GANNON lectures in English and literacy across the curriculum in secondary teacher education at the University of Western Sydney. She is a founding member of the Narrative Discourse and Pedagogy Research Group. Her current research explores the writing and pedagogical practices of secondary English teachers also published poets, novelists, and playwrights.

Susanne's thesis, *Flesh and the Text: Poststructural Theory and Writing Research*, wove creative and analytical writing around each other in textual performances informed by poststructural theory. It incorporated and critiqued poetry, collective biography, autoethnography, and drama as genres of data production and representation. The play that formed part of the thesis — "The Breast Project" — had a successful season in 2004 with Just Us Theatre Ensemble at CoCA (Centre of Contemporary Arts), Cairns, Queensland, Australia.

27. A Collage of Borderlands

by Sara Promislow and Ardra L. Cole

Borderlands

On the borderland between doctoral student and supervisor Sara's arts-informed thesis was formed. The metaphor of "borderlands" encompassed and guided Sara's doctoral thesis, *A Collage of "Borderlands": Arts-informed Life Histories of Childhood Immigrants and Refugees who Maintain their Mother Tongue* (Promislow, 2005). Borrowing the term from Gloria Anzaldua (1987) — for whom "borderlands" depict geographic and ethno-linguistic spaces between Mexico and the United States — it served to represent the multiplicity of reality as experienced and embodied in the subjectivity of childhood immigrants and refugees who become and are bilingual; the ongoing interaction among languages, cultures, and identities in their lives. "Borderland suggests a space where multiple cultures, multiple consciousnesses, and multiple possibilities exist — where a border is dissolved" (Delgado-Gaitan, 1997, p. 37).

At the root of Sara's doctoral research was her personal experience as an immigrant and a bilingual person, the difficulties she encountered as a child when she immigrated with her family to Israel. Her experiences as a second language learner, and later as a bilingual minority, resulted in deeply ingrained self-doubt and low self-esteem with regards to her intellectual and academic abilities. She could never really brush off the experience of having "failed" her first IQ test in Grade 4 (a year after she arrived in Israel); nor will she ever forget the day her Grade 11 homeroom teacher announced, before the whole class, that she would never succeed in life.

Being different and not fitting the mould was a hindrance to Sara's well-being. Not knowing the language of her surroundings and its implicit social codes was a source of pain and isolation for many years. She eventually did manage to assimilate to the culture of her surroundings but, as a young adult, she could never imagine herself in a context where she was able not only to fit in, but to flourish.

Sara carried forward this uneasiness to her doctoral program, struggling to find a space to grow intellectually with confidence and comfort. Eventually, she found a home within a community of researchers at the Centre for Arts-informed Research. There, with Ardra as her mentor and thesis supervisor, and inspired by the work of her peers, her talents were recognized and celebrated and she found promise and possibility through research.

A Collage of Borderlands

In this chapter we explore, through dialogue, the central role of the supervisory relationship in fostering not only research that matters but researchers who matter. We suggest that the cultivation of a borderland space defined by relationality is vital to the development of work that pushes boundaries, crosses borders, and expands possibilities.

Crossing Boundaries into Borderlands of Possibility
Ardra:

Sara came to my course in qualitative research methodologies full of big questions but with little confidence in herself as researcher and writer, and in research methodologies as pathways to answer those big questions. In what I intended to be a supportive yet challenging creative space, Sara's defensiveness and doubt about research developed into possibilities. She became excited by the prospects of the arts as a way to address complexity and make research meaningful.

Sara:

Ardra was a source of inspiration to me. She actually lived and researched as she preached, and this was one of the reasons I trusted in her. Also an exceptional educator, she recognized the wounded learner within me and provided me with the support I needed to grow and take risks in my research. Her belief in me as a student, novice-researcher, and writer and the gentleness with which she pushed me forward enabled me to envision my research. In recognizing my differences as strengths and finding ways to assuage my fears as a learner and emergent researcher, Ardra enabled me to overcome my self-doubt and gain the confidence I needed to succeed. It was her trust in me that led me to trust myself and my ability.

Ardra:

Because Sara's research was deeply rooted in her own immigrant experience, it was imbued with a passion defined by a strong sense of moral responsibility. She was determined to make her research matter, to find and make her own voice heard as well as the voices of her participants. Her history of difficult borderland experiences, particularly in education, left her feeling fragile and with little confidence in her many strengths as a writer, thinker and border-crosser. Ironically, it was this vulnerability that gave foundational fortitude to her work. From my perspective, it was easy to see the creative possibilities of this dynamic; however, Sara was the one who most needed the clarity to recognize the potential of her research.

Sara:

Ardra's deep presence and attentive listening in our meetings encouraged me to explore my own unique ways of knowing and being in research. Her intuitive responsiveness to my researcher / learner needs facilitated my emergence as a scholartist. The borderland space that we created in our relationship expanded to the dynamic community at the Centre for Arts-informed Research where I began to work and deeply listen and see the endless possibilities of using the arts in research through the works of others. My creative self stirred into motion and I wanted to go beyond my inner boundaries to create meaningful knowledge that transcends external academic boundaries. Ardra allowed me to fumble and fall and find my way as I worked within the complexities of researching human experience and explored artful paths unpaved.

Ardra:

Through an intensive meaning making process, with all the usual stops and starts, Sara recognized the need to find an art form that would take her and her research to a deeper level of interpretation and representation. All the advice in the world about ways of working with life history data could not take Sara to that next level. She needed to find her way and I needed to support her in that.

A Collage of Borderlands

Sara:

Ardra's teaching about the important role of serendipity in research — that inspiration, insight, and knowledge can be found anytime and anywhere — helped me to be open to the fluid and emergent nature of arts-informed research. The first time I attended the American Educational Research Association's Annual Meeting (AERA) I happened upon and enrolled in a pre-conference workshop where I was introduced to the art form collage as a research method (Butler-Kisber, Bodone, Meyer, & Stewart, 2003). As I flipped through magazines searching for images that attracted my attention, cut and pasted them together on Bristol paper, amid the laughter and excitement that engulfed my fellow scholartists, I returned to a long forgotten state of being — pure wonder. When I later proudly displayed to Ardra my first efforts at collage making, I was a child again, showing my Grade One teacher my latest masterpiece. It was crude and unfinished but full of meaning to me. Ardra recognized this, smiled encouragingly and asked me about the images that appeared in the chaos of my first collage. Her matter-of-fact acceptance of my process as well as her obvious pleasure in my discovery propelled me onward. I had an inkling that I had found an art form that would enrich and deepen my understandings of my data. A couple of months and a number of collages later I showed more rough works to Ardra. This time I was very nervous; my earlier carefree excitement was replaced with fear. The memory of a Grade 10 art teacher's response to a drawing I made of a group of trees ("that's not good") found a prominent place in my conscious mind. But, despite my trepidation, Ardra responded positively and encouraged me to continue to use collage in my research process and incorporate the collages in my thesis representation. I had found my art form.

Ardra:

Sara's interest in expanding the possibilities of life history research to include the arts, and particularly the collage art form, came not

329

from her experience or background as an artist but from her deep commitment to embracing the complexity both of her research topic and the research process. Determined to find ways to honour the richness of her participants' lives as well as the non-linear and un-reasonable quality of the analysis process, Sara took enormous methodological risks. Her main requirement at this point in the research process was emotional safety. As her supervisor, it was my role to provide the support necessary so that she could take those risks.

Sara:

During the research process, while working with my research data, I gained much insight and understanding through the art form collage and was able to move forward with the conceptualization of my research analysis, with the images I juxtaposed, at times when I was unable to move forward with words. My participants' experiences defied words and fixed categories. Linear analysis served only to block my way. In order to do justice to their experiences I knew that I needed to go beyond my habitual linear thinking and take risks. Ardra created a safe space for the exploration of my ideas and encouraged me to envision and re-envision my doctoral research, to think outside the box. She did not allow me to rest within simple solutions to the questions that my research raised; instead, she pushed me to welcome and trust the complexity of the research process, to find my own creative rhythm and embody it.

Borderlands in Transition

There were in our relationship the elements of "relationality" as described by Cole and Knowles (2001) and Lawrence-Lightfoot and Hoffman Davis (1997). Relationality refers to authentic and intimate relationships based on mutual trust, care, sensitivity, and respect. These elements can be found in any postive and healthy supervisor-student relationship and are not unique to an arts-informed context; however, they are essential to the support of creative endeavours and the level of risk-taking that undertaking an arts-informed thesis involves.

Borderland research that crosses boundaries to advance ways of understanding, knowing, and being in the world requires the customary attention to knowledge and skills associated with the creation of sound scholarly work. In addition, borderland research demands particular attention to the space in which the work is created. Dissolving borders and creating borderland spaces entails placing emphasis on the supervisory relationship. For Sara, this meant regaining sufficient confidence and trust to be able to take the considerable risks required to explore unfamiliar and uncertain terrain. For Ardra, this meant attending to issues of emotional safety and security as foundational to the creation of imaginative and inspired scholarship.

Sara:

Beige wallpaper — a shade lighter than the wallpaper that accompanied my childhood in Jerusalem — is interrupted by nail holes, holes my scholartist predecessors made in these walls, holes I now fill with nails of my own. Within a short time the institutional ambiance is transformed into a gallery of collages, my participants' lives, my research, old friends in a different context. I am comforted by their presence, reassured. I am ready to face the oral examination of my doctoral thesis.

The last question is Ardra's. She makes me smile. I am grateful for the opportunity to speak to my collages, previously unnoticed by the examiners. As I respond, the collages take on new meaning. I realize that they not only represent my research but myself as researcher. There is a part of me in each and every one of them. They are a part of me. It is Ardra who has made their presence here possibile in so many ways.

Looking back on the immense vulnerability I contended with throughout my doctoral research, I feel it again within me, in this

331

"moment in time". However as Matiss (2001) eloquently phrases:

> *Yesterday's ideas change in meaning when viewed*
> *in today's moment in time.*
> *And tomorrow — another moment, another time —*
> *will again bring new meanings,*
> *reinterpretations of moments in time. (p. 223)*

While I continue to carry the nasty voices of teachers of old, their shrill sounds are scarcely heard when I remember the melodies of borderland spaces, my relationship with Ardra, with my peers and colleagues at the Centre for Arts-informed Research. I am fortified by what I have learned and eagerly share my knowledge with others. In the face of barriers, I now embrace my vulnerability, my evolving uniqueness, the richness of my diversity. The belongings and borderland spaces I have found are with me wherever I go.

I sought to create research that transforms and I have been transformed.

References

Anzaldua, G. (1987). *Borderlands/La frontera: The new mestiza.* San Francisco, CA: Aunt Lute Books.

Butler-Kisber, L., Bodone, F., Meyer, M. & Stewart, M. (2003). *Artful analysis and representation in qualitative inquiry using poetry, theatre, and collage,* AERA Pre-conference Workshop, Chicago, IL.

Cole, A. L. & Knowles, J. G. (Eds.). (2001). *Lives in context: The art of life history research.* Walnut Creek, CA: AltaMira Press.

Delgado-Gaitan, C. (1997). Dismantling borders. In A. Neumann & P. L. Peterson (Eds.), *Learning from our lives: Women, research, and autobiography in education* (pp. 37-51). New York, NY; London, UK: Teachers College Press.

Lawrence-Lightfoot, S. & Davis, J. H. (Eds.). (1997). *The art and science of portraiture*. San Francisco, CA: Jossey-Bass.

Matiss, I. (2001). Moments in time. In A. L. Cole & J. G. Knowles (Eds.), *Lives in context: The art of life history research* (pp. 223-229). Walnut Creek, CA: Altamira Press.

Promislow, S. (2005). *A Collage of Borderlands: Arts-informed Life histories of Childhood Immigrants and Refugees Who Maintain their Mother Tongue*. Unpublisjed doctoral thesis, University of Toronto, Toronto, ON.

About the Authors

SARA PROMISLOW holds a PhD from the Ontario Institute for Studies in Education of the University of Toronto (OISE/UT). She was editor of the Centre for Arts-Informed Research's online publication *arts-informed* for five years. Her research interests include arts-informed and life history research methods, collage as method in social science research, diasporic languages, cultures and identities, minority bilingualism and biculturalism, and immigrant and refugee adaptation and identity negotiation.

A Collage of Borderlands: Arts-informed Life histories of Childhood Immigrants and Refugees who Maintain their Mother Tongue, Sara's doctoral thesis, explores the socially embedded experiences of four adults who migrated in childhood and maintain their mother tongue and culture. The research focuses on the ongoing process of reconciling languages, cultures, and identities at the centre of the process of mother tongue and cultural maintenance. The thesis combines stories of experience, poetry, collage and academic discourse.

ARDRA L. COLE is Professor and Co-director of the Centre for Arts-informed Research at OISE/UT. Most of Ardra's teaching and scholarly writing is in the area of qualitative research methodologies, particularly life history, arts-informed research, and reflexive inquiry. She has extensively published, performed, and exhibited arts-informed research, including the co-edited *Handbook of the Arts in Qualitative Research* (2008) published by Sage. Selections of Ardra's performative inquiry and installation art-as-research can be found at www.oise.utoronto.ca/research/ mappingcare.

28. Liminal (S)p(1)aces of Writing and Creating

by STEPHANIE SPRINGGAY, ALEX F. DE COSSON AND RITA L. IRWIN

The room glows purple warmth as the cold light of a winter day creeps through the windows. Inside, nurtured by hot tea, a group of artist-researcher-teachers gather to think through the "(s)p(1)ace" (de Cosson, 2002) of arts-based research and to continue defining and constructing a methodology called a/r/tography (de Cosson, 2003; Irwin, 2003; Irwin & de Cosson, 2004; Springgay, 2002, 2004; Springgay, Irwin, & Wilson, 2005; Wilson, 2000). This fluid group, composed of graduate thesis researchers and their mentor, Rita Irwin, gather together to work on publications, conference presentations, dissertations and theses, research projects and art exhibitions as a way of supporting one another's academic journey. These meetings are an integral part of creating and articulating an a/r/tographical methodology, as we think, write, and image with, in, and through one another's work. We come to the meetings with a series of questions or a project in mind that needs attention, intersecting our common goal with individual ideas. Alex usually brings an audiotape recorder and we spend our time weaving words and images together. We struggle in metonymic spaces moving through a tangled web of theories, contemporary artists' works, and our own personal challenges writing and imaging in the academe. The a/r/tographical process is one of intimacy and vulnerability; a living inquiry that breathes and moves through difficult spaces of un/knowing. As a collective we search for openings. We cut and stitch our lives and experiences into new patterns and meanings. While each of us in this research group worked on individual theses, our collaborative meetings became places to "come together" and "to pull apart" — to think through what it means to engage in evocative research. Our personal stories collide with each other and, although Stephanie, Rita, and Alex have collaborated for this chapter, the voices, images, and bodies of other colleagues reverberate through this text. We have chosen to imag(e)ine this chapter as a collective conversation with(in) a (s)p(1)ace of un/knowing. Our goal is to seek questions not answers, to find comfort in discomfort, and to collectively image the future of a/r/tographical research.

Rita

As the research supervisor for this group I have a unique vantage point. It does not seem that long ago when I completed my doctorate. I wanted to use action research as my methodology but was unable to do so given there was not a critical mass of supportive professors at my university. Four years later, after completing my degree and working at another university, I returned to my alma mater as an Assistant Professor. During the first semester on campus I stepped out of the mould and integrated action research into one of my courses. The students became so involved with their projects they wanted to continue after the course was finished. This group became my first master's level group of arts-based researchers (Irwin, Crawford, et al., 1997; Irwin, Stephenson, et al., 1998; Irwin, Mastri, & Robertson, 2000; Irwin, Stephenson, Robertson, & Reynolds, 2001). During those years we began to conceptualize what research would look like if it began from art and action research. We wrote articles, read theory and practiced our teaching and art making. Our monthly dinner meetings at my home became a very special time for all of us.

Alex

As I struggled to write my thesis I was buoyed by a lifeline to similar minded people. I remember well my committee member Carl Leggo telling me that I must cultivate a pool of support and allow time to take its course. "You most probably will not find it all in one place (I did not realize, at the time, he was referring to both time and people). You have to put it together as you attend conferences and meet others interested in similar issues." It was this liminal (s)p(1)ace of connection that slowly materialized and became a driving force in my thesis writing.

Stephanie

In my role as a new faculty member I recognize the need to create spaces for doctoral students to come together outside of formal class time. Some of my most rewarding experiences at the University of British Columbia (UBC) grew out of my participation in our a/r/tographical collective. In imagining a similar (s)p(l)ace at Pennsylvania State University, I asked myself to describe the key elements of this collaborative group. I remembered *laughter* being such an important part of our meetings. So often in academe we are presented with very "serious" expectations and endeavors: performing to particular standards, applying for grant funding, writing conference proposals, while also being in the midst of enacting "rigorous" research. Our collective meetings where marked by a sense of deep vulnerability, where each member was asked to step into the fold (Springgay, 2003), to experience un/knowingness, and to laugh and entertain our ruptures and passions.

As people in our action research group began to graduate, and life circumstances took other members elsewhere, I felt compelled to open up the group to others. Before I knew it, a new arts-based research group emerged. This time doctoral students were involved and the discussions grew deeper and more complex. We continued to meet regularly. This group transformed over the years to become a group of doctoral students willing to use our newly con-ceptualized methodology of a/r/tography as their methodology of choice for their doctoral research.

Today a student arrives in my office to speak with me about the possibilities of "performing" an arts-based thesis. To prepare for this journey she has undertaken the task of work-ing on an independent study, the outcome of which will be an artful comprehensive exam. She is excited by the prospects of thinking with(in) this (s)p(l)ace, but also heavy with hesi-tation. Later that afternoon as I walk across campus to teach a class, I find myself shivering against the warmth of a strong fall sun. When I arrived at UBC, arts-based research was alive and fever pitched. My first formal encounter with the research group was at American Educational Research Association (AERA) where I happened to volunteer to videotape a per-formance by Rita, Alex, and others. With a camera in hand, I eagerly stepped into the middle of an existing performative and evocative space. Today I shiver not from cold but the fear and excitement of the un/known. I am aware that, while there were few hurdles to face in presenting arts-based forms of theses within the Department of Curriculum Studies at UBC, in my new academic home I will face new challenges as I work my way through the tenure process, colleagues' words of rigour and standards brushing against my ears. But I also

question how I can bring this incredible journey to the students at Pennsylvania State University. Where do I start?
What questions should I ask? How far can I push? This
dis/comfort is splayed open knowing there are others who
struggle alongside me.

I met Gary Knowles at the first conference I attended in 1999. He stood in
the lobby area, between interconnecting corridors of one of the main session
blocks of the conference, animating a kinetic sculpture with controls held
behind his back (Cole, Knowles, Brown, & Buttignol, 1999). There were two
other sculptures on view in the same area. The intrigue struck me immediately. I stopped to observe as he called out to conference goers, "Does this
resemble your experience of teaching?" Some passed with a, "*Don't bug me,
I'm on a mission which doesn't include some harebrained piece of whatever
that is,*" expression. They hurried to their assignations; the idea that art could
have a place in these research corridors seemed foreign to some. There were
many who were interested, however, who stopped or came back after their
sessions and engaged with these wonderfully playful and insightful works.
They talked with Gary and others who gathered, conversations were traded;
the art was working as it should — creating (s)p(1)aces for new understandings to be co-created. Meanings unfolded for those present as they engaged
with the sculptures and each other. Dialogues of real-life teaching were heard
echoing from the ceilings. As this was my first conference, little did I know the
significance of what I was experiencing.

I have been to many conferences since and have yet to see something so
immediate, as sessions are presented behind closed doors, tiptoed into after
the assigned start time. I now realize that the use of the corridor, the medium
of expression, the delivery method, were all innovative and challenging to the
accepted norms of conference gatherings. That I was engaged in *living*
research has grown with me as an example of the powerful affect arts-based
research can have.

The person who operated these sculptural works also intrigued me. This
tall man with long hair seemed to be out of place and yet totally comfortable
with what he was doing. I struck up a conversation and found out he was from
the Ontario Institute for Studies in Education in Toronto, and that he was
deeply committed to arts-informed research. "Here is someone to add to my
list of like-minded souls" I thought to myself. I met with him and one of his

graduate students and found solidarity in our thinking about art as research, research as art; a methodological process fixed in praxis.

This was the beginning of a journey of finding like-minded scholars, trading Email addresses, and attending conferences throughout North America always building a circle of support. I looked for sessions that could breathe outside the regulation formats and allow for performative understandings. I am now connected to an ever-expanding community of scholars from all over the world. It is committed and relational time that has formed this community.

In a time span of 17 years since completing my doctorate I have witnessed an epistemological shift and a methodological transformation at UBC. Whereas I used ethnographic techniques in my doctoral research students are now participating in the creation of a methodology called a/r/tography as a precursor to their doctoral research work. The conditions for this fundamental shift can be attributed to several important points. First of all, as a faculty member, I was in a good position to experiment with new research methods and to support students. Secondly, while I tested the waters amongst my colleagues, I pursued my interests with like-minded graduate students. This supported our mutual desire to grow while giving all of us the courage to transform our research traditions. With that courage I was able to learn how to debate with those who were unaware of our innovations. Thirdly, and perhaps more importantly, our work was beginning to have an impact on others. Starting out in a small community of graduate students committed to change, we collaboratively gathered strength, ideas, and creativity from one another. We were stronger together than we were apart. As a result of the incremental development of the research methods within the Faculty as a whole, students were able to identify committees that supported arts-based educational research.

This was an organic process of growth leading naturally to the next (s)p(1)ace. What is easier in the writing, than in reality, is allowing the space for the process to happen (de Cosson, 2002). Sometimes the path was diffi-cult to discern, my confidence shaken by uphill sections or large detours, as I continued to formulate my own area of research.

During this time I was also meeting with my colleagues at UBC where we had formed a research group, one that was dedicated to understanding our own connections to the world of the arts-based theses. We met weekly for a number of terms, presented at conferences, together and debated the many issues that arose from what we were seeing and reading. As we were all visu-al artists it meant that our understandings were coming from a similar frame-work. This tightness of focus allowed us to conceptualize and formulate a/r/tography as a research methodology from which theses could be (art)iculated and defended.

At the time of writing my thesis I remember how frustrat-ing it was to be in a place of not only thinking through research questions on how youth understand and negotiate the lived experiences of their bodies but that, simultaneously, I / we were creating a new methodology. I recall the anxiety I felt trying to explain to faculty and students that my method-ology was not "complete", that it was not a package that I could apply to my research site and text. While struggling to analyze and grasp the effects of my research project in a local secondary school, I was also trying to articulate the intricacies of doing a/r/tographical research with others. There were so many moments of hesitation, uncertainty, and fear. I know that I often retreated to my studio where the texture of hair and red pigments that, stained by fingers blood red, allowed me new points of departure and helped me wade through the thickness of un/knowing in my research. This led me to think about the conceptual narrative I described in my thesis. At one point in my committee meet-ings, someone mentioned that my writing read like many "dropped threads". It was a wonderful metaphor that inter-connected with numerous conversations I had had with a classroom teacher.

In pondering this notion of "dropped threads" I discovered an image of Bronwyn, the art teacher, sitting in the class un/knitting. I also remember my grandmother having to unknit something because she had "dropped" a stitch, which meant that there was a mistake in her pattern, a place that she needed to return to so that she could re-knit her project. This form of unknitting is linear, travelling a path backwards to a place of origin, to a dropped, missed stitch, in order to repair and correct the knitting. Bronwyn's un/knitting was altogether different. These were not dropped threads that she was trying to mend but, rather, she was involved in an active process of "dropping threads" — intentional acts of disruption. Using previously knitted objects Bronwyn un/knits and I use the slash in this instance to "image" the idea of unknitting and knitting simultaneously, in order to create something new. Her knitted art pieces are interwoven combinations of "dropped threads", entangled wools of different colours and textures. Bronwyn's un/knitting is an aesthetic inquiry, it is a process of interrogation and, because she intentionally questions, examines, and reflects on its meaning in relation to her art practices and pedagogy, it also becomes an a/r/tographical gesture. Jean Luc Nancy (2000) articulates this concept of un/knitting when he argues that meaning is created when it "comes apart" (p. 2). This philosophical shift is important because common sense posits meaning as a linear assemblage, as something that is added to and built upon. Instead un/knitting insists that meaning is an exposure, a rupture that emphasizes an opening up.

Dropping threads and dis/repairing textiles are difficult metaphors to contend with given that education has often rewarded students and teachers for finding the correct answers or mending knowledge as opposed to searching for painful questions. The act of dropping threads, of dis/repairing my thesis (research), was intentional. To create separate boundaries between art making, research, teaching, and understandings of body knowledge would continue to perpetuate dichotomous relationships and impose a false sense of order. I encourage researchers to embody the gesture of dropping threads as a process of interrogation that un/knits new directions, new meanings, and folds aesthetic inquiry, intercorporeality, and a/r/tography together.

This chapter represents a collaboration with two talented and courageous doctoral students with whom I have worked over the last few years. They have produced the first two theses at UBC using a/r/tography. Together, we have taken arts-based research to a new level. Through our collaborative efforts we have managed to stretch our ideas collectively while maintaining our independent research, teaching and art making activities. What is incredibly exciting for me is to witness the development of these ideas over time and groups of people while cherishing the commitment by everyone to ensure that the conceptual and philosophical premises of our epistemological change projects resonated with our practices as researchers, teachers, and artists. We are committed to emphasizing our processes while including products; the evolution of research questions and forms of inquiry within projects, creation as a form of inquiry, and collaborative yet critical engagement as a research collective. As students embraced these, and other ideas, I felt compelled to participate to the same degree. Even though the academe might misunderstand our work and claim a lack of scholarship I found the courage to resist these views and invested my time and energy in this work despite my untenured status. I may have opened up a space for the students but the students also opened up the space for me. As I cultivated a sympathetic collegial community so, too, was I helping to nurture the community that would eventually grant me tenure and promotion. Colleagues in my subject area as well as in other arts areas and, indeed, in other fields became interested in our work and created their own forms of artistically enhanced, informed or based work. A synergy of energy could be felt across the Faculty. Now my colleagues are creating their own study groups, performing their own inquiries, and / or stretching their own fields. We are a community of artist-researcher-teachers engaged in re-thinking our research paradigms. It has been an amazing journey that still has many miles left, more study groups to enjoy, and more research / art / teaching to create and understand deeply.

My committee members were all aesthetically minded individuals, who recognized the value of my research plan. They encouraged me to navigate a course, often circuitous, to build my strengths. For instance, there were swirling debates on the validity of the novel as a thesis format, with Rishma Dunlop (1999) being the first to navigate that particular shoal. I attended AERA sessions where impassioned speakers appeared to want to hold the dykes strong for fear of the flood gate that could be unleashed if the artistic notions being advanced were allowed to move forward unchecked.

I listened. I formed my own judgment and realized it was up to me to grab what I could and venture forward knowing I was not alone, that my colleagues would be there to push the envelope with me (de Cosson, 2001). This I believe is one of the most important criteria a doctoral student can nurture, namely, a like-minded peer group. These colleagues created a powerful tool for concept advancement, all members chiseling away at their particular area and collectively nudging things along. One of our early dabblings in consensus and peer group building was to hold a conference in the very area we were interested in researching, namely, artists' praxis. Little did I know at that time that I was creating the foundations of my thesis. This not-knowing and being comfortable in that (s)p(1)ace for an extended period of time is something a student interested in arts-based research must be prepared for, as only time gives the understandings, threads, and connections necessary for the coalescing of new ideas and only a dedicated peer group gives the intellectual, emotional, and willing support to see it through to its fruition.

The room glows purple as another fall day dips below the horizon. I reminisce upon the many meetings that have taken place in this space. As I sit and gaze upon the oblong table, that has been the defining centerpiece for so much of this growth I contemplate the excitement, Stephanie and Alex will have as they go out into the world and create their own a/r/tographical study groups and learning communities. Perhaps in 15 to 20 years from now, when I complete my academic career, the three of us will revisit this space and reminisce upon the growth we will have experienced in the liminal years ahead. May we all be so lucky.

A version of this chapter appears in Four Arrows, aka Jacobs, D. T. (2008) The Authentic Dissertation: Alternative ways of knowing, research, and representation. London, UK: Routledge.

References

Cole, A. L, Knowles, J. G., Brown, B., & Buttignol, M. (1999, June). *Academic altarcations, (first installation in) Living in paradox: A multi-media representation of teacher educators' lives in context (version II).* Installation presented at the Annual Meeting of the Canadian Society for the Study of Education, Sherbrooke, QC, Canada.

de Cosson, A. F. (2001). Anecdotal sculpting: learning to learn, one from another. J*ournal of Curriculum Theorizing, 17*(4), 173-183.

de Cosson, A. F. (2002). The hermeneutic dialogic: Finding patterns amid the aporia of the artist / researcher / teacher. *The Alberta Journal of Educational Research, xlviii* (3), CD-ROM.

de Cosson, A. F. (2003). *(Re)searching sculpted a/r/tography: (Re)learning subverted-knowing through aporetic praxis.* Unpublished doctoral thesis, University of British Columbia, Vancouver, BC, Canada.

Dunlop, R., (1999). *Boundary Bay.* Unpublished doctoral thesis, University of British Columbia, Vancouver, BC, Canada.

Irwin, R. L. (1999). Listening to the shapes of collaborative art making. *Art Education, 52*(2), 35-40.

Irwin, R. L. (2003). Towards an aesthetic of unfolding in / sights through curriculum. *Journal of the Canadian Association for Curriculum Studies, 1*(2), 63-78. Available at: http://www.csse.ca/CACS/JCACS/ PDF%20Content/ 07._Irwin.pdf

Irwin, R. L., Crawford, N., Mastri, R., Neale, A., Robertson, H., & Stephenson, W. (1997). Collaborative action research: A journey of six women artist-pedagogues. *Collaborative Inquiry in a Postmodern Era: A Cat's Cradle, 2*(2), 21-40.

Irwin, R. L., de Cosson A. F., & Springgay, S. (Eds.). (2004). *A/r/tography: Rendering self through arts-based living inquiry.* Vancouver, BC: Pacific Educational Press.

Irwin, R. L., Mastri, R., & Robertson, H. (2000). Pausing to reflect: Moments in feminist collaborative action research. *Journal of Gender Issues in Art Education, 1*, 43-56.

Irwin, R. L., Stephenson, W., Neale, A., Robertson, H., Mastri, R., & Crawford, N. (1998). Quiltmaking as a metaphor: Creating feminist political consciousness for art pedagogues. In E. Sacca & E. Zimmerman (Eds), *Women art educators IV: Herstories, our stories, future stories* (pp. 100-111). Boucherville, QC: CSEA.

Irwin, R. L., Stephenson, W., Robertson, H., & Reynolds, J. K. (2001). Passionate creativity, compassionate community. *Canadian Review of Art Education, 28*(2), 15-34.

Leggo, C. (1999). Research as poetic rumination: Twenty-six ways of listening to light. *Journal of Educational Thought, 33*(2), 113-133.

Nancy, J. L. (2000). *Of being singular plural.* Stanford, CA: Stanford University Press.

Springgay, S. (2002). Arts-based educational research as an unknowable text. *Alberta Journal of Educational Research, 3.* CD-ROM.

Springgay, S. (2003). Cloth as intercorporeality: Touch, fantasy, and performance and the construction of body knowledge. *International Journal of Education and the Arts, 4*(5). Available at: http://ijea.asu.edu/v4n5/.

Springgay, S. (2004). *Inside the visible: Youth understandings of body knowledge through touch.* Unpublished doctoral thesis, University of British Columbia, Vancouver, BC, Canada.

Springgay, S, Irwin, R. L., & Wilson Kind, S. (2005). A/r/tography as living inquiry through art and text. *Qualitative Inquiry,*

11(6), 897-912.

Wilson, S. (2000). *Fragments: A narrative approach to arts-based research*. Unpublished master's thesis, University of British Columbia, Vancouver, BC, Canada.

About the Authors

STEPHANIE SPRINGGAY is Assistant Professor of Art Education and Women's Studies, Pennsylvania State University. Her research and artistic interests include the body, phenomenology of touch and desire, aesthetics, visual culture, feminist epistemologies, social justice in the arts, and a/r/tographical research. Her artistic installations incorporate human hair and felt. Stephanie was awarded the Gordon and Marion Smith Award in Art Education from the University of British Columbia in 2003.

Stephanie's doctoral thesis, *Inside the Visible: Youth Understandings of Body Knowledge through Touch*, is an a/r/tographical study that examines students' experiences of their body in and as visual culture. Body knowledge through touch poses proximinal understandings of knowledge production. During a six-month curriculum project participants created visual art works as a means to think through the body as a process of exchange and as bodied encounters revealing body knowledge as dynamic, generative, and vulnerable.

ALEX DE COSSON is a sculptor and earned a PhD from the University of British Columbia (UBC). Since 1989 he has been a faculty member of the Ontario College of Art and Design, Toronto and is concurrently a Sessional Instructor in Art Education, Department of Curriculum Studies, UBC. His research interests include arts-based and autobiographical research. Alex was awarded the Gordon and Marion Smith Award in Art Education, UBC in 2003.

In *(Re)searching Sculpted A/r/tography: (Re)learning Subverted-Knowing through Aporetic Praxis,* Alex invites readers to walk with him, a sculptor who wished to understand his pedagogical and artistic practice as an artist / researcher / teacher, through an arts-informed exploration into praxis. Alex takes the reader for a pedagogical journey utilizing writing as a metonym for building a sculpture. The thesis records, self-reflexively and interrogatively, the research site of Alex's practice as researched and his research site as practiced.

RITA IRWIN is Professor and Associate Dean, Faculty of Education, University of British Columbia. She is an artist, researcher, and teacher who is committed to the arts as living inquiry. As such, she continues to create art, conduct research, and practice her pedagogy in ways that are integrative, reflective, and full of living awareness. Her research interests include in-service arts teacher education, curriculum studies, artist-in-schools programs, First Nations, and gender issues.

29. Mirroring at the Borders: Strategies for Methodless Method

by ANTOINETTE OBERG and LAURA CRANMER

Imaginative art forfeits interpretation and calls instead for a compara-
ble act of imagination.... Along the mirrored border one does not hear
the language of meaning; understanding is not the aim so translation
falls away. There is instead a miming dance back and forth of the bor-
der guards, the greetings of images, exchange of gifts, ceremonies.
(Hillman, 1983, p. 30)

    For the four years between 1998 and 2002, Laura Cranmer and
Antoinette Oberg mirrored each other's creative processes across the

349

border between student and supervisor, in ways they were not fully aware of until they wrote this chapter. As a longtime supervisor of creative acts of inquiry (narrative, autobiographical, arts-based), Antoinette has always thought of her pedagogy as a creative act of improvisation as she responds to students' free-form writing on topics that interest them deeply. As a creative writer Laura applied creative writing skills to her inquiry and discovered a way of writing that also served to purge herself of the negative construction of identity imposed by powerful colonial forces. During her thesis inquiry she also became a playwright and produced a full-scale stage play called DP's Colonial Cabaret *(Cranmer, 2002).*

Conversations between Antoinette and Laura formed the temenos, that delimited space in which "special rules apply and extraordinary events are free to occur" (Nachmanovitch, 1990, p. 75), in which Laura's play was birthed. As well as being a post hoc representation, the play was the vehicle for Laura's inquiring into, through, on, and even beyond the effects of the colonization of her person. Containing seven characters, the play began as a play of ideas — a discourse between energetic presences that had contributed to her identity as a colonized Nam'gis woman.

Like all deeply interpretive inquiries, Laura's was an inquiry without method. Abjuring method places Antoinette dangerously close to, some might say beyond, the border of that territory called legitimate social science research. The marginalization she experiences as an academic who fosters and supports inquiry without method attuned her to Laura's experience of marginalization and equipped her to call forth Laura's inquiry into her experience of colonization. Each at her own border they mirrored each other's experiences subconsciously in the ritual call-response that is the core of Antoinette's pedagogy.[1]

They now weave together their recollections of this particular inquiry. Again they pick up threads of their conversation and in doing so, hope that their very specific experiences will open out in meaning for readers travelling similar paths. In that most common form of improvisation known as ordinary speech, they negotiated this recasting of experience as they each remembered it and then edited their conversations. Now, as then, they are curious about the nature of inquiry-without-method: how it begins, is nurtured, and flowers, and what it produces and leaves behind.

LAURA. My first graduate course with you [Antoinette] required not essays, not term papers, but journal pieces. After five years of writing formal essays to earn a bachelor's degree in English, imagine my delight at being in a place where my personal practice of informal journaling was recognized and valued. Although having the sense of embarking on a journey, I did not have a clear intention for my inquiry or a predetermined outcome. My intention became clear only with your close attention and careful questioning in response to the journal writing I submitted to you.

ANTOINETTE. As a medium of inquiry, journal writing gives students a space, free from the formal requirements of academic writing, where there is permission to immerse in that deep and often frightening pool of uncertainties from which a research topic eventually emerges. As students open themselves to the unknown and pay attention to what shows itself there I, too, must open and attend closely and without judgment to the unpredictable course of their inquiries.

LAURA. You noticed that searching was a constant in the dreams recorded in my journal submissions and asked, "Is the shape of your thesis the search for details which construct your identity both negatively and positively? What would be entailed in showing this search in the form of a play?"

ANTOINETTE. That question arose spontaneously, prompted by something more than my conscious mind. In retrospect, I can see that a play was the appropriate genre for your inquiry precisely because it allowed you to deal with that which resides beneath and behind rational mind. Moreover, the multisensory devices available to a playwright that affect play goers subliminally allowed you to communicate the messy underside of life to an audience (Artaud, 1958).

LAURA. My inquiry was embedded in my writings but not immediately apparent to me. What strikes me now, in retrospect, is that you picked up on signals from my dreams — the very stuff of subconscious desire. I understand now what you meant when you asked about my interest, that is, what was I in the midst of?

ANTOINETTE. Presuming that students enter graduate school always already in the midst of an inquiry not yet articulated, I ask this question to bring inquiry forward: What interests you? The etymology of the word "interest" indicates that I am asking, "What are you in the midst of?" This question invites students to pay attention to their embeddedness in matrices of meanings and memories that shape their lives and to pause long enough to notice which meanings and memories are particularly salient for them in the present moment. In contrast to academic writing that proceeds impersonally to marshal arguments to make a point, the writing called for by this question is autobiographical and open-ended; its aim is not to close in on an answer, but to stay open to the question. As Gadamer (1986) says, "To ask a question means to bring into the open…. The real and basic nature of a question…is to make things indeterminate" (p. 338). Learning to question in the sense of opening to the question is a matter of letting go of the desire for answers — even about method — in the same way that learning to float requires surrendering every attempt to swim and remaining perfectly still (Stafford, 1978). Students' writing in response to this question about interest invariably signals a deeply meaningful inquiry yet to manifest.

LAURA. I was in the middle of colonization and trying to regain my equilibrium. By mirroring the subconscious signals in my writing, you acted as a tuning fork — a diviner's willow branch in search of a deep well. Homing in on the interstices of my psyche, you tapped into my poeticizing consciousness. Your question served to simultaneously coalesce work I brought to the table and paradoxically enough, made indeterminate the very answers I thought I had. In other words, while your question finds the well, it also makes the well all that much more challenging to reach and draw water from. And perhaps more paradoxical is the fact that my writing was sabotaged by deep subconscious doubts about my ability which arose each time I accomplished a major section of the play or was about to take up another section. What stops the "stopping" of the mysterious writing process?

ANTOINETTE. My answer to this question is the same answer given by Gail Sher (1990) and other writing coaches and it is deceptively simple: "What stops the stopping is staying with the stoppage". Asking, "What is the stoppage?" is a way of going on. I share this insight with students in the form of an invitation to pay attention in writing to whatever they are in the midst of, whether it is the accumulation of years or the difficulties of the moment.

LAURA. Devoting a whole semester to journalling was important in creating the conditions (time and space) needed to generate enough writing to see what I was in the midst of.

ANTOINETTE. I promise a disinterested acceptance of students' responses to the invitation to write from the midst of not knowing answers. Their responses are usually initially hesitant and uncertain, always partial, and often somewhat cryptic. A patient, nonjudgmental acceptance of whatever students write opens a space of possibility for creative processes to unfold. The simplicity of this space is complicated by the psychological environment of the university, where social norms require not invitation but assignment, not disinterest but judgment, not patience but efficiency. Entering this conflicted space requires the mutual trust of student and supervisor.

LAURA. Your energetic attunement implicitly invited me to open where I was closed, to risk where I was fearful, and to voice the unknown in me. Throughout my program, I relied on the works of writers who provided guidance and inspiration for my own writing when venturing into unknown psychic territory. Many writers have been to that unknown space where they found treasures within themselves. Among these are Helene Cixous (1990) and Jack Kerouac (Charters, 1995) whose principles, of "writing from the body" and "spontaneous prose writing" (respectively), I blended together. A conscious application of Kerouac's stream of consciousness writing method to Cixous' "writing from the body" released powerful psychic materials that were profoundly transforming.

ANTOINETTE. That you were willing to do emotionally dangerous work in the academy, and I was willing to allow and support it, attests to the trust we had in our own and in each other's ways of working. We trusted your spontaneous writing and my improvised responding, both of which exist outside the realm of legitimate research procedure, to produce the material of legitimate research.

LAURA. Given that I was consciously using spontaneous writing in the aesthetic and therapeutic sense I could say with confidence that, this process, as difficult and frustrating as it was and is, led to my de-colonization. I could not have sustained the depth of the work without therapeutic support and would not recommend engaging in this method of inquiry without first establishing a solid relationship with an Integrative Body Psychotherapist.[2]

ANTOINETTE. Though you had, parallel to your graduate work, the support of a skilled therapist in your quest to reinvent yourself, as a teacher and inquirer I was not absolved of my responsibility to be constantly attentive to the possible effects of my invitations to you to re-examine and even to dismantle existing networks of meanings that held your life together. You were rewriting the dominant discourse in your life with conscious intent, but many students have no such intent and, finding themselves unexpectedly in the midst of such a project, might resist or be surprised at the disorientation that results. Always, and especially in these cases, I must continuously question the confounding effects of the power dynamic that is inevitably present in the relationship between student and teacher, giving my invitations more force than I might intend or wish.

LAURA. And as they say in theatre, intention is everything. Although I would not consciously apply the ideas and concepts of spontaneous prose writing for a number of years, I was deeply impressed by this kind of lawless writing, free of the shackles of the Queen's English. Dr. M. Soules (1994), who introduced me to Kerouac in his dissertation, *Sam Shepard Improvises*, theorized that

> improvised writing based on the jazz model is analogous to riffing — as a pastiche of phrases and inspired allusion…. Given that jazz sketching is the "undisturbed flow from the mind of personal secret idea-words", such writing must eventually accommodate confessional impulses. (p. 2)

Applying Soules' theory of "jazz riffing" to journaling my dreams, my writing surfaced "confessional impulses". Through the kind of writing I engaged in, I worked on many levels to throw off the colonial script inscribed upon my body and psyche. The dominant meaning you speak of was impressed on my body — my colonized body. As a Nam'gis woman, I was the by-product of some bureaucrat's vision of my erasure. Policies were designed to supplant my body's cultural memory with the dominant patriarchal meaning long before I was born.

ANTOINETTE. Similar to, yet, different from the improvisational writing theorized by Soules, my questions to students are improvised in response to their writing. I have no *a-priori* agenda and no investment in the outcome. My aim is simply that inquiry should move, that the autopoietic impulse to explore should be unfettered, and that what is implicitly there should be allowed to take shape. In enacting that aim, I ask questions that are intended neither to understand students nor to shape their understanding (although both of these may result). Rather, as I read what students have written, I notice what is called up in me and, without presuming or imposing, I formulate my responses as questions and offer them as reflections of what might be contained in their writing.

LAURA. Yes! In your reflective response to my work you acted like the border guard, who offers gifts in the guise of questioning, as opposed to the university's "guards" who simply protect their territory. Your questions in turn triggered responses in me that kept me moving. At the mid-point of my program, you asked whether my thesis was my life's work, which, at the time, seemed like a fairly benign question. I was also enrolled at the time in a paraprofessional therapy training course (Integrative Body Psychotherapy) where I learned about the concept of fragmentation. I realized I lived in a continual disassociated state, and if my Master's work was my life's work and if I was having an out-of-body experience all my life, I had to ask, "Then whose work and whose life is this?"

Bringing alive my deepest doubts, the question triggered a crisis of confidence serious enough to question the authenticity of my intentions, the import, and even the necessity of continuing the work.

ANTOINETTE. As often happens in the course of autobiographical inquiry that goes close to the bone, misgivings threatened to halt your inquiry. I expect this when it happens in students' inquiries and I allow whatever time is necessary for students to confront this stoppage. It is part of the creative process. In your case, sometimes I would not hear from you for months at a time. I trusted, however, that you would return when you were ready for, as Nachmanovitch (1990, p. 32) reminds us, the flow is always there. "We can choose to tap into it or not to tap into it; we can find ourselves unwillingly opened to it or unwillingly cut off from it. But it's always there".

LAURA. Your "close to the bone" comment hits at the heart of my inquiry in that the process of writing the play became my way of rewriting, in essence, purging my blood and bone of the colonial script. Since my writing process was also based on Cixous' concept of writing from the body, I had to learn to read my physiological responses to the work. I needed to pay attention and notice my own pattern of shutting down. Our relationship created a space large enough for my writing process to breathe, digest, and shape my lived experience in an aesthetic way.

ANTOINETTE. Your improvisational and poetic writing effectively challenged the dominant discourse by challenging the pretension of reason to universal jurisdiction. As Caputo (1987) describes it, poetic thinking is in touch with things long before the demand for reason. In contrast to propositional discourse, which requires reason and grounds, the space of poeticizing is groundless. In place of the solidity of ground there is movement. In this place, the notion of method as a set of directives or procedures is replaced by a sense of method as the suppleness by which thinking is able to pursue the matter at hand. Caputo says this sense of method is "an acuity which knows its way about even and especially when the way cannot be laid out beforehand, when it cannot be formulated in explicit rules" (p. 213).

LAURA. Many threads form the weave of the matrix of our work together. Exhorting women to write from the body, Cixous (1990) believed the unconscious to be "that other limitless country" where the repressed survives and where poetry resides. She also believed that *"new insurgent writing"* springs from this deep well (p. 484). Poetic expression thus becomes a way to disrupt dominant discourse. The movement of playful poetics necessitates improvisation with attunement. Again, attunement is really a way of seeing and engaging with the world on a daily basis. Rather than reading about attunement, you read your body and the body of the person in front of you. How else to read the body but through dreaming and streaming with writing, and when it flows, it flows.

ANTOINETTE. That flow is the stream every creative artist seeks. Nachmanovitch (1990, p. 32) calls it "the stream of consciousness, a river of memories…beyond the personal, from a source that is both very old and very new…a seemingly endless stream of dance, imagery, acting or speech that comes out of us whenever we let it."

LAURA. My means of tapping into this stream was through Kerouac's "Belief and Technique for Modern Prose"[3] (Charters, 1995). The most powerful monologues in the play were written on the basis of his technique. They began as stream of consciousness writing of my dream images, which then became part of the play. And, at certain points in the process, whether it came to introducing two characters in opposition to each other or a crisis in confidence about my work, I would become physically incapacitated and required days of bed rest. Even well into the process, your questions continued to prompt either getting out of resistance, or moving in another direction when I hit a dead-end.

ANTOINETTE. This pattern is a prime example of this work being "non-linear and contingent, difficult and humbling" (Caputo, 1987, p. 213).

LAURA. Your continual affirmations reminded me that despite my sense of being ungrounded, I was on the right track in a seemingly trackless land. Your questioning served to draw out the "new insurgent writing" deep within me and in a related vein allowed me to effect those "indispensable ruptures and transformations" which challenge the dominant discourse (Cixous, 1990, p. 484).

ANTOINETTE. As Caputo (1987) reminds us, authenticity in this work means owning up to the embarrassment of not knowing how to proceed and paying attention to where we close down and where we come up against dominant discourse, where the going gets too difficult to keep going. As I said earlier, asking at those times what stops us is a way of keeping going. This way of moving is non-linear and contingent; it is difficult and humbling. It is the mode of inquiry without method.

LAURA. Despite the dangers of this kind of writing, I had the profound sense I was traveling to Cixous' (1990) "limitless country" — my own subconscious — where I embarked on a hero's quest, fought my colonial demons, and came to my rescue to retrieve the treasure of my own authentic un-disassociated self.

ANTOINETTE. In the *temenos* of the mutually respectful relationship we forged as student and supervisor, we mirrored each other our's experiences of improvisation — you of playwriting and I of thesis supervising. We set the border guards dancing. Although the statement by Hillman (1983) that opens this chapter originated in a therapeutic context, it applies as well in our specific experiences, wherein we also mirrored our processes to each other, and exchanged gifts and insights at our own borders. Indeed, our border guards made friends and became allies in our parallel projects of dislodging the residue of dominant discourses deposited in our lives. Supplanting the limited form of reason purveyed by the dominant discourse, we employed a poetic rationality to rewrite the rules of colonial and academic institutions. And that has made all the difference.

Endnotes

1. This pedagogy begins with the question, What interests you? and proceeds by means of an ongoing series of written exchanges between teacher and student as the student seeks to articulate her not-yet-imagined interest. Each piece of student writing calls for (and calls forth) an imaginative response from the teacher intended to provoke a further act of imagination by the student.

2. An Integrative Body Psychotherapist (an IBP certified therapist) is a therapist who has at least four years of training in the experiential application of concepts (body, breath, and boundaries) central to the IBP model.

3. Kerouac's "Belief and Techniqe for Modern Prose" is a list of dos and don'ts for spontaneous prose writing which, if followed, allows one to process material from the subconscious to the conscious realm with a minimum of distortion and supplies rich material for the creative writing mill.

References

Artaud, A. (1958). The theatre and its double (M. C. Richards, Trans.). New York, NY: Grove Press.

Caputo, J. (1987). Radical hermeneutics: Repetition, deconstruction, and the hermeneutic project. Bloomington, IN: Indiana University Press.

Charters, A. (1995). Jack Kerouac: Selected letters 1940-1956. New York, NY: Penguin Books.

Cixous, H. (1990). The laugh of the Medusa. In P. Hoy II, E. Schor, & R. DiYanni. (Eds.), Women's voices: Visions and perspectives (K. Cohen & P. Cohen, Trans., pp. 481-496). New York, NY: McGraw-Hill.

Cixous, H. (1993). Three steps on the ladder of writing. New York, NY: Columbia University Press.

Cranmer, L. (2002). DP's colonial cabaret. Unpublished Master's thesis, University of Victoria, Victoria, BC, Canada.

Gadamer, H. G. (1986). Truth and method. New York, NY: Crossroad.

Hillman, J. (1983). Healing fiction. Putnam, CT: Spring Publications.

Nachmanovitch, S. (1990). Free play: Improvisation in life and in art. New York: Penguin Putnam.

Sher, G. (1990). One continuous mistake: Four noble truths for writers. New York, NY: Penguin Compass.

Soules, M. (1994). Sam Shepard improvises. Unpublished doctoral dissertation, University of Michigan, Ann Arbor, MI.

Stafford, W. (1978). Writing the Australian crawl. Ann Arbor, MI: University of Michigan Press.

About the Authors

ANTOINETTE OBERG is Associate Professor Emeritus in the Department of Curriculum and Instruction, University of Victoria where she developed and coordinated graduate programs in

Curriculum Studies. In 1995 she won the University of Victoria Alumni Award for excellence in university teaching. She teaches graduate courses in curriculum theory and interpretive inquiry. Her research focuses on inquiry processes that generate their own form through practices of imaginative, personal, reflective narrative writing.

LAURA CRANMER was raised in the 1950s and 1960s in Alert Bay, Vancouver Island, by her paternal grandmother, Agnes. She attained her BA in English and MA in Curriculum Studies from the University of Victoria. Both degree programs assisted Laura in making sense of her colonial history. She is a doctoral student in language and literacy education at the University of British Columbia.

DP's Colonial Cabaret, Laura's Master's degree thesis, is a two-act play expressing the energetic forces that contributed to her identity as a colonized Nam'gis woman. The action follows DP's struggle with substance abuse and ends with a confrontation between Anomie and Mother Bond, two characters competing for his allegiance. Imagining the characters and writing the play was Laura's way of understanding and purging harmful colonial influences — thus rewriting the colonial script handed her at birth.

Centre for Arts-informed Research

The Centre for Arts-informed Research is affiliated with the Department of Adult Education, Community Development and Counselling Psychology in the Ontario Institute for Studies in Education of the University of Toronto. It was created in early 2000 through the energies and support of faculty and students.

The Centre's mission is to articulate, explore, and support alternative forms of qualitative research and representation which infuse elements processes, and forms of the arts into scholarly work.

The Centre's goals are:
• to contribute to the advancement of the genre of arts-informed research
• to create a context for emerging and established researchers to explore methodological issues associated with arts-informed research
• to work toward the development of a local, national and international community of arts-informed researchers
• to promote open dialogue and collaboration among researcher, professional artists, communities and schools
• to provide opportunities and spaces for public access to alternative forms of research

The Centre's priorities include publishing as well as offering seminars, colloquia, exhibits, workshops and conferences. Although the Centre does not offer academic programs, student and faculty scholars of all departments within the Institute and beyond are welcome to participate in all its activities.

Contact Information:
Ardra L. Cole, Co-director
Centre for Arts-informed Research,
Department of Adult Education, Community Development and Counselling Psychology, University of Toronto
252 Bloor Street West
Toronto, Ontario, Canada, M5S 1V6
acole@oise.utoronto.ca
www.utoronto.ca/CAIR

Backalong Books
www.backalongbooks.com
nwcove@ns.sympatico.ca

Knowing Her Place (Neilsen)
ISBN 1-894132-02-5 $28.95

A Teacher's Life (Muchmore)
ISBN 1-894132-12-2 (CAN)
ISBN 1-880192-47-0 (USA) $28.95

Through Preservice Teachers' Eyes (Knowles & Cole)
ISBN 1-894132-26-2 $34.95

Arts-informed Research Series

The Art of Visual Inquiry (Knowles et al)
ISBN 1-894132-10-6 $34.95
Provoked by Art (Cole et al)
ISBN 1-894132-08-4 $28.95
The Art of Writing Inquiry (Neilsen et al)
ISBN 1-894132-06-8 $34.95

Scholartistry Series

Of Earth and Flesh and Bones and Breath (Thomas)
ISBN 1-894132-14-9 $34.95
Remembering Place: Domicide and a Childhood Home (Sbrocchi)
ISBN 1-894132-24-6 $28.95

Living and Dying with Dignity: The Alzheimer's Project
(Cole & McIntyre)
ISBN 1-894132-20-3 $19.95
RESPECT: A Readers Theatre about People Who Care
for People in Nursing Homes (McIntyre)
ISBN 1-894132-18-1 $14.95
The Alzheimer's Alphabet: Self-care from A-Z (McIntyre & Cole)
ISBN 1-894132-32-7 $10.00